THOM WHEELER

ONE STEPPE BEYOND

ACROSS RUSSIA IN A VW CAMPER

summersdale

ONE STEPPE BEYOND

Summersdale Publishers Ltd
46 West Street
Chichester
West Sussex
PO19 1RP
UK

www.summersdale.com

Printed and bound in Great Britain

ISBN: 978-1-84953-156-6

Substantial discounts on bulk quantities of Summersdale books are available to corporations, professional associations and other organisations. For details telephone Summersdale Publishers on (+44-1243-771107), fax (+44-1243-786300) or email (nicky@ summersdale.com).

For Jo

Estonia

Tallinn

St Petersburg

Vologda

Yaroslavl

Kostroma

Moscow

Suzdal

Nizhny Novgorod

Kazan

Ufa

Yekaterinburg

Omsk

Novosibirsk

Russia

Thom Wheeler studied Russian at university and returned to live in St Petersburg for several years after the 1997 trip, earning a living teaching and guiding, while also reviewing bands for the Russian *Big Issue*; he then lived and worked in Ukraine, Estonia and Georgia. He is now based in Brighton, where he teaches drama.

CONTENTS

PROLOGUE

St Petersburg had been a cold and bleak place when my sixth form history class and I arrived during the last days of the Soviet Union, its real identity disguised under its Soviet name Leningrad and several feet of heavy February snow. The city's residents were generally reserved and suspicious, or, conversely, overly friendly in an attempt to sell Red Army uniforms, Soviet badges, or cheap Sovietskaya champagne. Our itinerary had included the usual suspects on the tourist route: Alexander Nevsky Monastery, St Isaac's, the Hermitage, but also we were 'very lucky' to be taken on an excursion to a local school.

On arrival at School No. 81 on the Petrograd side, the district north of the Neva River, we were given a short tour around several gloomy-looking classrooms with dull lighting and bare grey walls, before congregating in a small hall, where some of the more senior students joined us. As a gesture of fraternity we had brought with us a loaf of bread, painstakingly sculpted to depict flowers and birds in bold relief on the top. The procedure planned was that one member of our party would step forward and formally present the symbolic loaf to a representative from the school – a simple enough task, which is why I had no misgivings when it was decided that I would take on the job of official diplomatic bread hander-over.

However, as this ceremony drew closer, I found myself unable to control a mounting fit of the hysterics, not helped by winks and nudges from other members of the group. The Russian recipient of the loaf stepped forward, a girl of about sixteen called Katerina. Katerina contributed to my barely suppressed hysteria by the fact that she herself was suffering from an all too obvious fit of the giggles coupled with mounting embarrassment. Her cheeks were reddening to such a shade of crimson that they looked fit to burst, her clear discomfort at being centre of attention adding to her awkwardness.

Then came the moment for the loaf to be exchanged. During the split second as it left my hands and was about to arrive in hers, it somehow slipped and merely clipped across the ends of Katerina's fingers. It then seemed to hover in mid air for an eternity, before commencing its downward plunge, performing a couple of somersaults before impacting on the floor. The beautifully sculpted ceremonial loaf divided into two uneven halves. My eyes had searched frantically for a face in which to bury my own embarrassment. Most of my group were laughing wildly, in marked contrast to our Russian hosts, who stood wearing uniformly blank expressions – apparently taking these loaf-exchanging ceremonies very seriously. Katerina was quick to rescue the bread. The atmosphere, which had crashed along with the loaf of bread, gradually lightened over refreshments of shortbread and blackberry juice, giving me and Katerina the chance to laugh about the mishap and exchange notes about our respective countries. We also exchanged addresses – and Katerina became my first and only pen friend.

Getting my first letter from the Soviet Union was very romantic. She wrote at length about her recent holiday in Odessa, and how she had passed her driving test; she even enclosed a picture of her behind the wheel of a Lada – looking supremely proud. The second letter was exciting too, as she was really looking forward to coming over to England to visit. All she needed from me was an official invitation. The third letter, which arrived shortly after the second, reiterated how excited she was about coming to see me, and that all I now needed to do was organise an official invitation for her mother and younger sister.

I was too old for pen pals. Especially when they came with so much baggage. The bureaucratic mountain that it was necessary to climb in order to get merely one Soviet citizen across Europe on an Aeroflot flight was significant, but a whole family would require more stamina than I could muster. Fortunately, Katerina apparently felt the same – as when I wrote back with a lengthy list of requirements, which included eight passport-size photographs and a not inconsiderable amount of hard currency, I didn't get a reply.

By the time my brief friendship with Katerina had become nothing more than a memory, the same was true of the Soviet Union. Almost overnight an entire country existed no more. At midnight on 31 December 1991, arguably one of the most important states of the twentieth century ceased to exist. As dawn broke on New Year's Day in 1992, the great socialist experiment that had imposed itself on the world for seventy years was over. No fanfares, no great battles – the hammer and sickle of the Soviet Union had already been replaced by the Russian Federation's tricolour – as a once mighty power left the stage without so much as a whimper. The leaders of the original 1917 revolution had aimed to rid the world of capitalism, and all the oppression and exploitation which capitalism entailed, believing the Soviet state to be 'the only sure way to bring about social and material contentment', sentiments which, wherever you stand on the political spectrum, are difficult not to be warmed by. However, once the presidents of Russia, Ukraine and Belarus had agreed to disband the union, it was that very capitalism that was to gush in to fill the vacuum. The USSR was replaced by fifteen independent states, all in varying degrees of chaos. Russia was to be dominant within the newly formed confederation, but this was still a long way away from the iconic images of Boris Yeltsin astride a Taman Division tank in opposition to the coup d'état months earlier.

In one of Katerina's letters she had included a flimsy, discoloured map of the USSR. It was a map given gravitas by its condition, torn folds held together with tape, faded coffee cup stains – suggesting it had visited every last place printed on it. The map found its way onto my wall and I spent much time marvelling at this huge country, hypnotised by the alien, impenetrable Cyrillic script, daydreaming about all the possibilities that lay waiting in the post-Soviet world. Beyond the exotic-sounding names of Kazan, Yekaterinburg and Vladivostok existed a world that somehow wasn't there before the collapse, when there had been nothing but Moscow and the distant spectre of Siberia. Now the whole of this vast space was alive again – a whole new world to explore. For the first time, as I gazed captivated by this abstract of lines and shapes, Russia became more than the romantic invention of cold war thrillers, and tour companies with snowy winter itineraries. It mutated into a geographical monster, now somehow accessible and tangible. The USSR had been little more than its capital, like a tree only part visible above ground, anchored by a hulking great network of subterranean roots. For the first time those roots had made themselves visible to me – and I wanted to see more!

My chance came a few years later, and took the form of Uncle Tony. Not really an uncle, he was one of those family friends who had always been there. From as early as I can remember, Uncle Tony had been drinking coffee at the kitchen table and laughing his deep, hearty laugh, enthusiastically recounting impossible tales. It was during one of his visits that he mentioned a forthcoming trip to Estonia to meet a business associate. When Tony wasn't pursuing life's pleasures with the gusto of a man half his age, his business was wood, a lot of which came cheaply from Eastern Europe. Without a second thought for ideology Uncle Tony was one of many now filling the void left by communism.

'I'll be staying with Olavi, he runs a timber yard in the south... Small town called Pärnu,' Tony said with a glint in his eye. 'You ought to visit some time, it's a really beautiful country.' I had never really given Estonia a second thought.

I knew nothing about it, and was all too aware that Uncle Tony's opinion was solely derived from it having a supply of cheap timber for his garden sheds – or whatever else he did with the wood that arrived by the ship load. Tony was silent for a few moments before adding nonchalantly, 'I'll get you a job out there if you want.'

This somewhat throwaway-sounding offer of a job was a little more potent than it may at first appear. Since that visit to the Soviet Union over five years before, my time had been spent completing a thoroughly amorphous course of higher education. Employment in my chosen vocation of community drama hadn't come easily; in fact, employment of any kind came with very little regularity. I was in my prime, hungry to make a mark on the world, yet I was making ends meet by delivering egg and cress sandwiches on a bicycle with a bent axle to condescending office workers – and getting a little bit too excited about my visits to the local job centre.

The highlight of my week was meeting with Jo – she too had graduated from the faculty of delusional education and we had both moved up to London, eager to put our newly acquired skills into practice. We used our time together comparing notes on soul-destroying McJobs and planning community productions to make the world stand up and pay attention. Unfortunately, the more we drank, the more outlandish and completely unrealistic these productions became. We did, however, succeed in one thing – exhausting most of our meagre earnings, and thus giving us no other choice than to wake up the next morning, bleary-eyed, ready to clamber back into our increasingly comfortable ruts.

Uncle Tony's words were a lifeline, a chance to kick-start my stagnant existence – OK, a little further afield than the 25 kilometres stated in my job search declaration, but a job's a job. Gainful employment in the ex-Soviet Union was a dream come true.

CHAPTER ONE
PÄRNU

'The world does not understand Estonians, and Estonians do not understand the world. The world can easily live with this, but can Estonians, that is the question.'

ANDREI HVOSTOV

The job was timber 'stress grading', which involved a lot of coffee, a lot of smoking and very little stress. I was to work alongside Janis, the yard foreman, an Estonian man of twenty-eight in a state of constant agitation – he couldn't stand still for a moment, either playing with an unlit cigarette in his hand, playing 'keepy uppy' with an invisible football or juggling objects only he could see. On my first day, between cups of coffee, Janis and an assembled group deliberated long and hard over the future of a burnt-out timber truck. Now, I'm no expert on aging Soviet heavy goods vehicles, but running my untrained eye over the ailing truck I concluded quickly that, largely due to the huge amount of daylight underneath the bonnet, there was no future for it. I couldn't understand what Janis and his friends were saying, but as the minutes turned to hours I got my first insight into the mindset of the *Homo sovieticus*. Why work when there are important decisions to be made? I found their attitude endearing, feelings probably not shared by the management.

THREE SOVIET PROVERBS

- The future belongs to he who knows how to wait.

- Initiative will be punished.

- We pretend to work; they pretend to pay us.

Janis had recently returned from the UK having completed a course in stress grading. However, he appeared in no hurry to show off his new know-how. When the gathering of men in dusty boiler suits eventually started to disperse, I noticed Janis anxiously searching the yard for further distractions, his eyes hunting high and low with the alertness of a meerkat for anything that might provide an opportunity to kill some more time. Failure to find anything was met with a childish resignation, and I'm sure I saw him stamping his foot as the realisation hit home that work would have to begin. But Janis was nothing if not resourceful. Having manoeuvred a split pine trunk into position, rather than scrutinise it for quality he sat himself down on it and reached for his cigarettes, muttering what could only have been the Estonian equivalent of 'A quick fag, and then we'll start'. A 1950s poster courtesy of the Soviet Union's tobacco industry had offered the simple message 'Smoke cigarettes'. Janis' smoking habit was living proof of the effectiveness of the Soviet propaganda machine.

Finally, with a fresh cigarette behind the ear, he clapped his hands together, rose to his feet and pushed a reluctant 'OK' from his mouth. Grading the timber involved dividing the wood into what we termed white and red – on the whole this meant spruce and pine, pine being the heavier and more likely to be exported to England for the manufacture of furniture – then dividing up the 5.5-metre-long slabs of trunk depending on the percentage of knots. After the planks had been checked they were bundled into parcels of twelve and piled up ready for the boat. Planks with too many knots, or which had been badly cut or damaged by worms, were put to one side. Janis set to it with fervour; despite earlier delays he now seemed to be in his element. The fresh Baltic breeze brought clean, vital, sweet-smelling air, and warm sun illuminated the surrounding woods, reflecting off the silver birch and the yellow timber in the yard.

The yard was a couple of miles outside the town of Pärnu, where the previous day myself and Jo had met up with Olavi and Roland, his old friend from university days and partner in the timber yard. Yes, that's right – Jo, my old friend from university days. She had done a lot of travelling in South East Asia, and Estonia would probably not have been her first choice of destination, but like me she reckoned anywhere was better than nowhere, and when the opportunity for a little adventure came about she had jumped at it. We had met our hosts outside the post office as planned. Olavi had been impossible to miss, a man of Viking stature whose physical superiority was somewhat offset by a fixed look of bewilderment. A thick strawberry blonde beard partially concealed his weather-beaten and ruddy complexion. When Olavi opened his mouth he revealed a set of teeth that wouldn't have looked out of place on an aging horse.

We had arrived in Estonia's second city somewhat fatigued, having crossed Europe in our ageing campervan, Max. Our journey had begun with us hurtling across France, arriving in Munich to be met by a raging blizzard. It was April, so we were both slightly bemused by the extreme conditions.

At some point during a visitor's stay in Munich, all roads will lead to the Hofbräuhaus. It is a magnet for travellers from all over the world – especially popular with antipodeans – over a fourteen-day period in October. This 500-year-old beer hall is allegedly the largest public bar in Europe, if not the world. It has welcomed such luminaries over the years as Paul Theroux and Vladimir Lenin, though probably not at the same time. Legend has it that long ago a certain German princess insisted her ladies-in-waiting go to the Hofbräuhaus for medicinal reasons, as the beer was believed to be necessary in maintaining a healthy constitution. Some of the girls were quite likely to consume up to 7 litres a day! Now, call me old-fashioned, but this being true, when did they find the time to plait the princess's hair?

Despite the venue's popularity with tourists and Germans alike, the day we went the crowds were few; in fact, at first we had an entire 20-foot-long bench to ourselves. By the time our second *Stein* arrived (for the uninitiated, that's an incredibly large beer), we had been joined by Bavarians Gustav and Leopold. Gustav wore an outfit of leather finished by a leather flat cap tilted over one eye, which wouldn't have turned heads if worn on a float during a Gay Pride parade. It didn't turn heads in Bavaria's foremost beer hall, either. Leo, meanwhile, was decked out in an off-the-peg suit and looked like he'd come straight from his job at the Munich municipal council headquarters. Gustav gently tickled a sprig of greying hair that had crept out from under his hat whilst the other rested on a glass of German beer the size of an average waste-paper basket, an image that would stay with us. We found much to guffaw about, and the sound of *Steins* crashing together accompanied by cries of *'Prost!'* could be heard throughout the evening as the benches filled. Encouraged by our companions and the curly-wurly sticks of salted bread we were persuaded to munch on by the ethereally beautiful and very agile waitresses in their dirndls, we consumed far more than what I assume is the recommended number of *Steins*. Come closing time, we stumbled out onto the streets of Munich, pale imitations of the hardy wanderers who had driven into town but a few hours earlier.

That was the last I saw of Jo that night. I reached the Hauptbahnhof – Munich's central station – where we had agreed to meet, and she was nowhere to be seen. I kicked myself a few times before jumping on the last train back to the campsite.

I was woken by Jo the following morning. Having missed the last train, and being in no fit state to convince *die Polizei* patrolling the Hauptbahnhof who she was and indeed what she was, she had been persuaded by the kindly police that it would be best for her to sleep it off in their office.

When Jo had finished making her night on a woven straw mat sound considerably more exciting than I suspected it was, I noticed the snow had gone. It was time to leave Munich.

Next stop was Prague – fast becoming a member of Europe's tourism royalty and for obvious reasons. Enthusiastic stags, who in times gone by were quite happy to catch the train down to Tenby, sink a skinful of mild, then cuff themselves to a lamp post, were nowadays favouring the option of having a shapely Slavic buttock rubbed in their face whilst drinking a skinful of premium Czech lager. Other tourists were drawn to Prague, of course, by the stunning, often fairytale medieval architecture – which, due to a lot of fast talking by a succession of Czech foreign ministers, had remained largely as it was the day it was built some six hundred years ago. Prague was indeed a lovely city and well deserving of its growing status as a tourist gem.

Whilst in a cafe in central Prague, watching an American passing by with a marionette in one hand and a copy of *The Trial* in the other (the obligatory Prague souvenirs), we met a man with lots of grey hair and a beard, who told us he was one of the last remaining Plastic People of the Universe. I later discovered this to be an avant-garde Czech rock band, often cited as the foremost representatives of Prague's underground culture between 1968 and 1988 when they split up, but not before getting arrested for their pro-democracy activities, which helped persuade their playwright friend Václav Havel of the need to enter politics.

The rest, as they say, is history – a history that led to Havel returning the favour and persuading the band to reform in 1997.

A few days later in Kraków, Poland, we watched the national football team lose a World Cup qualifier to Sweden. We'd found a cheap hotel on the outskirts of the town that for a few zloty had let us park Max up in their grounds. This gave us use of their cafe, which was showing the football, and the use of a cold trickle of water they were calling a shower. The next morning we headed to Kraków's centrepiece, the Main Market Square, which at 200 square metres is the largest medieval town square in Europe. It was also the largest town square in Europe to prohibit the entry of unauthorised vehicles. We didn't know this, and had successfully managed one whole circuit and were about to begin our second in search of a parking space when a policeman – who obviously hadn't broken out of a walk since his school days some thirty years since – charged towards us manically waving his arms about. We got the message, and got much pleasure in doing a lap of honour, before hiding Max down a backstreet behind St Mary's Basilica.

We returned to the square on foot to explore the Sukiennice (Cloth Hall), the fading landmark that dominates the square. As its name suggests, it was once a major centre for international trade, with such exotic imports as spices and silk, leather and wax found here. Nowadays, you were more likely to haggle over a pair of prickly socks or a wooden backgammon set. The only haggling we did was with an old lady wearing a Father Christmas hat (it was the middle of April) for a couple of thick woolly jumpers. She drove a hard bargain, but we still managed to walk away with them for less than five English pounds.

After all that excitement on the back of a late night, we needed to do something calm and soothing. So we went to the Gallery of 19th Century Polish Art, found in a small section of the Sukiennice, where we stared in wonderment at a picture called *Czwórka* by Józef Chełmoński. This life-size painting of four horses charging towards you with a cart in tow (the sense of speed was mind-blowing) perfectly captured for me a Poland of years gone by. Both of us sporting our new jumpers, we sat hypnotised by it for some time. By the time we eventually left the gallery, the evening service at the basilica had already begun.

We were just in time to catch the last two days of an 'eco' festival in Warsaw, with lots of tie-dye and sausage, before beginning the climb north through Lithuania and on to Riga. The last night of the journey had been a sleepless one listening to Latvian seagulls dropping excrement onto the plastic pop-up roof.

Unfortunately given our sleep-deprived state, Olavi now led the way out of town, and some 40 kilometres into the countryside, across terrain much more suited to his Japanese 4x4. The destination was Roland's farm. We passed through towering forests of thick conifer punctuated by bald and prickly fields. Roland spoke very little and laughed a lot – this hearty manner suited his rotund frame and rosy cheeks.

Dogs barked in the distance, perhaps wolves in the surrounding woods, and smoke meandered from the chimney of a small wooden hut, where we stopped. Inside, pine beams groaned with the growing warmth as the fire in the oven roared, devouring newly sacrificed logs. The cabin belonged to Roland's laughing brother – he didn't seem to have a name, he was referred to simply as 'the brother of Roland' – and was used by Swedish and Finnish hunters who came in search of boar and elk during the season. As both were out of season we were in luck and able to stay in the vacant cabin. It was only metres from the edge of a forest, close to the sound of a trickling stream.

We had a cluster of neighbours in the hamlet of Pootsi. An old couple lived in the wooden house opposite and they kept themselves to themselves; occasionally I would catch them observing us from behind a window, or from behind a pile of logs. A few farmers acknowledged us with reluctant waves from their tractors. And there was Almo, an elderly man who spoke good English, having spent many years in Bradford. He didn't seem to have a house, but appeared to live a micro-nomadic existence, as we only ever saw him wandering amongst the trees of the nearby forest. On the rare occasion he engaged in chit-chat he was quick to sing the praises of Massey Ferguson and their contribution to farming in his country.

Some 50 metres up the aspen-lined road from our cabin, a Marlboro sign dangled precariously from a tree, as if part of the set for a western. It indicated the local pub, which was no larger than a garden shed yet was something of a Tardis, as inside there was a bar sporting every spirit imaginable and some best not to imagine, and three varieties of Saku beer – strong, stronger and too strong!

Four tables and a collection of stools managed to fit into the claustrophobic space. The gents' was out the back, and comprised a rotting dinghy leaning against a tree. There was no ladies'. This was our local, and well reflected the local community, in size and appetite.

A FEW FACTS ABOUT ESTONIA

- At Saaremaa in the west of the country, you can find the biggest meteorite crater in Europe – legend has it that the huge hole is the sun's grave.

- In Otepää there is a museum devoted entirely to the Estonian flag.

- Traders have been decorating the Christmas tree in the old town square in Tallinn since 1411.

- In October 1996 Scotland were due to play Estonia in a World Cup qualifier in Tallinn, but the Estonian team didn't turn up.

Janis and I understood very little of what each other said, which wasn't really an obstacle as most of his talking was done with his body. I was able to gather that he had a four-year-old son and a young wife, and despite first impressions, when he set his mind to it he was able to handle several metres of thick, very heavy pine trunk with ease. His face carried a weary look, beyond his years. I wasn't surprised. He had experienced things I couldn't even imagine, having grown up in an occupied country in which it was necessary to go back two generations for a glimpse of independence (and even then independence had been fleeting). He had served for two years in the Soviet Army and then lived as a good, hard-working Soviet male, before the revolution came in 1991. Since then he had played his part in rebuilding a nation, a very proud nation whose identity had been stripped from them by Sovietisation.

All three Baltic states were still clawing their way out from beneath the oppressive shadow of Russia, the neighbour from hell still able to wield its often spiteful influence. Six years had now passed since Estonia had gained sovereignty, and she was enjoying the first flush of the free market and all the hope that entailed. Independence hadn't just happened, however, it was the conclusion of a hard-fought battle that had gained momentum in the late eighties. At 7 p.m. on 23 August 1989 around two million impassioned people had joined hands to form a 373-mile human chain. The Baltijos Kelias (Baltic Way) started in Lithuania and continued through Latvia and on into Estonia. It had been triggered by a demonstration marking the fiftieth anniversary of the Molotov–Ribbentrop Pact – responsible for dividing up Eastern Europe between the Nazis and the Soviets, resulting in fifty years of occupation for all three Baltic countries. The human chain was a symbol of the Baltic states' solidarity in their struggle for independence, not to mention a playful way of bringing attention to their pro-democracy stance.

The struggle for Estonian independence reached its zenith with the 'Singing Revolution' – a great source of pride for the northern Europeans. Their old tradition of singing folk songs at any given time, waiting for a bus or in the pub, became a form of political protest, and was used to great effect in building morale and momentum amongst the people prior to the revolution. Crowds regularly gathered to blast out hymns and other verses, as the democracy juggernaut built up speed. Unfortunately for the rest of Europe, this was also the seed for their fanaticism regarding the Eurovision Song Contest and, judging by subsequent Eurovision entries, it had been a canny ploy for getting rid of the Soviets. I'm surprised that Dave Benton, winner of the 2002 Eurovision for Estonia, wasn't unleashed on an unsuspecting Kremlin earlier – how different history might have been.

At the end of that first day Olavi had given me directions to School No. 37. I didn't question why in a town of only eight schools, this one was so-called. Jo wasn't able to work in the timber yard, as physical work involving machinery was apparently not deemed suitable for young English women. Instead, Olavi had promised her another form of employment. Jo was waiting outside the entrance to the school looking quite perplexed. She climbed into the van. Minutes of silence passed before a smile crept onto her face.

'These people are totally weird!' she exclaimed, then with furrowed brow proceeded to tell me about her day. Olavi's wife Seri had arranged for her to do a tour of the local schools. Pärnu had five junior schools, so her remit was to visit one each day for the first week, and if successful she would move onto secondary schools in the second week. Well, that was the plan.

'I was paraded around like a celebrity... or nutter, take your pick. The headmistress dragged me into all the classes and told me to talk about England, then she stood behind me occasionally prompting me with a poke and saying "some history please" or "perhaps some culture". After about an hour there was a question-and-answer session. The kids looked at me as if I were some sort of alien, asking me if I'd met the Queen or if I lived in the same town as the Spice Girls. Then they all wanted me to sign bits of paper for them. One of the form teachers even got a camera out so the class could be photographed with me.'

We both laughed about this, but the truth was that Jo was more than likely the first English person the children of Pärnu had ever met – not surprising, as Olavi had been the first Estonian I'd met. She embodied all that they had to look forward to – the freedom, the wealth of the West, and, of course, girl power. We went back home to the cabin, showered – using water which was pumped into the cabin via a network of rusty, groaning pipes from the nearby stream – fired up the log burner and settled into slightly bemused reflection on our first day in Estonia.

Olavi and his circle of friends were very attentive, and, in their peculiar way, very hospitable and gracious hosts. It became clear that the role of entertaining us was being passed around the group. After a couple of days it was Elo's turn to entertain the foreign guests – and we were to be taken to the beach. Pärnu was proudly labelled Estonia's Summer Capital, a title of which we were constantly reminded. I was looking forward to seeing what all the fuss was about.

I didn't really like the look of Elo on first meeting her. Her deep-set eyes were close together, which gave her a look of constant suspicion. I immediately thought 'informer'... and it stuck. However, Jo had met her before whilst out and about with Seri and Roland's wife, and seemed to get along with her OK. Elo was a middle-aged lady who owned an ironmongery in the town centre. She worked with her husband, who kept the books for the shop and also other businesses in the town. Jo had assured me that Elo was less of an informer and more of a gossip, but nonetheless something of a character. She certainly didn't stop talking for a moment. She was what I would have considered to be a typical Soviet lady – forceful and domineering. Her femininity had been suppressed by Sovietisation, and as she constantly reminded us, she was an 'independent woman'.

A FEW WORDS ON THE SOVIET WOMAN

Article 35 of the Soviet Constitution clearly states that women and men 'have equal rights': equal access to education, training, employment, promotion and remuneration, plus all participation in social, political and cultural activities. In the 1980s, women made up over half the workforce. However, in 1983 women only made up 27.6 per cent of the Communist Party, and only 4.2 per cent of the Central Committee. It was women who were seen clearing the roads of slush and snow – with a work ethic that would put most ants to shame – whilst the blokes played at being good communists.

Our feet melted into the fine white sand as we trudged along Pärnu's chief asset. The beach was indeed beautiful, riding up into the tree-sheltered dunes on the edge of the town and rolling down into clear blue sea, an image befitting any seaside holiday brochure. However, the neglected climbing frames and corroded metal seats attached to cracked concrete bases we passed were probably best left out of said brochure – unless it was peddling beach holidays for Soviet nostalgia buffs.

'In Soviet times,' said Elo, 'you had to wear clothes on the beach and if you went to the shop, you for sure had to wear clothes.' She laughed with a melancholy shudder at her joke. I thought of a picture of Kenneth Williams wearing a three-piece suit on the beach in Tangier. This image was fast replaced by the reality of Elo's words, a haunting image, made more so by the beauty of the place we were walking in. A beach was no place for rules. Elo seemed to have been taken away in a capsule of memories. Her face was suddenly less threatening. Looking around, the beach was empty, although it was a pleasant evening in April. Elo read my mind: 'The beach had to be cleared for official use by five o'clock.' Old habits die hard.

Jo was incredulous. 'People weren't able to come here in the evening?'

'People did, of course, but it was not officially permitted until after 1991. There were events here, often, which all people could attend.'

We continued walking out to sea along a narrow natural jetty made of rocks and seemingly running to the horizon. Elo walked a few metres behind us, as if giving us time to appreciate the beauty of our surroundings. But I was finding it harder and harder to see the beauty, and when we eventually turned back towards the beach, I found myself relieved, just wanting to be alone with Jo – with every minute the mood had become more sombre, in keeping with Elo's increasingly gloomy narrative.

We wandered back to the centre of Pärnu, down enchanting streets lined by wooden slat buildings of green, yellow, burgundy and brown. The town was undeniably charming, yet somehow cold, lacking spirit, and lacking people too. Lush greenery filled the parks, splashes of colour provided by daffodils, violets and daisies.

A statue of the town's greatest poetess held pride of place in one such park: Lydia Koidula, who had left a substantial body of work close to most Estonian hearts. We passed by St Catherine's, an ornate green and white church, strikingly Russian with its dazzling golden cupolas. The occasional yelp from a drunk reminded us that we weren't in a fairytale, and it was a breath of fresh air to see a young guy with an angry Mohican wearing insurgent boots laced up to his knees.

Elo led us up a spiral staircase into a dimly lit restaurant, empty except for the glum waitress who hovered impatiently whilst we sat down.

'We will now have some traditional Estonian coffee.'

I wasn't quite sure what Elo meant but it fast became clear she simply meant 'bad' coffee. As we sipped hesitantly, Elo seemed to sense that she should be highlighting Estonia's present and not dwelling morbidly on its Soviet past. This didn't come easily for her: 'Lydia was our greatest and favourite woman. Her life was short and tragic.'

No surprise there. Jo managed to turn a giggle into a choke.

'She wrote about nature and her love for nature, but she died when she was only sixteen, after falling from a horse.'

Later research revealed she died from cancer when forty-three, which led me to believe Elo wanted to make Pärnu's greatest woman seem even more tragic – as if being struck down by cancer in her middle age wasn't tragic enough. I remained unsure of Elo's motive, but our guide certainly seemed to thrive on woe-mongery. In any case, Pärnu's choice of favourite daughter, regardless of age of death, seemed to reflect the place perfectly. The light in the restaurant appeared to be getting dimmer as Elo spoke, her face across the table soon reduced to a silhouette. It was time to go.

Arriving at the yard one grey and overcast morning later in the week, the smell of damp wood filling the moist air, I passed Janis heading off in a forklift, cigarette in mouth, with a look of desperation on his face. I spent the morning shredding wood in the sawmill before being introduced to the 'green monster' – a superior shredder, used to dispose of all junk wood in the yard. Its product was bagged up and sold as fuel to a local power station. Olavi had only recently been able to afford the machine, so they had been renting a second-rate equivalent, which simply hadn't been able to keep up with demand. This had resulted in piles of junk wood rising uncontrollably, blotting out much of the surrounding skyline. I started working with two hardy Russian men, who brought to the job the traditional Soviet work strategy: half an hour on, half an hour off.

They worked for thirty minutes then took a coffee break, joining a constant stream of men coming and going from the yard, which made it difficult to concentrate on any work. It wasn't until maybe the fifth break that I was given the nod to join a small group, and was led conspiratorially to the staff room located in a concrete building hidden away at the back of the yard. The room was jammed, faces distorted by a haze of smoke as men were packed in like sardines. If that was what they put themselves through during their breaks, I would sooner be working, and it was with great relief that I got the nod to return to work.

On the second day working with the green monster, one of my Russian comrades was sacked. I never gathered the reason why; when I asked about him his mate simply ran a finger across his neck. He was replaced by a fresh-faced young Estonian who went slightly easier on the breaks, and whose eagerness to work was only matched by his enthusiasm for swigging beer all day. The remaining Russian was no fool and just sat back and let me and the new boy do all the work. By the end of the week we had cleared up most of the yard, and I thought I had certainly earned my weekly wage of 500 kroons – about 40 pence an hour. Meanwhile Jo had completed her tour of Pärnu junior schools and seemed to be enjoying her new-found celebrity status, which was just as well, for when she received her brown envelope, she realised that at 600 kroons for the week, Estonian celebs were never going to get rich.

As the second week progressed, the initial interest in me from my fellow workers turned to suspicion. One week was a novelty, a bit of fun for me and something for them to talk about. But why was I still there? The yard was now pretty much clear of the junk wood and it was hard to see what work there would actually be for me to do when the spring clean was finished. I was beginning to have motivation issues myself; it was always at the back of my mind that I was getting out of bed for £3.20 a day. The gainful employment I had invested with so many hopes and possibilities was fast turning into, at best, ungainful employment and, at worst, not far off slave labour. I also had a growing feeling that my fellow workers thought I was patronising them by being there voluntarily.

It was half past eight in the morning and the sun was already generating a burning heat, not unusual for the end of April. Children were walking past the perimeter of the yard on their way to school proudly sporting baseball caps. We had been working on the green monster for only half an hour, but my two comrades had slowed right down, drawing the work out, and I sensed that they too had realised that there might well be no more work when we were done. Unlike me, if there was no work they would have to leave – which meant making no money. At that moment fate intervened and with a coughing and spluttering, the grating roar of the monster ceased, replaced by distant sounds caught on the breeze.

My two friends muttered something before sitting down and lighting up. Within moments a group had gathered around the unconscious beast. Men were appearing from nowhere, having quickly caught on that there was a bona fide time-wasting opportunity in the offing. I looked on as cigarettes were passed around, along with various diagnoses.

One of the men, his new blue overalls giving him an air of some importance, eventually stepped forward and began fiddling with the monster's undercarriage. He was fast to conclude: '*Kaput.*'

For the next hour members of the assembled group took it in turns to make an assessment of the ailing wood shredder. It could have gone on for much longer as the group was definitely growing in size; however, it was Janis who took the decision to inform the suits upstairs of the problem, and soon no less than Olavi himself made an appearance. He was closely shadowed by another smartly dressed man, with the look of an accountant about him – wiry physique, and matching wiry spectacles perched on the end of his nose. Since being at the yard I had seen him around and about and he had always had a warm smile for me.

Whilst Olavi was taking control of the situation, I had found a log to sit on, taken a piece of paper from my pocket and begun to write. The bespectacled man, obviously having decided he had little if any contribution to make, made his way over and sat down next to me. He introduced himself as Yens and proffered a skeletal hand to shake.

'What are you writing?' he asked.

His directness surprised me, so I replied as a joke, 'I am writing bad things about Estonia in a letter home.'

He looked put out and became defensive. 'I sorry, no you must not,' he said, without a hint of irony. I was quick to reassure him, 'I'm not really.'

His body language was strong yet shy at the same time, his English wasn't good, and whatever he did say was turned into an apology. He looked on at the green monster.

'I sorry, this is not good, it cost us much money.'

Perhaps he was indeed the accountant.

'What is your job here?' I asked, slightly concerned that I would receive a prickly response. He simply replied, 'I work,' accompanied with a deep sigh. I thought it was probably best not to ask any more questions as Yens apparently had other things on his mind. Or maybe conversation was awkward due to a lack of language, as a few minutes later he turned and said, 'I sorry, I not so good, but play basketball.' This brought a smile to his face and began a pidgin-English conversation. What came out was that Yens was exactly the same age as me, having been born on the same day in 1971. So there we were, two people sitting on a piece of wood in a timber yard, having grown up in completely different worlds, living completely different lives, but having been given the same time in history in which to do so. The bond I had with this man was probably greater than I knew, certainly greater than Yens knew or cared – as the discovery provoked no more than a barely audible grunt.

Our talking was interrupted by Olavi raising his voice above the chatter from the group. I don't know what he said, but it had Yens jumping to his feet and the rest of the group slowly dispersing – back to whatever they had been doing several hours earlier. Olavi came over to my log and merely said, 'It's dead,' with an expression that suggested he spoke of his new-born baby, rather than a wood shredder, before walking back towards his office with Yens closely behind him.

We had been in Pärnu nearly three weeks and the longer we stayed the harder it became. Our circle of hosts had done all they believed they should do as such but we sensed that our novelty had gradually become an annoyance. After Jo's second week of celebrity her appearances had dried up and I was pretty much just standing around the yard all day like a spare part, hoping that someone would ask me to do something – which didn't happen. I had even given up collecting any money at the end of the week – it didn't feel right. I had begun to ask the same question that everyone else at the yard must have been asking, from Janis to Olavi… What was I doing there?

The truth was we were both still there because we simply weren't yet ready to face the inevitable, the crushing disappointment of what was staring us in the face… that 'things just weren't working out'. The taunting voices in my head from people back home who had asked, 'But why Estonia?' or even worse, 'Where is Estonia?' started to get louder. Our expectations of the complete unknown had simply been too high. Neither of us had made any contingency plans. Neither of us had a Plan B, hence our reluctance at letting go of Plan A. We had invested heart and soul and some into this new start. It was nobody's fault, it simply wasn't the dream we'd both signed up for; that is, having jobs that would enable us to save some money in a part of the world that accepted us and didn't look upon us as curiosities. We had failed on all of the above.

I still felt an obligation to Uncle Tony. I couldn't help but feel like something of an ambassador for him after he had organised the job, as he couldn't have known what it would be like. He had been running a timber yard and manufacturing wood products for decades back in the UK.

His business was solid and safe, and possibly in reaction to that security he had cultivated an enthusiasm in his dealings with his new 'friends'. He was a risk taker by nature and a gambler at heart, and his advances into the ex-Soviet zone had been purely opportunistic.

Straight after the collapse of the Soviet Union, the old party hierarchy and factory chiefs had begun privatising the organisations they controlled; by the mid nineties over 60 per cent of all state enterprises had been privatised. These 'bosses' channelled raw materials and money out of Russia and into private banks – not illegally, as there was no law to prevent it at the time. It is believed that an average of one billion dollars left Russia in this way every month during the nineties.

Whilst this was going on, the ex-Soviet zone was awash with Western experts preaching the Western model – which was still highly regarded – and tapping into business opportunities when they appeared. I think secretly Tony liked being part of that 'anything goes' wild East, especially as it was making him money and he could bail out as and when.

I had known that Tony would make a visit at some point, I had just hoped under different circumstances. Seeing Olavi bounding along shoulder to shoulder with Tony somehow made me feel even guiltier about telling him that we would be returning home. I had never really associated Olavi and his timber yard in Estonia with Tony, the man at the kitchen table back in England. For the first time Olavi appeared submissive in the company of the booming Englishman, who was decked out in a garish brown and orange check suit, his trousers tucked into his socks, which in turn disappeared into a pair of patent brogues that possessed a flipper-like quality – as if Tony was bounding up the beach having spent the morning snorkelling.

Jo had as yet not met Tony so introductions were necessary, which left me witnessing a 'Monty meeting I' type moment from *Withnail and I*. Tony breathed down on Jo's diminutive frame, invading far too much of her personal space – made more uncomfortable by Tony's very obvious interest in Jo's chest. My laboured response to Tony's initial enquiries about how things were going quickly produced a questioning look. Having deduced that I was holding back in front of Olavi, a drink was suggested.

'So where's the local hostelry? I'm parched!' Tony barked, and we all simultaneously looked over to the Marlboro sign just visible through the trees. Olavi led the way with Jo, and I dropped back with Uncle Tony.

'What's the problem?' Tony instinctively began.

Tentatively I responded, 'Look, everyone's been really good to us, it's just not what we expected – we're going to have to come home.'

'Anything I can do?' Before I could answer, a warm smile came over his features and he continued. 'Look, don't worry about a thing, you do what you have to do. The truth is, I've never spent more than a couple of days here – I fly in, get drunk with Olavi, say all the right things and probably plenty of the wrong ones, toast his family a hundred times and fly out.'

I was off the hook – and now I felt even worse. It looked like we were on our way back home. All I could think of was egg and cress sandwiches and a bike with a crooked axle.

We joined Jo and Olavi at the tiny pub. There was just enough room for Almo, who soon came to meet us. After two Sakus' worth of hearty small talk we left Pootsi's pub and headed into Pärnu for some dinner. Olavi led us down some uneven stone steps into a dimly lit cellar restaurant just off the town's central park. The stone walls were adorned by skins and antlers on which hung tankards of pewter and, surprisingly, wood. Heavy wooden tables – gnarled and distressed, yet more attractive for it – added to an atmosphere that led us back several centuries. Perhaps the Tardis back in Pootsi had time-travelling qualities after all. The most mouth-watering aromas of roasting pig wafted in from the open-plan kitchen area, where a bandana-ed chef was hard at it. Estonian dining at the time was a long way from haute cuisine but if meat and potatoes were your thing, disappointment wasn't likely. Which was the case for us all – with the exception of Jo, who had recently become a vegetarian. Her timing was bad. As we were fast discovering, the ex-Soviet Union was no place for humane sentiments in the kitchen – 'vegetarian friendly' still had a long way to go. So when the rest of us sat back stuffed and thinking about coffee, Jo was still glancing through the menu hungrily.

Coffee arrived at our table just as Tony cleared his throat. 'I'm afraid, Olavi, I'm going to have to take these two off your hands.' His eyes passed over me and Jo. Olavi said nothing, simply nodded his head. Not even an 'oh, that's a pity'. He genuinely appeared not to care. (What it is to be wanted...) Tony continued, 'I've got a business partner in

41

Vladivostok, who I need them to visit.' I had only caught the name Vladivostok, as egg and cress sandwiches drifted back into my grey matter. Getting no reaction, Tony turned up the volume: 'How does that sound to you two?'

I re-engaged. 'What – how does what sound?'

'Taking that old rust bucket of yours to Vladivostok.'

CHAPTER TWO
TALLINN

The sun sat high in the sky, reflecting off the many puddles left by the previous night's storm that patterned the road north. We shared the short drive to Estonia's pocket-sized capital with a light breeze that joined us from the looming coastline. Effervescing with anticipation for the exploration that lay ahead, having eagerly and thus unevenly parked up, we were drawn towards Tallinn's old town, signs of which peeped out from behind its protective medieval wall.

Quickly lost in its network of winding cobbled streets, eventually we emerged onto Pikk Jalg, a narrow road that cuts through the city's historical heart. The cobbles of Pikk Jalg, which translates as 'long leg', would have been traversed by German and Danish merchants using the town to trade goods from Scandinavia as far back as the fourteenth century. The street runs from the lower part of the town up to Toompea, a limestone outcrop which looks out over the rooftops below. Toompea started life as a wooden fort before the Danes captured it and built a more substantial castle in the thirteenth century. The castle is still there, along with the invitingly pink hue of the Riigikogu – the Estonian parliament. *The Book of Cities* says that Toompea 'represents less than one per cent of Tallinn's area but possesses all its charm', which is a bit unfair as there was plenty of charm to be found all over the city. It also says that Tallinn is 'the most beautiful German city in the world'. In appearance at least, it was hard to argue with this. With the old town's plethora of spires, steeples, turrets and Hanseatic town houses it could have been plucked straight out of Bavaria.

Once our cursory investigations were complete, and we concluded that we had probably exhausted much of the town's sightseeing potential in only a couple of hours, we settled into a car park a skip and a jump from the old town, behind a newly built Statoil twenty-four-hour garage. It was a location where we thought we wouldn't draw too much attention to ourselves, overshadowed by articulated trucks, and insignificant below the cranes that decorated the nearby docks. Tram tracks close by provided a pleasant soundtrack as trams clattered past. From our vantage point in the car park we were able to see the ferries coming and going to Helsinki and Stockholm. The Tallink line regularly delivered Finnish booze cruisers travelling to Estonia for cheap shopping and drinking. Booze was cheaper in Estonia than Finland, and even cheaper on the ferry. Many Finns didn't bother or were simply too drunk to go ashore, while those who did could be seen trudging unsteadily, weighed down with spoils, between the docks and the town like a battle-worn army in retreat. The best thing about the

Statoil car park was that we were anonymous again, like the Scandinavian truckers who frequented it. Beholden to nobody.

TWO ESTONIAN PROVERBS

- Beauty does not fill your tummy.
- Make fun of the man, not of his hat.

We didn't plan a particularly long sojourn in Tallinn. The truth was, we were only really still in Estonia because of Uncle Tony, in a somewhat misguided belief that to remain in the country for a little longer was something of a debt that had to be paid. For better or for worse we were driving to Vladivostok – well, in the direction of Vladivostok, for neither of us was entirely convinced at that point whether we'd reach the Estonia–Russia border, let alone get to the Far East. Tony's suggestion had bought us some more time away from England, and a rather fragile plan had been conceived around it. Tony had worked with Nikolai from Vladivostok in the capacity of consultant – helping Nikolai set up his timber business.

'Delightful man, you'll get on like a house on fire!' Um, now where had I heard a similar sentiment...?

'OK. So why do we want to go all that way to visit Nikolai?'

'Because he should be able to give you both some work.' Tony paused, realising the thin credibility of this statement, before continuing with the customary glint in his eyes.

'And you'll have a bloody good time getting there! I'll call ahead and let Nikolai know you're coming – once you're there I'm sure he'll find you something to do.'

Jo listened with a 'here we go again' expression. I was inclined to agree but the desire not to return home with my tail between my legs had now become so strong, I would probably have driven pretty much anywhere on such flimsy intelligence...

'And look, if it doesn't work out you can always pop across to Japan – teach some English or something,' Tony added with satisfaction. Japan was in fact a forty-eight-hour ferry crossing from Vladivostok. However, the nonchalance in which he managed to neatly wrap his suggestion and the confidence with which it was dispatched were entirely infectious. He made it sound so simple. We *hop* across to the Russian Far East, and if no joy with work there, then we simply *pop* over to Japan! As unlikely as this all sounded, the fact that it was somebody else's idea and not mine somehow made it more plausible, and we had already been carried by it as far as Tallinn.

There was a more immediate complication blocking our road to Russia, and that would have to be resolved in Tallinn. To enter the Russian Federation we would need visas. As a tourist, one of the delights of the ever swelling European Union was that as a member you had an ever expanding area in which to freely drive your campervan. In theory it was possible to glide over borders that until recently would have involved much paperwork, time and patience to cross. Time and patience still figured in the trans-Eastern-Europe equation but all the paperwork had been consigned to the dustbin of history. Nowadays, it was quite possible to bowl up to the checkpoint, flash your passport, and be happily on your way. Driving into Russia, however, was a different story and one that involved the above three factors in abundance.

I soon decided that getting visas took precedence over marvelling at how many bottles of hard liquor the average Finn could squeeze into a plastic bag, so I went in search of the Russian Embassy. If it's not stating the obvious, Russian embassies differ the world over. Organised travellers planning to travel to Russia whilst resting in Prague might well go to Warsaw with the purpose of procuring the services of an altogether more efficient and reliable visa section. Even back in the UK it is widely believed that posting your application to the consulate in Edinburgh is a much more astute practice than so much as driving past the oak-panelled door of the consulate on the Bayswater Road. In the same way, the good people at the consulate in Helsinki are held in relatively high regard. Something you're not likely to overhear in the common room of the Travellers Guesthouse in Moscow is 'Get your Russian visa in Tallinn – I'd never go anywhere else!'

The embassy, located down a leafy street in the new part of town behind the imposing Hotel Viru, was on first impression quite user-friendly. A young man wearing a grey uniform, the jacket of which ended just short of his waist, lending him the appearance of a rather insipid bull fighter, greeted me with a warm smile then directed me to a small window counter, behind which sat a well-presented young lady with grey, shoulder-length hair. Her face was somehow too young for her to have naturally greying hair, yet it suited her.

'I'd like to get a Russian visa.'

'OK,' she said, producing a form from beneath the counter.

'I need two, please.'

She looked about for signs that I wasn't suffering from multiple personality disorder. Finding none she smiled sympathetically and produced another form.

'Complete these then return with your passports and photographs. Thank you.'

'How long will it take?'

'Five days perhaps!'

'How much will it cost?'

'Twenty dollars each.'

Well, that was easy enough.

My optimism regarding the smooth procurement of visas was, however, misguided. It would have been more rational to back Estonia's chances of winning the World Cup. But for a short time anyway I was able to enjoy the sense of belief I had allowed to be instilled in me. I dropped our completed forms into the embassy resplendent with mug shots the following day, paid up and left, pleasantly satisfied with the apparent ease of a process I had convinced myself would evoke comparisons with something written by Kafka.

With the visa wheels in motion, we had five days to fill. Jo and I agreed that rather than waste time and money in a futile attempt to suppress the boredom, we should really be trying to make some money. To this end we flexed our entrepreneurial muscles and, a few bottles of Saku later, a plan was in place. Jo would put on day trips for tourists to Lahemaa National Park. She would drive people the seventy or so kilometres out to the park, provide them with a lavish packed lunch, show them around a stately home, and then return them to Tallinn. The house in question was to be the recently restored Palmse Manor dating back to the eighteenth century, once home to the von der Pahlen family. Intelligence revealed that it was complete with a park full of rare old trees, a lake with swans and a visitors' centre in the stables – enough to get any self-respecting day tripper's mouth watering. If that wasn't enough, a few kilometres down the road apparently a museum could be found sporting a collection of chainsaws and hunting rifles. With the right marketing she would be able to put on at least four tours by the end of the week. Max Tours was born.

It's easy to say Jo did it first, but I'm pretty sure she did. Lahemaa National Park is now day trip champion's league for the Tallinn tourist board. Fleets of Mercedes Vitos plough the route, bulging with tourists. So what's all the fuss about? Well, with a small country such as Estonia, you have to make the most of what you've got.

It is arguably 700 square kilometres of the most beautiful scenery to be found in the country. The region became the Soviet Union's first national park in 1971, to protect the impressive north Estonian landscapes and the area's heritage. Lahemaa translates as the 'land of bays', and is distinctive with its four peninsulas jutting out into the Baltic Sea – Juminda, Pärispea, Käsmu and Vergi – all with long sandy beaches. Further inland the forests of Lahemaa are home to much wildlife including moose, brown bears and wolves – more than enough to satisfy the visiting naturalist.

In order to get some punters for 'Max Tours', Jo put a small advert, with space for signing up, in the tourist information bureau in the old town square. When the day for the first scheduled tour came about, two names had found their way onto the list. I'm not exactly sure how events followed the course they did; however, it must be said that the preceding evening was spent in Diesel Boots, a Tex-Mex in the old town that did a mean margarita…

I was woken to Jo bellowing in my ear, 'Time to get up, I need the van!' The lines that dictated at what times Max stopped being a bedroom and became a tour bus were still a bit blurred – at that moment he was very much my bedroom.

'I can't move.'

Jo came back with even more energy in her voice.

'OK, don't move, I've got an idea – you can come on the trip.'

'Won't that just look daft?' I grumbled.

'Not if you pretend that you don't know me.'

And so I arrived at Hotel Viru at the appointed time, my head full of splinters. There was no sign of Jo but two others waited impatiently at the meeting place. Keith introduced himself with a firm handshake, Jilco with a soft one, both from Japan.

'You here for the tour?' Keith asked with an American twang. 'You're twenty minutes late, but you're OK because so is the guide.'

What a relief, I thought.

After a few minutes of stilted conversation, my hangover getting the better of common civility, the guide made an appearance.

'Hi, I'm Jo, sorry I'm late.'

She looked at Keith to divine the same information.

'Hi, I'm Keith from Japan via the States.'

'I am Jilco, also from Japan,' said Jilco, disconnecting herself from a pedometer. Then it was my turn. Jo looked at me without any hint of farce. I considered for a second the implications of just walking away from the situation and regaining normality in a cafe round the corner, but Jo had a serious expression on her face that suggested forgiveness wouldn't come readily.

'Thom, England,' I blurted out.

From that moment I was in character, one that needed very little work. I was a bolshy git from Blighty, who cared very little for national parks and even less for Estonia.

We all piled into Max and headed north-east along the Narva Highway. Keith took the front seat and entered into enthusiastic conversation with Jo, whilst in the back I had the benefits of measuring your footsteps explained to me by Jilco. This didn't last very long, so we found ourselves listening to the chatter in the front.

'I am now twenty-five and must return to marry in Japan,' Keith was saying. 'And I will work for my father, this is the way it is in Japan, but it won't be easy as I've been in the States for five years now working for my uncle.' Keith noticed that I was listening.

'Hey Thom,' he shouted, 'what about you – what brings you here?'

I instinctively looked at Jo, but got no response – I was definitely on my own.

'Oh, you know, just having a short holiday.' Keith's eyes insisted that I continue. So I did, 'I've left my wife behind at the hotel, she's not very well today. We're chemists, interested in the effects of acid rain on Hanseatic architecture...' and on I went. The more I said the easier it got. I continued until Keith's face signalled that he had heard enough and was quite keen to carry on talking about himself.

By the time we arrived at the park the temperature was well into the thirties. We pulled up into a small opening in the forest.

'OK guys, if you follow that pathway, it leads you along an ornamental track. There's some great flora and fauna to see – keep your eyes out for elk and wild boar. I'll meet you at the other end. It should take you an hour or two.'

Jo failed to mention it would be possibly the longest hour or two of my life.

The ornamental track (a glorified name for a barely noticeable path through trees and bushes) certainly traversed some beautiful woodland, though it was hard to tell due to the persistent clouds of mosquitoes that smothered us all the way – quite an international showing of fresh blood. If that wasn't bad enough, Keith insisted on darting off into the undergrowth every few minutes and surprising us with missiles of varying shapes and textures – why was anyone's guess; perhaps the untamed surroundings were responsible for bringing out his inner warrior. He often underestimated the power of the damp mud bombs which he launched in our direction – one such bomb actually brought Jilco to her knees. Eventually the mozzies cleared off and Keith tired of running about, so we had the chance to look out for all the wildlife we'd been promised. But the only creature I heard during the walk was the great crested moaner. The moment Keith stopped throwing mud about he became hungry – and did we hear about it! For the remainder of the walk there was a litany of, 'Do you think it's much further, I'm starving...' In over an hour there was time for much repetition. So it was with more than a little relief I spied Max waiting in the distance, Jo with her feet up close by.

As time went on I was fast gaining the impression that I was bugging the hell out of Keith, which I suppose was only fair as he was certainly bugging the hell out of me. With his tight trousers, leather jacket and long hair, I sensed that a boring scientist from England was simply not rock 'n' roll enough for him. Furthermore, as the day progressed and I became more and more prickly towards Jo, half deliberately, Keith picked up on it. His natural Japanese sense of honour meant that he had to step in and defend her against me. At one point after I had mumbled my disdain for Jo's enthusiasm regarding German sausage sandwiches, Keith had suggested I 'take it easy'. Meanwhile, as the day wore on, Jo was becoming more and more irritated by Keith, her champion. So convincing must have been our performance that at one point Keith actually said, 'At least after today you won't have to see each other again.'

On the way back from the park, after a visit to the Palmse Manor house that had taken all of ten minutes due to most of it being closed for restoration, and not a swan to be seen, I exchanged places with Keith and found myself in the front of the van. Thankfully, very soon Jilco and Keith were totally engrossed by one another.

Jo sprang a badly needed treat on us by stopping at the historical seaside village of Käsmu. The village was all wooden slat houses in pastel shades attached to neat little gardens. A little church and village school sat side by side, the icy blue of the Baltic their backdrop. Käsmu was built in the early nineteenth century and quickly became known as the 'millionaires' village', such were the profits being made from salt smuggling. In the 1920s, nearby Finland attempted to impose prohibition on its population. So, seizing the chance to make money from a desperate Finnish populace, Käsmu's smuggling shifted from salt to alcohol. When in 1932 Finland gave up on the prohibition idea, Käsmu was to suffer considerably, such had become its reliance on the alcohol-smuggling revenue. However, smuggling in one form or another continued – in 1940, it was people that were smuggled out of Estonia in readiness for the Soviet occupation. In the post-Soviet Käsmu, businessmen from Tallinn and other Baltic cities were buying up former 'captains' houses', which was returning some prosperity to the village and surrounding area.

The most impressive building in Käsmu was the centrally located Maritime Museum, previously the navigation college and then later the coastguard station during the Soviet period. The museum had no entry fee and was always open. The owner, Arne Vaik, a long man with a greying bob straight out of the Middle Ages, had spent twenty years collecting material in secret – at a time when there was little if any chance of displaying any of it. Arne chatted with us as we marvelled over his hand-carved canoes and other bits of seafaring memorabilia, claiming to have the largest collection of wooden rudders anywhere in the world. I certainly wasn't going to argue with that.

Beside the church was the Baron Bellinghausen memorial – unique in that it was built by the man himself in order to feign his own death. The baron had been implicated in a failed plot to kill Tsar Alexander II in 1881 (an increasingly unpopular institution in nineteenth-century Russia, the tsar was successfully blown up later the same year), and as a result he fled to Germany, but not before erecting the memorial in order to shake off any police on his trail. It didn't take long for his cover to be foiled, yet he still managed to elude the police for the rest of his life, eventually dying of natural causes in Germany.

We all left Käsmu glad of the unscheduled stop. Even I was really starting to enjoy myself. The fresh sea air had cleared my head and I was genuinely impressed by the day trip Jo had stitched together. Keith no longer seemed to care what was going on between me and Jo; Jilco had become the only person on the trip for Keith. They had drifted about Käsmu as if advertising match.com, and for the rest of the drive back to Tallinn all we heard was the sound of their whispers. Who knows – perhaps Max Tours had been responsible for getting Keith hitched.

I returned to the embassy at the end of the week, confident that I'd soon be able to flash Jo a splendid new visa and break the news that we were finally getting out of Estonia that evening. The young guy in the short jacket never gave anything away – he looked at me as if he'd won the lottery, and I suppose with his job, compared to many of his countrymen, he had. But I knew it would be a different story the moment I set eyes on the lady behind the glass.

'Ah yes, you want your visas.'

'Yes,' I confirmed, going over all the other possible reasons that I might be there in my head.

'One moment – I make one call.' She picked up a phone, dialled a number, pressed the receiver to her ear for some moments, said nothing and replaced the receiver.

'Your visas are not ready yet – perhaps Monday, I think.' It was Friday – she didn't fill me with confidence but she had only ever said 'perhaps' they would be ready in five days; perhaps this had been wishful thinking by both of us. I did, however, consider for the first time how often Russians used the word 'perhaps' when speaking in English.

I went back on Monday and the young guy enthusiastically shook my hand this time. The girl with the grey hair now had red hair that was also considerably shorter. She clenched her teeth and shrugged her shoulders. 'Sorry.'

I decided to leave it a few days before going back again. Jo now had Max 'Dating' Tours to keep her entertained – after the success of her debut she had since done two more trips up to Lahemaa, and had bookings for a fourth. Since my own debut there had been no further requests to make up the numbers, and not wanting to cramp Jo's entrepreneurial style I took myself off to investigate Tallinn's more conventional job market. My first port of call was a hotel located in the old town square called 'Eestitall' which translated as donkey stable – a function the building had once held. On enquiring about the possibility of some temporary employment, I was directed to the restaurant manager, a camp, unhealthily thin Estonian man called Titte. A glass of cognac in one hand

and a cigar in the other, Titte had enthusiastically welcomed me into his poky office. This space he shared with a pale-skinned, nervous-looking Finn called Suzanna, whose main responsibility was the management of the hotel's garden terrace cafe, soon to open for the summer season. Suzanna had an obsession and that was France and all things French. Her plan was to give the terrace a French theme that year; she wanted to deck it out in a style that persuaded guests they were in fact drinking their coffee in the heart of Paris. On discovering that I was English, Titte and Suzanna believed I was the ideal person to get the place up and running, possessing that Western sophistication that as yet hadn't reached their corner of Eastern Europe. I got a little caught up in the moment and, distracted by their gushing enthusiasm, not to mention flattery, I didn't quite manage to tell them that I only planned to be around for a few days or that my knowledge of drinking coffee in Paris was probably considerably smaller than theirs. After a couple more cognacs, Titte seemed convinced that he had his man.

I set to work, and having quietly ignored Titte's suggestion that I wear a string of onions around my neck, I managed to persuade the Toompea accordion player to provide some gentle atmospheric melodies in the background. OK, he was Russian not French, but he did wear a tatty beret, and who was to know that he hadn't been lured from the cafes of Montmartre? The promise of a free lunch had been all that was necessary to secure his services.

For the three brief days that I spent on the terrace, customers were slow to pick up on the delights of the cafe. Yuri the accordion player was punctual, however, arriving at midday on the dot. He headed straight for the kitchen from where he would re-emerge with a tray laden with food. Having savoured every mouthful he reluctantly hitched up his instrument and began a set of sufficiently jaunty melodies that, to the untrained ear, sounded as French as they were indeed Russian. My assistant on the terrace was Kenny, a fifteen-year-old boy who had recently finished school. His great passions in life were beer, The Prodigy, juggling (or trying to) and English swear words. So whilst Yuri pumped out his tunes we worked together juggling lemons, listening to The Prodigy and practising English swear words on the few unsuspecting punters that trickled onto the terrace – much to Kenny's delight.

By my third day, however, Yuri was not alone on his stage, having been joined by just about every drunk who made Tallinn their home. The vodka flowed, the gathering was raucous, overshadowing any hint of sophistication that might have previously existed. Yuri himself was soon very drunk and his set fast declined from simple Russian folk songs into morose Russian folk songs. The Russian heart unfortunately left very little room for the French one. It was about time that I returned to the business of visa acquisition anyway, so it was with some relief that Titte appeared and squarely sacked Yuri. With my second Oscar-winning performance in so many weeks, I informed Titte that I would have to accept all the responsibility for the chaos, and had no alternative than to give him my reluctant resignation.

I returned to the embassy, my optimism restored, as it had been now well over two weeks since the applications went in. I'm sure that anyone who ever tried to get a visa for a country on the axis of evil will be smugly thinking, 'That's nothing, mate.' However, this was my first trip along the rocky and heavily cratered road that is Russian bureaucracy for foreigners.

I had started to look forward to my regular dose of effusively warm smiles from the guy at the embassy door, which went some way to compensating for all the gloomy faces about town. But when I turned up this time he had been replaced by a new man who simply eyed me up and down with an ice-cold gaze.

I shuffled quickly past him, and thought I saw the receptionist trying to hide below her counter. Too slow, she muddled about before resuming her position, then looked at me with a blank expression suggesting she had no idea who I was. I timidly asked, 'Any luck with the visas?', trying to be as nonchalant as I could, when really I could have quite easily throttled someone.

'Your passports.' She handed them across to me impassively. My immediate reaction was to search for the visas inside. As I did she continued, 'We can not make your visa, only the consulate can make your visa.'

I took a moment to consider what she was telling me.

'So where is this, if it's not the consulate?' I tried to remain calm.

'This is the Russian Embassy, you must go to Russian Consulate.'

She whipped out a photocopied map and handed it to me.

'But you… you… you… said…' The truth was she hadn't said very much – only 'perhaps' quite a lot. In the last two weeks we'd got absolutely nowhere, except for several return trips to Lahemaa National Park. She on the other hand had changed the colour of her hair and taken forty quid off me.

As I left the embassy, scrutinising the map I'd been given with something verging on hatred, I quite literally bumped into Colin. I hadn't met him before, but his accent gave his Scottish roots away and he was quick to reveal that he was in town extending his visa before returning to work in Moscow. After I had told him about my frustrations with the embassy, Colin calmly said, 'There is a simple way of getting a visa.' He wrote down the address of a travel agent in the old town. 'They'll do it all for you, you won't have to set foot within a mile of any Russian embassies.' I thanked him enthusiastically, slightly curious as to why he had himself set foot within a mile of the embassy, and armed with the address and bucketloads of doubt I headed directly for the old town. Once there and in the capable hands of the beautiful Lilya, I paid out roughly four times over the odds – worth every penny – and within a couple of hours our Russian visas were in place.

CHAPTER THREE
ST PETERSBURG

'Petersburg is both the head and heart of Russia...
Even up to the present Petersburg is in dust and
rubble; it is still being created, still becoming.'

FYODOR DOSTOYEVSKY

With visas safely attained we wasted no time in filling up with petrol at the garage for what would be the last time. The blue and gold of the Statoil flag had become familiar and strangely homely. The high-pitched seagull chorus, the rattling trams, the groans of Finnish and Swedish trucks parking in the darkness of night – all these sounds we left behind. On a hot day in July we headed east again along the single lane and heavily potholed Narva Highway, but this time we passed on through the Lahemaa National Park and on towards Russia.

A few hours after leaving Tallinn we arrived at the border, relieved to be wasting no more time and excited for the adventure that lay ahead, impatient to give life to our daydreams and unmask all our speculation. What we hadn't counted on was the ten hours it took to pass through the checkpoint.

On the positive side, the excruciatingly long wait had the effect of building up the suspense. Thanks to the hassle of getting a visa and now being confronted with a border crossing that made smuggling explosives past Ben Gurion Airport security seem simple, Russia was now a lot more than just another country. Such was the frustration of getting a van and two passengers into the country, there had to be something in there worth seeing, some suitable reward. It also gave us the chance to consider how reliant we had become on Max. Until we left Pärnu we'd taken our campervan somewhat for granted. In Tallinn, Max had really become home.

THE VW TRANSPORTER

Many would argue that the VW Type 2 (aka Transporter) has often been imitated but never equalled. Dodge, Ford and Chevrolet have all produced alternatives over the years, but none have looked or sounded as good. It all began at the end of World War Two, when the British found themselves running the Volkswagen factory in Wolfsburg, Germany. Stripped down Beetles (Type 1s) were turned into little transporters to convey parts across the huge factory floor. The idea of the Type 2 is accredited to a Dutch VW importer, Ben Pon, who drew the first sketches in 1947.

The transporter started life as a box on wheels. The first models left the factory in 1950, and over the next five years ninety different body combinations were tried out, including refrigerated ice cream vans, bakers' bread vans, mobile milking machines, beer wagons, mobile butchers, police wagons and fire engines... and then the campervan. The Type 2 really caught on in 1960s America, fast becoming a symbol of the counterculture. It made a statement, being something that all the American cars of the day weren't – small, compact and one of the first vehicles to have the driver positioned above the front wheels, in stark contrast to the humungous bonnets of the day. By 1963, America had bought 150,000 campervans.

In 1968 the second generation of Type 2 was introduced and continued to be built in Germany until 1979, production then shifting first to Mexico and then Brazil in 1996. Models built after 1971 were called T2B and, having lost the distinctive split windscreen, were commonly known as the Bay Window. Other nicknames included the Kombi – popular with antipodeans – taken from the German, 'Kombinationskraftwagen', meaning 'combined use vehicle'.

By 1975, the factory in Hanover had turned out four million Bay Windows – and the van was a resounding success. Not bad for a vehicle that started life as a box on wheels. When the Bay Window arrived, VW had to end their gesture of giving away a gold watch to anyone who reached 100,000 miles. They had given away in the region of 160,000 watches, such was the van's reliability. The Bay Window, as we would be able to testify, lived up to its reputation – it was as tough as old boots.

It had been a wet day in January that I met Jo outside the Ladbroke Grove Tube station, before hurrying on to Jack's Garage, a popular place for buying and then selling aging campervans. We were met by Grant, a softly spoken New Zealander, who led us down an alleyway that got narrower and darker before opening out into a car park, where Grant came to a halt.

'There she is – a facking beaut!' he exclaimed, his outstretched arm pointing to the far side of the car park, where, under a railway arch, it was possible to just make out the shape of a vehicle in the gathering dusk. Even after closer inspection it was impossible to tell whether it was a 'facking beaut' or whether it was 'totally facked'. It didn't matter – our excitement at being confronted with what we saw as the first tangible realisation of our proposed odyssey was too much. We bought it. It had an immaculate interior decked out in varnished wood. The electrics weren't so good, and the cooker was knackered. The exterior came with plenty of rust. This was the most expensive purchase either of us had ever made, and we weren't convinced that it would get us very far, but that didn't matter. Max was ours.

The cheerless atmosphere of the border at Narva was heightened by nightfall, as we joined a line of some thirty cars – beaten Ladas, bulging vans and the odd Japanese import. Having passed through the Estonian side we began a slow crawl along a wrought-iron bridge that linked the two countries. Hours passed on that bridge as we watched fireflies and listened to distant sounds of barking dogs and car horns, hours for which in theory we were between countries – officially not in any country, bound by no laws or conventions, completely free to do what we liked. So with such a liberating opportunity handed to us, we stood expectantly by the side of Max drinking cups of vegetable soup.

As night was making the transition to early morning we pulled alongside the Russian barrier, brightened up by orange ribbons that fluttered along its length. Three soldiers proudly brandishing their Kalashnikovs pounced on Max, grateful to be presented with something different. They muttered in Russian amongst themselves, laughed deep tobacco laughs and then looked at our passports, pretending that they understood what they saw.

'*Angliski!*' one of the soldiers bellowed, before turning to his mates to share the joke.

I confirmed this by a nod of the head but they weren't interested.

'*Angliski!*' the soldier repeated handing back our documents.

'Welcome to Rossiya.'

The barrier was lifted and Estonia was quickly a memory.

In the concrete suburbs of St Petersburg, smoke stained the horizon as it wafted from tall solemn factories that rose up unevenly from the surrounding landscape. The industrial backdrop ran for several kilometres before giving way to downcast tower block upon downcast tower block, which in turn gave way to blocks of grand Stalinist apartments closer to the city centre.

The streets became livelier, with more colour and frisson, the closer to the nucleus we got. Still evident were the official slogans and murals of the Soviet Union, like the embers of a furnace whose flames might yet return. However, now vendors lined the pavements, squeezed together like sunbathers on a Spanish beach, selling anything from ice cream to newspapers. It didn't seem to matter what or how much they had to sell, they were selling: a pair of old shoes, a tube of Colgate, packets of cigarettes.

The heavy rush-hour traffic carried us across a palatial square and past the lavish exterior of the Oktiabrskaya Hotel with a solid line of magazine sellers on its steps, people stumbling through and over them to enter and exit the building. The traffic thinned out at the top of Nevsky Prospekt – 4 kilometres of majestic grandeur and stately dereliction lined with palaces and more palaces.

The pavements were jammed with people scurrying, weaving, somehow moving, the ground invisible beneath the pulsating organ that was the crowd. This Nevsky was unrecognisable from my memory of it. It was now summer, warm, and the flavour of the street life was like a potent cocktail, the women had stylish sex appeal, the men were uniform in black and leather.

We left Nevsky Prospekt and drove down a network of smaller roads in varying states of disrepair. The road into the city had been good, but in the centre several roads simply vanished into huge craters, while fluorescent ribbon flapped about too far from the holes to be anything but pointless. (We were only able to guess that its purpose was to warn of danger.) We passed dark, dank courtyards. Archways framed dimly lit spaces at the foot of tall pre-revolutionary apartment blocks, some of faded splendour, some of near decay, offering a tantalising glimpse as we passed by of a world I'd only ever read about.

Pulling up to get our bearings we saw the sun bouncing off the turquoise and white of the Mariinsky Theatre. Behind us was the gleaming dome of St Isaac's. We were on the bank of the Moyka River, part of the city's lattice of waterways that lend the city its nickname, the 'Venice of the North'. Only yards away was the palace of Prince Yusupov, and we were metres from the spot where Rasputin had been dumped into the Neva River, having been poisoned and shot on the fateful night when a collective of the city's aristocrats decided they had had enough of the Siberian giant. We were ready to sleep like the dead so it was as good a place as any to park up.

WHO WAS RASPUTIN?

Nobody really knows the date of his birth. He was born in a small village called Pokrovskoye in Tyumen Oblast, not that far from Tobolsk in Siberia.

Maria, his sister, drowned in a river. His brother Dmitri drowned in a pond. Rasputin would of course eventually follow in his sister's footsteps and be drowned in a river.

After spending a few months in the St Nikolai Monastery at Verkhoturye as a punishment for theft, he came in contact with a banned Christian sect called the Khlysty. Khlysty cells existed all over pre-revolutionary Russia and were especially common around the city of Perm, where there were some forty thousand followers. It is thought that it was during his association with the Khlysty that Rasputin's dark and seedy reputation as a seducer and hedonist developed. However, it was as confidante to the tsarina and healer of Alexie, her haemophiliac son, that Rasputin gained favour with the Russian royal family – that is, until certain aristocrats who felt threatened by his powerful position in court conceived a plot to do away with him. Thus to this end Rasputin was poisoned, then shot before being thrown in the Neva.

After the relative containment of Tallinn, St Petersburg was a very different proposition. It was chaotic and felt untamed, a little intimidating and at that point completely inaccessible. We were content simply to soak it all up at first, drifting around in something of a daze through passageways, along the banks of the canals and rivers, wandering up and down the length of Nevsky Prospekt, stopping for coffee and people watching. Being understood was the first problem, which made getting our hands on food (or anything else) not as simple a task as it could have been. Sitting in a cafe, our shamelessly ordering in English was met with a quick volley of incomprehensible Russian, or a facial expression that left you thinking you were insulting the waitress's nearest and dearest. Either way, whatever eventually arrived, if anything, was completely arbitrary. We learnt fast that survival Russian would be essential. We made a start with the two words universally acknowledged to be the most appreciated – please and thank you – as yet unaware that these were in fact the least used words in Russia. In the absence of a common vernacular we needed a friend. An unexpected one would do.

On the evening of our third day in the city, we hadn't been asleep long when there was a knocking on Max's window.

'Is anybody home?'

The voice came from the street in heavily accented English. I drew back the curtain to be met by a pair of large curious eyes peering back in at me. A man with floppy strawberry blonde hair and a sharp beard continued to stare, a soft smile gently breaking onto his face.

'There are only six of these in the city!'

I had no idea what he was talking about at first, but it soon became clear that the man referred to Max. How he'd got his hands on such statistics was anyone's guess.

'And I have one of them.' His smile grew; he was obviously very pleased about this. He began to stroke the paintwork lovingly. I was quick to join our visitor by the side of the van where he warmly introduced himself as Sebastion.

'That is my flat,' he told us, pointing up to a third-floor balcony only a few doors down from the palace. 'We are going out to drink like Russians tonight,' he said, introducing his friend Kristoff, who had been lurking suspiciously in the background – a visiting German scholar, as he described himself.

'You are welcome to join us.'

So we did.

Sebastion was born of a Dutch mother and a German father, and styled himself as a journalist, currently scheming the launch of a St Petersburg *Time Out*. He was a mine of information regarding the city, his relationship with St Petersburg obviously still very much in the honeymoon stage, as he offered endorsement after gushing endorsement. We were fast to realise that Sebastion had stumbled on his own little piece of Elysium and was earnest in his enjoyment of it.

He took us to the classically designed House of Culture on Pravdy Street just around the corner from the ornate and musty Vladimirskaya Metro station, gateway to Dostoyevskyville – the area where the writer spent the last years of his life.

We entered a courtyard lined with columns of crumbling pink stone. A golden eagle, wings fanned, was mounted at one end of the square yard, while at the other in stark contrast was a burnt-out Lada shell. We passed through a glass door attached to a thin splintered wooden frame hanging off its hinges and ready to fall at any time, and continued to follow Sebastion across a damp and dusty hallway and up a slated staircase, passing an old lady, cloth in hand, furiously scrubbing the steps whilst immersed in conversation with herself.

At the top of the staircase we stepped out onto a brightly lit landing. The faint sound of a piano could be heard from above, growing louder as we progressed. We followed a corridor illuminated by a red light. Sebastion bought us tickets from a man squatting like a chimp by the doorway before leading us through into the thick smog – a product of cigarette smoke. It was impossible to see beyond the length of your arm in any direction.

As my eyes adjusted a young girl appeared and spoke – at least, her lips moved, but the piano, joined by bass and drums, drowned out her words. A tug on my sleeve suggested she wanted to hang my coat for me. I took my jacket off and offered it to her, but she continued to stare at me with the sort of pathetic doe eyes that would melt the heart of even Genghis Khan. I then noticed that her clothes were ripped and she wore no shoes on her feet. I gave her ten roubles and she took my jacket. It crossed my mind I'd perhaps just paid her to steal it.

Waitresses were flitting about with large jugs of frothy beer. Sebastion had been quick to get the attention of a surly-faced girl, dressed in something that looked like the Dutch national costume. There was a bar at the back of the room and at the other end a stage was set for more musicians. Guitars and mics were at the ready. Tatty sofas were littered around the place as if as an afterthought.

'Kvadrat,' Sebastion said to me, shaking his head and still smiling. 'The best makeshift jazz club in town,' he informed me whilst nestling into a space at the bar.

The glum barmaid produced four beers before snatching the couple of banknotes with which Sebastion had been fumbling. The club was an assault on all the senses: the music took care of hearing, or made it impossible, vision was close to non-existent, touch was a warm glass of beer, and the smell was a blend of cheap tobacco and cheap perfume with a heavy sprinkling of body odour. Despite the noise, Sebastion attempted to talk.

'So what are you doing here in Russia?' I was just able to make out the question, more from lip-reading than anything else.

I had to think about a reply. Up until then our plans had been unspoken – they were like a secret that only Jo, Tony and I were privy to. Deep down we weren't sure how far we'd actually get in Max; you only had to look at the map and it all seemed a bit unlikely. Furthermore, we weren't sure of the reliability of Tony's 'partner'. When pressed, Tony hadn't been too sure that Nikolai had very much money, making us question whether he had work even for himself, let alone us. So we had been reticent about openly declaring our ultimate ambition because the simple truth was we weren't convinced by it ourselves. It was just much easier to not think about the next week, month, year – and if things worked out, then all the better. Since arriving in Russia, however, something had changed – things had somehow become more serious. Russia almost imposed the need to have a purpose, it didn't feel like the sort of place you could just 'be' for the fun of it. So when the next dip in the music arrived I blurted out, with an air that suggested it was quite a normal thing to do, 'We're driving to Vladivostok!'

He looked at me as if I was quite mad. Which was obviously what he thought, as my declaration received no response. However, despite Sebastion's lacklustre reaction, by sharing it with him I had somehow validated our journey to myself.

Any ideas of further conversation with Sebastion ended with the roar of applause and the arrival of a new musician on the stage. A young guy with strikingly pointed features gripped a harmonica. He proceeded to play a twenty-minute set, every facial muscle committed to the frenzy of his performance. He twisted and turned, ducked and looped with his instrument. At one point he crouched down on one leg and span round like a corkscrew – I half expected him to disappear into the stage beneath. His mouth at once longingly caressed the harmonica and seemingly chewed it like a tough piece of meat. He held the audience captive as his energy passed among us. Finally, to rapturous cheers, he plucked the instrument from his lips and dropped red-faced into the darkness of the audience. Reappearing by the doorway, he proceeded to do a roaring trade in selling his cassettes. Jo bought one, having been quite taken by the man and what he was able to do with his lips; unfortunately, she would find out later that the recording was pretty crude and consisted of forty-five minutes of a baby crying. It was certainly not a deliberate addition – more a hazard of home-recording studios.

SOME FAMOUS NATIVES OF ST PETERSBURG

Peter Carl Fabergé – jewellery maker
Anna Pavlova – ballerina
Vladimir Nabokov – writer
Vladimir Putin – politician
Dmitri Shostakovich – composer

The following morning we joined our new host for breakfast in his turn-of-the-nineteenth-century bachelor pad. The flat was only his second choice, Sebastion told us. He had been keen to buy a place on Vasilyevsky Island overlooking the Neva – St Petersburg is made up of a cluster of islands jutting out into the Baltic Sea, the largest of which is Vasilyevsky. He had been close to closing the deal when he discovered – in the nick of time – that the vendor had already sold the property twice that week. One of the other buyers had gone to the trouble of having the flat watched, and had caught up with Sebastion after seeing him look around said flat with the vendor. Apparently this was not an uncommon scam. I'm not an expert in such matters but I'd say it had something to do with bags full of cash and, strangely for Russia, very little paperwork. Despite it being second choice, Sebastion was pleased with the flat he had ended up with, and he had Brian Eno as an absentee neighbour. The musician made regular visits to the city and had bought the next door flat as an investment.

Sebastion was just as enthusiastic as he had been the previous night. His friend Kristoff looked on indifferently as he held forth, every now and again fumbling for a cigarette from the packet of Bond Street on the table. Occasionally he met Kristoff's gaze and a smile broke onto his face that suggested they were more than just friends.

'Things change quickly in St Petersburg – two, three years ago, say 1994, westerners were still flooding in. Investment from outside was high, it was the land of opportunity.'

He seemed to drift off to another place, a place he looked upon with fondness, but quickly pulled himself back.

'Have you heard of Dva Samoleta?' he asked. We both shook our heads.

'They are a ska band, very popular in the city, they run a cool club as well. I have some.'

He rustled through a pile of CDs resting on the stained fridge that looked like part of a Jean-Michel Basquiat exhibition. Having located the music he poured us all more coffee from a saucepan.

'The mafia controls much, all the kiosks that are dotted about, and the rouble – one day it has value the next none. If you put dollars into the bank you are throwing it into the Moyka.'

He glanced over his shoulder in the direction of the balcony that looked over the river. There was no chance of us opening a Russian bank account. Kristoff looked on as if he had heard these things a thousand times before, then, using the table to lever himself to his feet he said, 'I must now go and stand in a queue for the rest of the day.'

Sebastion looked at his friend quizzically.

'I have to go and register my visa at the OVIR.'

'Good luck,' Sebastion offered. 'I will see you next week,' he chuckled knowingly.

The heavy door slammed and footsteps could be heard disappearing down the stairwell. The OVIR, or the Office of Visas and Registration, with its frustrating ways, was the death of many a foreigner's sanity. Or so Sebastion got much pleasure from telling us, before adding, 'Hadn't you better do yours?' Remembering Tallinn, I quickly put the thought out of my head.

'I was one of the first westerners to come to the city in 1992,' Sebastion told us with pride. 'I came over to work with the Lutheran Church... it's halfway down Nevsky Prospekt. I still do some work for them now; it's pretty much the only service industry on Nevsky that hasn't come and swiftly gone in the last five years. Shops come and go, cafes, people come and go. Even the swimming pool a few blocks down has reverted back to the church it was meant to be, before the Soviets got the Olympics confused with religion... I love this place – but if it's stability you want, no way.'

Again his voice drifted off.

Sebastion, like most of the other foreigners, was there for the excitement – not actual running-around-shooting-people excitement, but being there to soak up the aftermath – an action junkie once removed, a James Bond wannabe, who'd got that little bit closer than I'd ever done. He reached for a newspaper that had been sitting on the table.

'Look, have you heard about this guy being shot?'

The previous morning, less than a mile away, Mikhail Manevich, the chairman of the city's property committee, had been shot five times as his car rounded the corner onto Nevsky Prospekt from Rubinstein Street. The sniper had been positioned in the attic of 76 Rubinstein Street, opposite the golden arches of McDonald's. I read, in the English-language newspaper, that the Manevich shooting was at 9.00 a.m. – breakfast time. Now that was exactly the sort of excitement we had previously yearned for. But when it's actually staring you in the face...

I waited for Jo to read it, and then listened to her exclaim, 'Shit! We would have been there about that time.'

I nodded in agreement, 'We must have been there just after.'

'This stuff happens all the time, people are used to it – it gets cleared up and everyone just gets on with it.' Sebastion sighed, then, as if to emphasise his point, swiftly changed the subject.

'On Monday night we go to the *banya*, you must join us. You can't visit Russia without making a visit to the bathhouse.'

That gave us the weekend to get all we needed for the onward journey and to follow one of Sebastion's other recommendations: 'The only way to spend a summer's weekend in St Petersburg is outside St Petersburg,' he had told us with a conspiratorial smile. It became clearer what he meant when he gave us directions out to Pushkin, one of the city's satellite towns and home to the Catherine Palace and park.

Our day out, which both myself and Jo were very excited about, began under a light drizzle at Vitebsk Station. It was the starting point for Russia's first railway line, opened in 1837 to carry the royal family from St Petersburg down to their summer residence in Tsarskoye Selo. In 1937, Tsarskoye Selo, meaning 'tsar's village', had its name changed to Pushkin after the nation's favourite poet, Alexander Pushkin. The station was awash with travellers lugging overflowing holdalls and other possessions across the tiled floor of the striking style moderne (the Soviet take on art nouveau) hallway and along platforms alive with the expectant buzz of a journey. We found the correct train and settled into one of the few available wooden slat bench seats, which gave no consideration for comfort. Moments later the train pulled away from the elegance of the station and was quickly engulfed by the tired-looking southern tower blocks.

It wasn't long before I'd lost feeling in my buttocks and the first of the on-board traders arrived. Through the swing door that separated the wagons appeared a squat man, breathless as if reaching the finishing line of a marathon – or at least having run for the train. He stood still, resplendent in stonewashed denim, waiting for the door to clatter shut. After clearing his throat he held aloft a plastic bag full of multicoloured paper clips. I didn't understand the proceeding monologue that he bellowed down the wagon; however, judging by the delivery it was a rehearsed speech that he reeled off to a largely indifferent audience, the majority continuing to chatter amongst themselves. The man spoke like a seasoned orator, totally impassioned as if rallying the passengers for battle. I was more than a little intrigued as to the relationship between what he was saying and the paper clips he held. After several minutes he paused and searched the occupants of the now jammed wagon for some kind of response to his exclamations. The penny eventually dropped when a man sitting close by wiggled his finger as if at an auction, the stonewashed orator pounced towards him – faster than a cat hunting a vole – and before you could say 'Alan Sugar!' he had exchanged the paper clips for a handful of roubles. Once the transaction was complete, the salesman hurtled down the aisle and out of sight into the next compartment.

He was quickly replaced by an elderly lady in a flowery frock, brandishing a can of Rexona deodorant. I was tempted to suggest she kept it herself, as she wafted a potent aroma of stale sweat. Perhaps our fellow passengers agreed as she didn't share the luck of her predecessor and, after an equally zealous pitch, left the wagon muttering under her breath, Rexona in hand. During the course of the journey I counted ten sellers of various shapes and sizes pass through the swinging doors, and all helped make the thirty-minute journey seemingly pass a lot quicker. The last man to appear before we entered the station at Pushkin was holding a pair of insoles – now that's a pitch I'd love to have understood.

Whilst the continuous procession of vendors had our full attention, Jo and I had in turn captured the attention of the man squashed into the seat opposite, legs crossed in an oversized suit, messy hair perfected into dishevelled chic. He made no secret of his interest in us, maintaining a constant gaze. Eventually, as the train was reaching its destination and the insoles peddler was beginning his patter, he took the opportunity to satiate his curiosity.

'Where are you from?' is probably one of the more common conversational openers when addressing persons who look more than a little likely to be from another country, and one I was quite ready for as the man gathered himself to speak. I was a little thrown, however, when he asked in perfect English, 'Have you read Carlos Castaneda?' All I managed in response was an inane smile and a barely audible, 'No.' The man was quick to expand, 'I have read all twelve of his books.' Uncertain whether the man was simply showing off or hinting towards something more sinister, I continued to smile. Carlos Castaneda was a Peruvian-born American author who wrote about Mesoamerican shamanism; however, the value of his work has been questioned, critics citing internal contradictions and discrepancies in his books. Despite his critics he had still managed to sell some eight million of his twelve books in seventeen different languages, not least in Russian – with the end of Communism leaving such a large vacuum in the area of belief systems, the likes of Castaneda and his particular blend of shamanism had become hugely popular with Russian people. Aware that he was not going to get very far with his chosen subject, the man introduced himself: 'I'm Sergey. I have a small language school located in the Kochubey Mansion, once home to Count Kochubey, the last master of ceremonies in the court of Nicholas I.' Sergey was obviously very proud of his connection with royalty. 'I'll show you some of the town's sights, and then I would be very pleased if you came to my school for tea.' His offer seemed non-negotiable, but one we were both happy to have received, so we obediently followed his diminutive frame as he wearily dragged his worn suit from the train. He led us away from the faded ochre shades of the station building for about half a mile, until we reached an entrance into a fenced-off park. We walked past an old lady defiantly guarding the entrance. Sergey bid her good day, without a response, before turning to us with a chuckle.

'You know foreigners have to pay to walk in these grounds.' He glanced back at the woman. 'They say the money goes towards the upkeep of the palace and the park, but you can see how much upkeep this place actually gets.' Around us, the park did look particularly wild. 'No, it's only pocket money for her.'

'So we got away with it?' I quizzed.

'Yes, but only because you are with me. It was a long time before she would let me cross the park without paying.' He made another uncertain glance back. 'It's a short cut to Kochubey and when I first arrived in Pushkin, we would have terrible arguments. You see, I'm from Siberia, a little town not far from Krasnoyarsk. That old girl was convinced I was a foreigner because of my provincial accent. These Petersburgers are snobs.'

'So what happened?' I was now intrigued that the whole business had made such an impact on him.

'Well, I wasn't going to pay on principle; it's the quickest and most attractive route to my school. So I started charging past her at a sprint.' It was hard to imagine the man standing with us in his baggy suit sprinting anywhere. 'At first she yelled blue murder, but eventually she stopped even getting out of her chair, and the day came when I thought I'd try passing at a more sedate speed. I approached the entrance somewhat apprehensively – it was to be a landmark stage in our relationship. She remained seated, and victory was mine.' Sergey's English reminded me of an early black and white newsreader's style – crisp pronunciation, structured, very formal – seldom heard these days.

'Next stage – talking to each other, perhaps?' Jo added, but Sergey had spotted something of interest and was pointing furiously.

We had reached the edge of an oval lake, presently being used by a family of geese to practise their landings. And they weren't the only family in the park that day – there was a prevalence of pram-pushing weekend strollers, an energetic celebration of family. It wasn't difficult to see why so many made the journey out from the city. Despite the many people there was a rehabilitating sense of release from the clutches of the dirty metropolis, the air was fresh and clean and there was plenty of it.

Between 1744 and 1796, empresses Elizabeth and Catherine the Great were responsible for creating the parks and palaces of Pushkin, and the Catherine Palace was the baroque centrepiece. It was designed by Rastrelli, an Italian architect favoured by the eighteenth-century Russian royals, and named after Peter the Great's second wife. Unfortunately, the exorbitant entrance fee to the palace was something even Sergey wasn't able to dodge, at the rouble equivalent of £40 for one foreign adult ticket, or £2 for one Russian adult ticket, and we decided to merely marvel at its sumptuous exterior. Sergey declared our decision a wise one, there being very few rooms on view to the public, so we settled down on the gravelled terrace in the shadow of the palace for a lukewarm milky coffee served by a lady with a flask of hot water and a box full of Nescafé sachets, and let Sergey fill us in on the mystery of the Amber Room.

The whereabouts of the coveted Amber Room is one of the greatest mysteries to come from the chaos of World War Two. The original Amber Room – sometimes called the 'eighth wonder of the world' due to its incredible beauty – was a collaboration between the German sculptor Andreas

Schlüter and the Danish craftsman Gottfried Wolfram. It began life at the Charlottenburg Palace in Prussia, until Friedrich Wilhelm I presented it to his then ally Peter the Great in 1716 – lock, stock and gold leaf panels – as a diplomatic gift. After several renovations by the Russians, it came to rest in the Catherine Palace, containing over six tonnes of amber. During the Nazis' siege of St Petersburg, then Leningrad, the Amber Room in Pushkin was looted and taken to Königsberg, later Kaliningrad, which with all the chaos of the end of the war is where the trail runs cold. The Amber Room has never been traced, and the one that was currently residing at the Catherine Palace was a work in progress, as craftsmen painstakingly recreated the original. As with all unsolved mysteries, theories abound as to what came of the treasure. It was widely believed that the Amber Room was destroyed when the British bombed Königsberg, while others suggest that it was burnt during a fire at Königsberg Castle. Some believe that it sunk whilst travelling on a German boat that was torpedoed, others that Russian soldiers destroyed it. One of the wilder theories is that Hitler's body was never burnt and was in fact buried with the Amber Room. Whatever the truth was behind the mystery, the palace's popularity appeared undiminished by the absence of its star treasure, as testified by the queue to get in, which I noted was made up largely of Russians.

We spent some more time wandering the park, enjoying the calm of our surroundings and following the progress of a bedraggled pony pulling a heavy carriage weighed down with a group of sharply suited men quaffing from wine glasses. 'The new aristocracy,' was Sergey's disdainful comment, made as he plucked a hair from his sleeve, drawing attention to the contrast between his worn attire and the tailored wardrobe of the group. He led us out of the park and into the centre of the town with its cratered streets and scruffy buildings, now a shadow of its imperial past, yet still showing glimpses of the one time majesty. The imposing cracked pillars holding up the baroque palace of culture, now home to the local council, a splattering of neglected stately houses and the wide central avenue somehow managed to elevate Pushkin above the hard times upon which it had fallen.

We never got to the school for tea; however, as the shadows grew longer, Sergey bundled us both down some steps into the 'Butterfly Cafe'. Even Jo, who I had at least a foot on in the vertical department, had to bend her head down to fit through the doorway, beyond which it all became a bit *Alice in Wonderland*. The Butterfly Cafe was positively miniature – especially compared to all that had gone before it in Pushkin. The yeasty smell of pies baking filled the air. We sat at a table covered by a white linen tablecloth, on which were little glass bowls all filled to the top with a variety of fruit preserves, glistening like gems.

'Raspberry, apricot, plum, cherry and strawberry.' Sergey pointed proudly to each in turn. Next to the jam was a mountain of sweet pastries smothered in sugar-coating.

At one end of the table was positioned a samovar, sparkling as if it had never been used. Sergey was quick to see my admiring glances.

'The samovar translates as "self-boiler". Traditional samovars like this one are made from copper or brass and are lined with tin. A narrow tube runs its length filled with pine cones to perfume the tea, and wood and coal are burnt to heat the water.'

It was during Catherine the Great's reign that tea drinking became a popular pastime for the Russian nobility. Tea was a status symbol and the wealthy threw large tea parties. It was another century before tea drinking became affordable and common amongst average Russians. Sergey, with this gesture of afternoon tea, I suspect, was trying to keep up with the Karpovs. Nevertheless, the delicately proportioned cafe was a world away from the street outside and a welcome rest, and to see Sergey filling up the dainty bone china cups from the samovar only using his thumb and forefinger, whilst pushing his narrow chest out like a robin, was something I wouldn't have missed for the world.

Back in St Petersburg, refreshed from our trip to Pushkin and glad to have a new friend, we followed the Fontanka River in Sebastion's bright yellow VW Transporter on our way to further revitalisation... but of a very different kind. We were heading towards Public Bathhouse No. 9, its number reflecting its location rather than its status amongst the city's other *banyas*. Sebastion was in his element as tour guide, authoritatively pointing out anything he considered of interest through the van's dusty windows. 'The Anichkov Bridge, decorated with magnificent horses – the work of sculptor Pyotr Klodt. During World War Two the horses were buried underground in the gardens nearby – as were many of the city's famous statues. The Beloselsky-Belozersky Palace on the corner of the river – look over there! Over there! Dark red like roses... Beautiful! Now home to a puppet theatre.' As we followed the river round the Sheremetev Palace became visible, its pale columns set back from the rippling water and the passing boats that conveyed ice-cream-licking tourists. One of its outhouses was home to the literary museum of Anna Akhmatova, famed for her poems about the siege of Leningrad during World War Two.

Sebastion appeared quite oblivious to the attention his van got from the people on the streets. Their interest was not surprising, as for the first time I became aware of the dowdy collection of vehicles on the roads. Such was the prevalence of the Lada (brought over from Italy and adopted by the Soviets as their own) that anything else was something of a head turner. The brightly coloured Western van we now found ourselves in was positively capricious.

The trip to the bathhouse was a weekly get-together for Sebastion and a few of his expat mates, and it was his job to get them all there. First was Fred, a short man with a bald head and round spectacles. Sebastion pulled into a courtyard and Fred bundled himself into the back next to Jo, cradling a leather bag tightly to his chest as if it were full of money. Fred worked for a German bank (so perhaps the bag was full of money) in the city and after initial introductions said very little all evening. Next was Matt, with a very high-pitched Finnish accent – he was from Helsinki and was in the city writing a book, about what he never actually said... which was surprising as he rarely stopped talking. The bathing crew was completed when Sunny Marcus clambered in through the sliding side door, after waiting in the middle of a busy intersection. Sunny was a tall man, with a not insignificant stomach region, and greeted the other two men as if he hadn't seen them for much longer than the week it had actually been.

Another ten minutes and we pulled into a long leafy avenue enclosed by pre-revolutionary buildings on either side. The van came to a stop opposite one such building where displayed on its crumbling brickwork was a number nine in faded blue paint.

The earliest description of the Russian *banya* was documented by the Apostle Andrew in a chronicle dating back to the first century. He said:

I saw the land of the Slavs, and while I was among them, I noticed their wooden bathhouses. They warm them to extreme heat, then undress, and then after anointing themselves with tallow, they take young reeds and lash their bodies. They actually lash themselves so violently that they barely escape alive. Then they drench themselves with cold water and thus are revived.

If we had read Andrew's summary before our visit I think we may have had second thoughts; as it was, I think Jo was having second thoughts anyway as she considered the collection of men she was about to be taking a bath with.

We all followed Sebastion up the steep steps to the entrance. After several fierce thumps on the iron door, silently we were beckoned into a damp passageway by a hunched man, who led us to the reception. Roubles were exchanged for towels, felt bath hats and soap. And, most surprisingly, our fellow bathers took the opportunity to stock up on bottles of Baltika beer, of which there was a huge supply, crates and crates piled up to the ceiling. At that point I was unable to equate drinking beer with melting at seventy degrees Celsius in a sauna, but that would change.

NOTES ON THE BANYA

- In Bulgaria 'the *banya*' refers to any type of bath.
- In Serbia a *banya* is a mineral water spa.
- In Russia 'the *banya*' refers to any kind of steam bath that involves much pain and much alcohol.

As I adjusted to the dim lighting, it became clear that the evening generally kicked off fully clothed drinking beer around plastic tables in a makeshift cafeteria.

After several beers, Sebastion stumbled to his feet, grabbed as many bottles as he could carry and vanished through another heavy wooden doorway. With some reluctance the rest of the group followed. Matt grabbed hold of my shirt and as good as dragged me in his wake; I in turn grabbed Jo. Once through the doorway the temperature rose dramatically, so it didn't somehow seem that surprising to be met by Sebastion standing stark naked in front of me. Fred was also quick to discard his clothes and lead the way into the sauna. I looked at Jo, she looked at me as if to say 'I will if you do!', so I too ditched my clothes and followed.

Inside the sauna, I took a seat on the lowest of the tiered wooden benches and noted the collection of men and women we had joined in the engine room of the *banya* number nine. There were all shapes, sizes and ages represented, and without exception everybody was starkers. There was a party atmosphere, which I suppose made me the party pooper as I sat rather self-consciously feeling increasingly nauseous as a result of the heat. I worried how Jo was going to handle the situation as I waited for her to come and ease some of my discomfort – but I needn't have worried as she soon arrived, skipping across the concrete floor like a newborn lamb, a Baltika bottle swinging above her head. Her exuberant entrance went unnoticed by everybody but me. Everybody else was fully engaged; some chatted energetically, some paced zombie-like about the room drawing in the now not inconsiderable heat, one couple even appeared to be doing the waltz. Two men were using a felt *banya* hat to have a game of frisbee.

Occasionally a little beer was poured onto the hot coals, producing a pleasant aroma of freshly baked bread. Exactly the same smell was produced when Matt started to pass urine onto the coals. I soon began to notice that as the temperature climbed and the more beer I drank, incredibly, the less nauseous I felt – there was method in our new friends' madness, I was pleased to discover. I had begun to think that Russian *banya* Sebastion-style was a heart attack waiting to happen, but the sheer vehemence with which Seb and his pals went about their weekly trip to the bathhouse had obviously been thoroughly tried and tested – an attitude very apparently shared by their Russian hosts.

I had just about adjusted to the whole experience, even started to enjoy the diminished state I found myself in, when I noticed something quite unsettling. Many of my fellow bathers seemed to be carrying bushy sprigs of birch – some as long as a metre. Now where had they come from? In some instances they were being used to gently slap the glistening bodies of other bathers. Matt was whacking Fred across the back as if delivering him from the devil, and Fred had an expression close to agony on his face – his road to purification would be a long one. I was just considering that I was now probably clean enough without putting myself through such an ordeal, when Sunny appeared in front of me armed with the biggest birch branch I'd seen yet. I hadn't really been introduced to Sunny, and considering we were both as bare as the day we were born it seemed a little strange to be shaking his hand and saying 'Good to meet you.' But that didn't stop us. Sunny was English, born and bred in Wolverhampton.

'I've been living here for seven years now, I married a Russian.'

'How do you find it?' I asked, still not sure whether polite conversation breached *banya* protocol.

'I love it, I'm a musician, just bought a small flat in the centre of town.' Sunny began fidgeting with the branch, menacingly tapping it against the bench as he continued, 'It's in an old Kommunalki block in the Liteiny district; shared kitchen, shared bathroom. There are only a few left as developers are buying them up – offering prices that just can't be refused.'

It was difficult to know where to look as my eyes kept settling on the large belly just inches in front of me. I was saved from my dilemma by Sebastion, who came prancing over waving his sprig of birch like a demented cheerleader, and with an accent more brusquely German than I'd noticed before exclaimed, 'Anyone want arh gute beating?'

There was nowhere to hide, nowhere to run, so I got to my feet, turned my back on Sebastion, and thought of England.

The next day, we said our goodbyes to St Petersburg and left much cleaner than when we had arrived. Sebastion kindly gifted us a selection of handwritten cards with useful phrases in Russian that he maintained could be easily adapted for a variety of situations we might meet on our journey, from angry Siberian farmers demanding we get off their land to fierce babushkas trying to sell unwanted vegetables. Jo suggested that the Russian translated more along the lines of 'We are stupid British tourists and need all the help we can get.' Unfortunately they got lost early on, so to this day we're completely ignorant as to what exactly they said. Whatever the truth, they had been a nice gesture to go with Sebastion's sizeable chunk of cynicism regarding the likely success of our venture. I think secretly he would have gladly come too.

After filling up with petrol at a garage opposite the Mariinsky Theatre, we headed out of town as the rain poured down. We set off early morning; however, it took us the best part of the day to find the correct road out of the city. Beyond the film-set centre, the repetitive sprawl of tower blocks became maze-like. With Russia so big and right in front of us, we could only laugh at our inability to get onto the Murmansk road and get driving in the right direction until mid afternoon, when we got ourselves caught up in the rush-hour traffic.

For the next 530 kilometres, it was just us and the road to Vologda, and the occasional truck ploughing past carrying timber. Forest and farmland, farmland and forest gently drifted past, as it gently sunk in that we were both now completely out of our depth, embarking on probably the longest commute ever...

CHAPTER FOUR
VOLOGDA

'Nowhere else can you find such a place like the Vologda land. When all Vologdian temples start to chime to the vespers, there is such a pacification, harmony and stillness spreading.'

(WORDS FROM A RUSSIAN TRAVEL WEBSITE)

Two days after leaving St Petersburg we reached Vologda. The journey through the north-western province had taken us past a handful of settlements, which interrupted mile upon mile of ravaged flatlands. Isolated industrial plants on the distant horizons had added colour to the often haunting canvas. The heavy rains – not uncommon at that time of year in this part of Russia – followed us into town late on a Friday afternoon. We entered along a wide boulevard, with the last remnants from the day's market being packed away. Crawling past a statue of Lenin with fresh roses placed at its foot, suggesting the local Communist Party had a good membership, instinctively we pulled up alongside the Sukhona River that cut through the middle of the town. With all the congestion caused by the market, it was the only place we could find to park, offering up a view of a church on the opposite bank that seemed suitably metaphoric for Russia itself – the golden onion resplendent on top yet the body completely gutted by fire.

During the worst years of Stalin's terror, Vologda had been used as a transit town for deportees. Forty-seven churches had been used as transit prisons, and multi-tiered sleeping platforms were erected, where the prisoners remained until onward transport arrived. In March, April and May of 1930, 25,000 children were reported to have died in the churches of Vologda. Starvation was the main cause, the locals too scared of their own arrest to help the prisoners with food. The persistent rainfall persuaded us to get some sleep. It was an inauspicious beginning to our visit.

The following morning I emerged from the van to benefit from the calm after the storm. The clouds had departed, leaving behind a crisp sunny day. The streets were empty but for a heavy air of expectancy – like the streets of an old western town before a gunfight. I waited for the Earp brothers to appear in formation in the distance; they didn't, but as if on cue somebody else rounded the corner and headed towards me. At first I was relieved by the presence of another human, as the growing 'pacification' I was feeling was quite alarming. However, as the lonely figure came into focus, he quickly became a source of alarm, not of 'stillness spreading'. He wore oversized trainers that complemented his grubby shell suit, the pale blue of which was decorated with blood stains, matching the angry hue of the blood that coloured his menacing swollen eyes, which gave him an insect quality. He came to an unsteady standstill with the burnt-out church as a backdrop, which somehow added to the desperation of his appearance. He stared at the ground as he groaned a barely audible request for a cigarette – we could have been the only two people alive, and it was quite possible that he would soon not be alive. The few kopeks I placed into his scabby hand seemed pointless.

I followed the clear ripples of the river round to a comely knoll that wouldn't have looked out of place in an English village. The only difference was this particular knoll, located beneath the Resurrection Cathedral, had been turned into a cardboard city inhabited by more depraved and helpless men and women. Alcohol and weather ravished in appearance, gripping onto existence but only just, they looked like a single organism, mutating in form as they huddled together for warmth. I was metres from the gathering – but went apparently unnoticed as I looked on, their presence in turn making the cathedral invisible to me.

Standing there I became engulfed by a sense of melancholy, a sadness – a sense of hopelessness I hadn't been aware of before in Russia. The men and women outside the cathedral were merely representative of a greater despair. It flowed down the shabby streets visible from where I stood, every rundown single-storey house, half-finished building project, rotten bit of scaffolding.

Plastic bags joined forces with plastic bottles, filling potholes and spilling out to create anti-ecological sculptures.

Random benches – one of the few concessions to civic pride
– sheltered used condoms and broken glass. Vologda should
have been quite the imperial spectacle, but it wasn't. It was
able to boast a rich history which had left behind a startling
number of churches and cathedrals. The kremlin built in the
seventeenth century had been designed to compete with that
of Moscow. Such was Ivan the Terrible's fondness for the
city, he wanted to make it his capital. It was from the kremlin
in Vologda that Peter the Great launched his campaign
against the Swedish, remaining there until the founding of
St Petersburg in 1703. Tanpinar, an early twentieth-century
Turkish writer, wrote:

> I see the adventures of these ruined neighbourhoods
> as symbolic. Only time and the sharp shocks of history
> can give a neighbourhood such a face. How many
> conquests, how many defeats, how many miseries did
> the people have to suffer to create the scene before us?

Perhaps the ghosts of Stalin's transit camps lived on, or
perhaps the reality of the Russia that now existed beyond
the Soviet Union wasn't to be what my imagination had
prepared me for. Either way, I had no wish to stay longer in
Vologda, and unlike the people who made the city's streets
their home I still had the opportunity to leave. Or so I
thought.

Whilst Jo was rummaging through our already much
played collection of cassettes, planning the soundtrack for
the next leg of the drive, I nipped over to a nearby kiosk to
stock up on Bonaqua and chocolate. The former, despite the

packaging, tasted like it had been collected from the puddles on the street, but the KitKats were always delicious and had something of a monopoly over other chocolate bars in the kiosks that decorated the towns we passed through. When I pushed my hand expectantly into my trouser pocket to gather the necessary change to pay for the supplies, to my horror I found only a few kopeks and a couple of Estonian coins. There was just enough to make the purchase but it fast dawned on me that was the last of my cash. I sheepishly returned to Jo, who seemed quite pleased with herself, having dug out *Neil Diamond's Greatest Hits*. My fears were realised when Jo confirmed that her pockets were also bare, with the exception of the Barclaycard that had carried us all the way from Tallinn.

How could we have been so stupid? How could we have left ourselves with only a few kopeks to rub together? Simple, really. Up to and including in St Petersburg, there always seemed to be a selection of service stations courtesy of Eurasian oil companies Neste and Lukoil on the roadside when we needed them. In said havens we were able to buy petrol and food using Jo's card and thus not worry about carrying thousands of Estonian kroons or millions of Russian roubles around. (The rouble was liable to change in value dramatically overnight due to Russia's then unstable economy, and several times during the trip we woke up as millionaires – a good feeling until we realised our millions in roubles were worth little more than a few English pounds.)

Having gotten used to the service stations, we'd casually drifted into a false sense of security, and armed with a Barclaycard and a jangling pocket of coins we had headed into the unknown. Still, presumably now that we had arrived in a town of significant size, we could simply find a bank and stock up on enough roubles to carry the three of us to our distant destination.

On Saturday afternoons, not just in provincial Russia but probably anywhere in the world, banks are closed. This further realisation hit us as Jo violently shook the locked door to the Central Bank of Vologda. It was obviously not going to open as Jo carried on tugging at it for several moments, leaving me to guess at what she had planned once she had forced her way into the dark hall beyond. No, the bank would be closed until Tuesday. (Not much work was done on Mondays in Russia: as in France, it was part of the weekend.) The ATM which teasingly flashed at us would only accept Russian bank cards; there was nothing we could do.

Dejected, we returned to the van and sat staring out, watching fresh rainfall trickling down the windscreen, remembering with fondness that last pan of pasta we'd cooked up the previous night. We had been spoilt. By the time we reached the other side of Russia we would probably be taking nothing for granted, but at that point, sitting there in Vologda having already decided we didn't want to stay, Tuesday seemed a long way off.

Jo managed about fifteen minutes of despondent rain watching; I managed about the same amount of time thumbing through *Essential Russian*, kidding myself I would master the language before Tuesday. It was no good: we had to take action. It was Jo's brainwave that sliced through the mounting frustration.

'We'll jump the train to Moscow.'

I considered her suggestion for a few moments – I liked the sound of that.

'Why Moscow?'

'To get some money of course!'

'I know, but wouldn't it be quicker to go back to St Petersburg?'

Jo dug around for the map. On our map the two major cities formed a perfect equilateral triangle with their country cousin Vologda.

Jo picked up a scrumpled, and in Russia worthless, five kroon note that lay on the dashboard. A picture of the handsome Paul Keres – a grandmaster chess player – was displayed on one side, the other offered a view of Tallinn's spires. She threw it into the air: 'Keres and we go to Moscow.'

The note fluttered onto my lap, Mr Keres glaring up at me.

'What about the van?' The thought of leaving Max for twenty-four hours, the time it would take for a return journey to Moscow, seemed to be the only flaw in the plan.

'I'll go alone,' Jo offered. I glanced over at the *Essential Russian* book I had discarded – perhaps I would be speaking Russian by Tuesday after all.

'All right. Let's do it.'

This was by far the best idea as Jo travelling alone without a ticket stood a better chance of succeeding in the mission. Being a girl she had charm and the sympathy vote on her side, should it be required – together, we'd be clumsy and get caught. Plan in place we left Max by the riverbank and nervously followed signs down to the station.

I took my place on the platform and tried to look inconspicuous, pretending I was a POW about to make my escape. The overcast skies and pending darkness helped forge a quite sinister atmosphere, which certainly helped my fantasy. A train soon arrived. Jo, as planned, joined a disorderly queue at the base of the steep iron steps leading up to the dusty green wagon. A formidable-looking *provodnik* (the wagon hostess) stood guard at the entrance to wagon fourteen. With the cunning of a seasoned jailbreaker, Jo slipped in between a very tall man and a woman with a look at least equal in ferocity to that of the *provodnik*.

Two militia patrolling the platform at that point asked to see my documents; I fumbled around in my pocket for my passport, my gaze momentarily diverted from the scene at the wagon. Satisfied, the two men moved on. However, looking back over at the wagon, I saw that Jo was by now involved in a heated exchange with the guard. Her until then polished performance was not working; she didn't win the sympathy vote and apparently the *provodnik* wasn't susceptible to being charmed in any way. Soon Jo was down the steps and being marched away by the patrolling guards along the platform until vanishing into an austere concrete building, where the gates closed behind her.

Well, that hadn't gone so well. I spent the next thirty minutes proving to myself that in a crisis I was pretty useless, unable to come up with a suitable recovery strategy. Fortunately, the responsibility of making a decision was taken away from me when the two platform patrollers returned and instructed me to follow them. I was led into the same bleak building Jo had entered earlier. They guided me into an open-plan room. Jo was seated behind a desk, tears streaming down her face. Seeing me, she darted over and dispensed a firm hug. At another desk sat a man with smoke billowing above his shiny bald head, as if he was on fire. Whilst one of his hands rested limp to the side, the other alternated between dragging on a cigarette and taking sips from a liquid in a small clear glass. The two other men – both in uniform – largely ignored us.

The police in Russia don't have a good press. As a Russian policeman, where do you begin? If your job is to uphold the law, in a country where the rule of law is pretty much an alien concept, you're going to have to make it up as you go along. The police do serve a purpose, it's just unclear whether it's a good one. They seem to be there to emphasise the irrational and subjective use of power in Russia. The Soviet Union had been particularly accomplished at keeping its residents in a permanent state of paranoia. The police were simply there to remind the good people of Russia that at any time and for any reason, they could lose their liberty and all their rights. So far we had only ever had contact with the traffic police, or GAI, found lurking in dog kennels at regular intervals along most major roads, who having flagged us down were usually content with a small contribution to the Stolichnaya benevolent fund. Some even smiled.

The desktop was littered with scraps of paper with drawings and signs scribbled on them, evidence that attempts had been made to cross the language barrier. Despite their reputation, Jo's uniformed companions appeared pleasant enough, and the atmosphere that greeted me seemed cordial. I was aware, though, that our visas were for St Petersburg only, and despite the earlier inspection, I still wasn't sure if this factor had been noted. We didn't want to give them any ammunition. However, it appeared that if I'd passed over a loaded gun and a belt full of grenades, that still wouldn't have been ammunition enough. There was no getting away from the fact that this bunch of coppers weren't bad at all.

We didn't want them to know about Max, believing that having a van would only complicate matters, so I wove them a tall story about how we had both arrived in their small town. This involved lots of pictures of stick men careering across north-west Russia on trains, accompanied by lots of grunts. The gist of the story:

- Lost our tour group in St Petersburg.
- Got on wrong train.
- Need to get a train to Moscow to meet group.

We had been travelling on a group ticket according to our story, and we therefore needed to get to Moscow for free. Given my largely confusing artwork and the look of bewilderment on Jo's face, we could probably have told them anything. With the benefit of hindsight, catching the wrong train is not the easiest of things to achieve, more than anything due to the *provodniki* that guard the wagons with special-forces style efficiency.

Whether the chief of the Vologda police believed us or not, or understood us or not, he certainly took pity on our incompetence. A long discussion took place amongst the assembled Russians and several phone calls were made, before with some urgency we were bustled out onto the platform once more. We were led across some tracks, down the length of another platform, over a bridge, along another platform just in time to see a train pulling in. After some talk between the policeman and the babushka guarding her wagon, we were beckoned up the heavy metal steps. The babushka showed us to our first-class accommodation, and asked if we would like tea in the morning. We had both got a free ride to Moscow.

Arriving in Moscow the following morning, our moods were more than a little elevated at having succeeded in our mission. Carrying a warm glow, a result of the kindness shown by the Vologdian police, we headed straight for a bank. We didn't have to deal with the chaotic Moscow streets for long, as we came across an ATM minutes from the station. We stopped for a coffee, concluded we would return to Moscow one day – but it wasn't for this trip – before jumping on the first train back to Vologda (second class, this time, as we were paying). We hoped that our benefactors from the previous night had all gone to bed, as even with tickets our return would have been more than a little suspect.

In daylight the chilling feel of the night before had been replaced by an uplifting ambience, as the sun was hoisted into the sky and the town stirred into life. We scrambled across to the riverbank and Max. With fuel in the tank we left. The suburbs soon gave way to arable fields as we followed the rising sun, joking about the Vologda militia sitting around chatting about the sudden popularity of their town with British tourists – albeit accidental tourists.

CHAPTER FIVE
THE GOLDEN RING

The Zolotoe Koltso (Golden Ring) is the collection of old towns north-east of Moscow, the old heart of Russia – picturesque, with a pull capable of drawing hundreds of tourists away from Red Square and the souvenirs of Arbat Street for a day's sightseeing. The ring manages to transport you back to a Russia of Tolstoy and Turgenev. Churches and monasteries dating back centuries are prolific. Monks with long orthodox beards are the rule, not the exception. This was the romance Russia of my imagination, from a time before the Bolsheviks enforced their questionable equality. A certain innocence floated in the air, a million miles from the atmosphere of St Petersburg and its provincial cousin Vologda, notwithstanding that we hadn't yet travelled that far from either.

Working from our map we wanted to join the main road east, unremarkably labelled the M7. So far the roads identified by the map as 'main' had been a long way from the quality of autobahns, so we really didn't want to risk anything less than what the map classed as a main road. Physically we were travelling in the wrong direction, but this was unimportant as everything was new. Our working schedule was more than a little relaxed as our sole time restraint was reaching Vladivostok before the weather turned nasty – which would also coincide with the need for unskilled hands in the timber yard. Such moderate ambitions gave us the opportunity to visit some premier league tourist sights of the ring.

YAROSLAVL

I once saw a documentary about Yaroslavl, the Golden Ring's largest town by population, which revealed it to be one of the worst for heroin addiction in all Russia. For two hours the film followed the day-to-day lives of an extended family caught in the post-Soviet poverty trap. Most of the action was set in a poky two-room flat, which was home to parents, brother and sister, sister's new husband, occasional wife of brother and their two children. Sister was addicted to heroin and would spend most of her day zonked out or having sex with strangers, behind parked cars or down alleyways. Brother was a very small-time crook, stashing stolen goods under his parents' bed and hanging out with other small-time crooks on street corners. Both parents, well into their sixties, went out to work in factories every day. The dramatic crest came when it was discovered that daughter had stolen money, money that her father had been putting aside for urgently needed drugs for mother. It made very depressing viewing.

The only thing that depressed us in Yaroslavl during our visit was persistent drizzle. We didn't see prostitutes or any petty crooks. We saw the Monastery of the Transfiguration – the cathedral which towered over the town, resplendent with a fresh coat of paint. Dating back to the twelfth century this great hulk of a church, comparable in size to Salisbury Cathedral, was the town's centrepiece. Its overpowering grandeur and ostentation seemed to scoff at the rundown communal flats, housing extended families living on the brink of despair. As a foreigner, it quickly became apparent that it was possible to exist in a parallel Russia, completely blinded by churches dripping with gold, oblivious to the contemporary realities uncovered by the roving eye of the documentary maker. After a potato pancake and a strong coffee, it was east to the next link in the ring.

KOSTROMA

By the time we reached Kostroma the town was basking in sun. A food market was raging in the central trading arcades on Susaninskaya Square – named after Ivan Susanin, whose statue kept watch on proceedings from upon a large, dusty plinth. Susanin was something of a Russian folk hero, having become a symbol of the Russian peasants' devotion to the tsar in the early nineteenth century – a useful propaganda tool at a time when the imperial family was doing pretty badly in opinion polls. It makes a good story which goes a bit like this:

When the brutal Ivan the Terrible was murdered in 1584 rule fell to his hopeless son, Fyodor; fourteen years later

Fyodor died, leaving no children, so ending the 700-year Rurik dynasty. Boris Godunov, already in the court of Ivan the Terrible, took over as tsar until he died in suspicious circumstances a few years later. So began the Time of Troubles – a period of leaderless chaos, with different factions vying for the throne whilst foreign invaders tried to take advantage of Russia's anarchic state. In 1610 the Polish managed to take control of Moscow, until a group of noblemen from Nizhny Novgorod successfully removed them. With power back in Russian hands these noblemen, needing a tsar and fast, chose the sixteen-year-old Mikhail Romanov. His credentials for the job were a little flaky – but being some very distant blood relative of Ivan the Terrible he would do. Mikhail was living in a small village near Kostroma at the time. Polish soldiers still roamed the Russian countryside, not yet having found their way back to Poland after defeat in Moscow, and were very keen for their man Sigismund Vasa to take the throne. To this end they headed to Kostroma to track down Mikhail and kill him.

The story goes that when looking for the young prince they met a logger in the wood, Ivan Susanin, who proceeded to lead them deep into the forest, where the Polish got lost and perished. Whilst Ivan was leading the Polish a merry dance he sent his grandson on ahead to warn Mikhail, who was kept safe by the monks of the St Ipaty Monastery. As a result of Susanin's loyal actions, Mikhail went on to rule for thirty-two years – founding the Romanov dynasty.

After buying bread and milk, both sold in plastic bags, we headed out of town to find the main attraction: the St Ipaty

Monastery. The monastery was to be found on the bank of the Volga River and a more perfect setting you'd be hard pushed to find. It was easy to imagine monks having an afternoon nap in the shadow of an apple tree, listening to the water burbling past only feet away, the bell chimes rippling sweetly from the shimmering onion-domed cathedral tower.

I'm the first to admit to being something of an ecclesiastical architecture bore, enjoying nothing more than marvelling at the devotion and sheer labour that goes into creating a place of worship. Yet despite the soothing serenity of the scene, we found ourselves unable to muster more than a sigh, before turning our thoughts to getting petrol and the next stretch of road. From that moment it became clear: we had contracted 'ecclesomnia'. My apathy towards St Ipaty and the beads of sweat creeping down Jo's brow confirmed the diagnosis. Apparently this is quite a common complaint, nothing that a long period away from Russia can't cure. But we would have to be careful, as that wasn't on the cards any time soon.

From the Alexander Nevsky Cathedral in Tallinn to the onslaught of churches in St Petersburg and Vologda, we were completely saturated and we hadn't even got to Suzdal – which is something of a museum town for all things old and Russian. It was with some relief that the next town we passed through was the industrial and very ugly Ivanovo – just the antidote after all that old world culture. Ivanovo was grim and menacing, not an inch of godly inspiration anywhere to be seen. And ooh, it felt good! Gratefully we passed by downtrodden and battered natives, hopelessly scuffling along, clinging onto life in the very real present.

SUZDAL

As soon as the 'ecclesomnia' kicked in we knew this place would be a problem. Fortunately, the gloom of Ivanovo had neutralised things somewhat, so we felt up to having a little skirmish into Suzdal. The town was rammed with coaches and day trippers, old women peddling copies of ancient icons and *Palekh* spoons, and plenty of churches. It was to Russia what Toledo is to Spain. After five minutes the sweating returned and I began to shake. We left.

BOGOLYUBOVO

We drove straight on past the town of Vladimir, the last of the danger spots, and pulled over in a tiny hamlet just outside. Why we did this is anyone's guess; I put it down to one of the following:

- A moment of weakness brought on from the knowledge that we were through the worst areas of concentrated religious buildings.

- The uncontrollable urge to look our tormentor in the face.

- The opportunity to visit the true site of Russia's earliest capital.

The small village of Bogolyubovo was dominated by a white monastery. However, across a lush green meadow 100 metres from the monastery located at the junction of two rivers was the real reason for visiting Bogolyubovo – the Church of the Intercession on the Nerl.

Four pale walls climbed to meet a dark blue cupola. The church perched at the top of a gentle hillock, brushed by the swaying branches of nearby trees, reflected in the river just metres away. Its cloudy stonework merged effortlessly with the soothing surrounds, immediately casting a spell. We sat on the bank and watched the Nerl joining with the Klyazma River and basked in the magic of the setting, for those moments oblivious to where and how we were in the world, detached from Russia, just floating in the cosmos.

Legend has it that Andrey Bogolyubsky, one time ruler of Russia, was returning home from Kiev sometime in the late twelfth century when his horse stopped on the site of the church, and as a result of such a divine interruption, Andrey decided to make the town of Vladimir some 11 kilometres down the road the capital of Russia, rather than Suzdal which had been his father's first choice.

After some time in reflective trance we set off back across the meadow, the long grass dancing with the light breeze. Ahead of us a large group of people appeared, moving in our direction. As they got closer it became apparent that they were tourists.

Soon the group broke into a run – heading straight for us. I could only think that they were in a hurry to reach the church, and why not? It was gorgeous. It wasn't long before a great mass of oriental features engulfed us both, and the sound of cameras clicking filled the preceding silence. Whilst I was spun in circles, Jo was bundled to one side and snap-happy Japanese took it in turns to have their photo taken beside her. She took it in her stride, no stranger to celebrity.

Possibly the most awesome vision of divinity that Russia had to offer was just metres away, yet it was Jo who was the priority photo opportunity. Perhaps it was her blonde hair or the jacket she wore, either way she was happy to take a few moments out; pouting, striking poses and all in all giving her fans what they wanted. Was there no end to her fame this side of Warsaw?

We were finally heading east across Russia and wanted to get to Nizhny Novgorod, the first city beyond the Golden Ring, before nightfall. We didn't set ourselves targets but we did avoid driving at night. This wasn't always easy, as the temptation to carry on that little bit further was always there and finding a place to park up that we were both happy with was becoming harder. It was more nerves than anything. Towns were fine, but out in the open, we both had to feel 100 per cent comfortable with the place we'd stopped – it became something of an OCD, an inch to the left, a couple to the right.

The drive was as straight as the flight of an arrow along a recently gravelled road, the sun was high in the sky and for the first time it really felt like we were covering some ground. Dusk was setting in as we reached the outskirts of the city. The suburbs were unending, wooden shacks and hovels each side of the road, bonfires glowed orange as sweet-smelling smoke filled the air. Reaching Nizhny Novgorod we joined the Volga River again, which we'd last seen back at Kostroma. It had now morphed into a wide business-like waterway, large container vessels ploughing its course. We parked up with a view down across the river.

Nizhny Novgorod, not to be confused with Novgorod, the once capital of Russia, is the federation's third largest city. During Soviet times it was called Gorky after the writer Maxim Gorky. It is home to the GAZ car manufacturing plant, Russia's second biggest car producer, making Nizhny a bit like Dagenham – but with the Volga running through it.

GAZ, the Gorky Automobile Plant, came into being in 1929 – a joint venture between Ford from the United States and the Soviet Union, an unlikely blend of American know-how and Communist labour. Volga is the brand name of cars from GAZ and throughout the Soviet world the Volga were seen as symbols of high status, commonly used by party officials and the security services – in spite of their American connection. They were built to last on bad Russian roads, having high ground clearance, rugged suspension and some serious rust-proofing.

Volgas had been produced since 1956 – and currently there are three models in the range. Top was the 3102 in production since 1982, ubiquitous, especially in the cities – although occasionally you might see one driven by a farmer, stuffed full of potatoes and his extended family, faces pressed up against the window like fish in a tank. Then came the 310221, just gliding off the production line as we arrived in town in 1997, and finally the 31105, then still a glint on a designer's sketch pad, came into production in 2004, available for a mere snip at $7,000. A year later it would be announced that production of the Volga would be phased out.

After a good night's sleep we performed our ablutions in the Volzhsky Otkos Hotel, which overlooks the river with an air of authority, then went to the post office to send postcards back to England, postcards that would never arrive. Although we didn't know it at the time, posting a letter in Russia was like throwing it in the bin. In all the time I've spent in Russia, I've never once seen a postman, which is strange as all the post offices make Leicester Square Underground Station on a Saturday night seem quite tranquil. This one on Gorkogo Square was no exception as I joined the tail end of a 'queue' that had reached the street. The minute I passed through the doorway I realised that the street was the best place to be. A few more thickset women had tagged on behind me, and so began the shoulder-barging, knee-clipping, toe-stepping and general physical intimidation that I should have been used to by then. I think being English I somehow have a heightened sense of 'queuing'. Standing in line in an orderly fashion is about much more than arriving at the front and buying a stamp; it is what arguably defines civilisation! It provides us with an opportunity to display a patient dignity on the outside, even if we don't have it on the inside.

Faced with a 'queue' in Russia there is only one way to behave, and that is the Russian way. Should a twenty-stone babushka who wouldn't have looked out of place in Saruman's army of Orcs in *The Lord of the Rings* happen to take exception and pin you up against the counter, start speaking quickly in English alternating pitch and tone, she'll conclude you're an idiot, and at the worst you'll escape with a few bruises. You may even get your stamp. Another option is to just drop your postcards in the nearest bin.

On this occasion, having clawed my way to the front through a feeding frenzy of old hags, I got the stamps and kept a modicum of dignity. I think they were all so stunned by my audacity that the worst I suffered was someone swiping the hat from my head. I retrieved it on the way out.

Research in a guidebook revealed Nizhny to be the famed dissident Andrey Sakharov's place of exile, and the Sakharov Museum to be well worth a visit. However, the museum was closed and nobody knew when it would be open, or if they did unfortunately we hadn't quite mastered the twenty-four-hour clock in Russian. Over a coffee at a pavement cafe on the leafy main street, with itchy feet and nothing to keep us there, we decided to bid Nizhny a swift farewell, but not before I bought a chicken for dinner from a lady located across the street from where we sat. We had watched her guarding her brood, waiting patiently for the anticipated comedy of a customer making a purchase and walking off with a very much alive clucking chook in their holdall. Unfortunately, our patience wasn't rewarded so we decided to become the protagonists ourselves.

She had a whole gobbling pen full of them and, we discovered, offered a pretty comprehensive service. I was able to choose a chicken. My instinct was to go for the fattest; however, after studying the ten or so chickens clucking away for some time Jo decided that the fattest was indeed her favourite. I did point out that if I didn't eat him somebody else would, and that we were probably doing him a favour by taking him away from the crowded pen sooner rather than later. She wasn't having it so we compromised on a bird less cuddly but healthier looking than most. Once selected the chook was taken behind the scenes into a wooden shack. After about thirty minutes, having had its neck rung and been plucked and tucked, the chook returned in a plastic carrier bag. The smell wasn't so good, and was even worse by dinner time, yet was largely diffused by the prospect of a tasty chicken supper.

We followed the road out of town and drove for several hours before we found a place on the edge of a small hamlet to settle for the night, on some rough ground nestled into the shadow of a stubbly mound. We shared the spot with an abandoned refrigerator, piles of rubble and a rusty old garden climbing frame, as well as a multitude of overflowing bin bags. It was obviously used as a dump, but it was off the road and secluded and felt safe enough. We erected the folding table and chairs that we carried in the back of the van, and sat by Max's side amongst the rubbish to enjoy the evening's transition to night. Gentle breezes cooled the heated earth, leaving the colour and the outlines of the panoramic hills to soften out into a warm patchwork. A group of men passed by with their herd of goats and singing a cappella, endearingly out of tune.

I cooked the chicken on a disposable BBQ, and it was deliciously washed down with a bottle of Armenian wine. Then we watched the dying embers blend in with the lights of the nearby town. As the darkness became thicker, Jo put together a fire made of brittle fir cones, and we watched the crackling wood etching out in flame a series of flickering faces in the darkness, casting light on the wind.

'Fancy a game of Strip Jack Naked?' I offered. A wry smile appeared on Jo's face, as if to say 'now you're talking'. I dug around in the van for candles and a pack of cards, which along with a small chess set were the only concessions to parlour activities that had been packed. It was a simple enough card game with seemingly little relation to its name.

STRIP JACK NAKED – RULES AND OBJECTIVE

- Each player must have three cards in their hand at anytime.

- Any necessary replenishment is from the deck.

- Cards are placed face up (just like with Snap).

- Each card carries an instruction, e.g. a nine must be followed by a lower card.

- The objective is to get rid of all your cards first. (For best results the game should be played at pace.)

'If you're going to pick up from the pack whenever you like there's no point in playing, you cheat!' came Jo's reprimand a few rounds into the game. I was a little bit rusty but that was a bit harsh, I thought. What was surprising was her tone; it wasn't light-hearted.

'Sorry,' I timidly replied. 'I need to warm up a bit.' I took Jo's words on board and managed to lose the first two games convincingly. What was becoming fast apparent was a side of Jo I'd never previously seen; she had taken the humble game of Strip Jack Naked way beyond drunken student games and apparently acquired the sort of competitive mindset that raises everything from the egg and spoon race to origami to Olympic status. Eventually, after losing three more games I got my eye in. 'About time, I thought I was playing the world's biggest Jack!' I wasn't sure Jo was joking; beneath the reluctant grin, I thought I glimpsed a latent irritation being exorcised. We had been together living in the tight confines of the van for nearly three months now. If Jo was releasing frustration it wasn't surprising. We played one more game in silence then it was time to sleep.

We awoke early the next morning with the sun beginning its ascent from behind the distant hills, offering us a warmly lit arena of expectation for the coming day. These chilly, somewhat dazed early mornings – waking up in Max, condensation trickling down the windows, a long day of possibilities ahead – I wished they could continue forever.

I scrambled Max back onto the nearest road, surprised at how far off road we'd come the previous night. Little was said, just a few mumbled words – both of us aware of the tension of the previous night. We motored for several hours along a wide gravelled surface bordered by mathematically aligned trees that could have been planted by Napoleon, before breaking out into lush pastures grazed by rugged ponies with a distant backdrop of clear blue skies. Villages of any kind were scarce, but that morning we passed through three dusty settlements, the largest of which was called Tsivilsk, which consisted of a dozen wooden slat homes with brightly painted window frames – green, blue and yellow dominated – and a general store stocking bread, cheese, tinned fish, tracing paper tissue and bottles of Fanta. Malnourished dogs roamed the street outside like vultures circling a carcass. As we broke from the ramshackle cluster of buildings Jo spotted a rusting water pump. Water was high on our list of vital commodities, coming second after petrol. We kept a 5-litre canister in the van which we would fill at any opportunity.

As we pulled up a grisly old woman was pumping some water into a bucket; when it was full she braced herself for her onward journey. I waited patiently for her to make space at the pump. On seeing me she turned her head in the other direction. Seconds turned into minutes and still she hadn't budged, leaving me no way of getting to the pump. There was an outside chance that she hadn't seen me and wasn't just being deliberately obstructive, so I cleared my throat and inched forward. When I was just within reach of the handle, just about to position the canister, without any warning whatsoever the hag spun round and walloped me with a clenched fist. She caught me full on the arm, and it quickly deadened. I was immediately overcome by shock – shock that I'd been hit in the first place and shock that the fist had come from a woman well into her seventies. There were a couple of litres still in the canister, so quickly taking stock I made the executive decision that water would have to wait. I retreated to the safety of the van and considered how very lucky I'd been back at the post office in Nizhny Novgorod. I was no match for the elderly Russian female. When I relayed the story back to Jo she simply looked at me as if I was making it up – the next pump we came to, she was getting the water.

CHAPTER SIX
THE TWO STANS

TARTARSTAN

Whenever I had thought of the word 'tartar' it had always been in association with either food or teeth. But the tartar found printed all over toothpaste tubes (a generic name for the salt deposits of tartaric acid, more commonly known as plaque) and tartare sauce, or *sauce tartare* as it is called by our neighbours across the channel (a mix of mayonnaise, mustard, chives and tarragon often served with fish), have no known link with the descendants of Tartarstan. Steak tartare's association probably comes closest; a gourmet dish of minced beef, eggs and seasoning, it may be descended from original Tartar food. The Tartars are said to have eaten the raw, tough meat of the Asian cattle that grazed on the steppe.

Probably the purest descendants of Genghis Khan's Golden Horde existed for many years in the Khanate of Kazan, the capital of Tartarstan, a true thorn in the imperial side of Muscovy – as Tartarstan is to Moscow today.

In the sixteenth century, Ivan the Terrible, then ruler of Muscovy, took an army east from Moscow and captured Kazan. To strengthen his hold he kicked out most of the Muslim population, who may have had hidden loyalties to the Khanate, and relocated Russian Christian artisans and merchants to Kazan. To celebrate his victory Ivan had a cathedral built in the centre of Kazan, and not content with just one, he also built the Intercession Cathedral, or St Basil's, in Red Square, Moscow – a building that many view to be the most powerful symbol of Russia.

Probably Kazan's most recognisable symbol is the Söyembikä Tower, named after a Tartar princess who is believed to have leapt from the top rather than go through with a marriage to Ivan the Terrible when he captured the town. Princess Söyembikä was a direct ancestress of Prince Felix Yusupov, best known for his part in the murder of Rasputin, and one time wealthiest man in Russia. At the beginning of the twentieth century the tower had an inclination of 194 centimetres, not far off the 3.9-metre inclination of the leaning tower of Pisa. Ivan treated Kazan as later tsars would treat Siberia – as a dumping ground for anyone to whom he took a dislike.

SOME FACTS ABOUT IVAN THE TERRIBLE

- Such was his fondness for St Basil's Cathedral in Moscow that he had the two architects responsible for designing it blinded, to stop them ever repeating such great work.

- When Ivan fell out with the archbishop of Novgorod, he had him sewn into a bearskin and hunted down by a pack of hounds.

- Ironically for such a violent man, Ivan died whilst playing chess.

The long snaking approach into Kazan took us down through a forest of thick evergreens. The full-bodied trees and smooth tarmac road offered the suburbs of Kazan a faux sense of opulence as we glided gently downwards towards the city and the fast approaching nightfall. Closer inspection revealed shabby wooden houses and rickety barns peering out from behind the trees, some with broken windows, some with roofs missing, some buildings so ramshackle they simply defied the laws of gravity and looked like the creations of Tim Burton. The atmosphere turned increasingly eerie the darker it became. By the time we had reached what we believed to be the centre of town, we had seen only a handful of people and the starless night, hidden moon and lack of street lighting gave the blackness greater resonance.

We'd had a good day's driving, but neither of us had really let go of the 'weird card incident'. So what we both needed was a good wash. The act of full body washing had become a source of much pleasure on our journey, like eating a meal long in preparation. Greatly anticipated and usually much needed, both had evolved into particularised rituals, with Jo and I falling into our roles with little if any discussion. It was the job of the person not washing to supply saucepans of hot water to the washer – who in turn stood upright in the van, the pop-up roof fully elevated, and poured water over themselves. Surfaces located close by were protected with towels set aside for the task, as was the floor. It was not as liberating an experience as it could have been, as you were always aware of splashing water around the inside of the van; however, generally the whole endeavour had the effect of lifting the mood.

I had the job of water supplier on this occasion, but my mind wasn't really on the job and my rate of supply provoked an impatient 'Hurry up!' from Jo. A little flustered, I managed to direct an entire saucepan of long-heated water all over the van's interior. Jo's response took me somewhat by surprise as she hurled the pan and what was left of its contents right back at my head. I managed to dodge the missile but my instinctive reply was to cover Jo in cold water. Jo fixed me with a defiant glare which I waited to mutate into a smile. Instead, rather more worryingly, she ripped a knife from the cutlery drawer close to hand and lunged at me. I darted away from the van, closely followed by Jo, who grabbed a towel on her way and, her face red with rage, sprinted after me, knife in hand. The Benny Hill style chase that ensued must have been hilarious for any onlookers – and I have to admit the sight of Jo in pursuit, her towel barely covering very much at all, shrieking obscenities, provoked a little chuckle in me. Unfortunately, Jo wasn't laughing.

I made good my escape and spent the next hour pacing nearby streets, biding my time before cautiously returning to the van. Jo was asleep in the back. Washing would have to wait, as I thought long and hard about dealing with the rot that was setting in between Jo and me. The frustration that had fuelled her attack suggested a deeper concern. I spent a very long and very upright night in the passenger seat.

In the Tartar language Kazan is pronounced 'Quazan', which roughly translates as cauldron – an ancient cooking pan, a variant on the wok – so named because of its geographical situation in a u-shaped lowland. Kazan, like Rome, stands on seven hills and, as I discovered whilst walking around groggy and agitated from lack of sleep, has evolved into two distinct sections: the upper town, where the Russian merchants and craftsmen lived, and the lower town, where the Tartar tradesmen and merchants lived. Ivan wasn't one for social cohesion. The Bulak canal at one time provided a distinct dividing line between the two sections, and indeed the two cultures of East and West. Alexander Herzen, the man considered to be the father of Russian socialism, a pro-Western writer and thinker, wrote of the city: 'The significance of Kazan is very great, it is a place where two worlds meet. It has two origins, the west and the east, and you can see them at every cross roads.'

Perhaps it is Western insecurity, but some would say that the Tartars have never really forgiven the European Russians for stripping them of their capital and then taking their lands in Siberia away from them. Rumour has it that the Tartars still have great plans of winning back Siberia – and legend has it that a giant white wolf will one day emerge from the Irtysh River and frighten away the Russians. The Siberian Tartars still call Tyumen (the last town before Omsk) Chingistora, after Genghis Khan.

The Kazan State University is the second oldest in the Russian Federation. Witnessing the university's grandeur first hand, I was not surprised that on a couple of affiliated websites the university is argued to have hosted a formidable list of academics:

> The history of Kazan State University is associated with many world-renowned figures, like the father of non-Euclidian geometry, Nikolai Lobachevsky; Leo Tolstoy; the discoverer of the Antarctic, Ivan Siminov; the founder of organic chemistry, Alexander Butlerov; a father of modern linguistics, Ivan Baudouin de Courtenay; the discoverer of electron spin resonance, Evgeny Zavoisky and the Soviet leader Lenin (Vladimir Ulianov).

Lenin was almost added on as an afterthought.

We drank milky coffee outside the university, suitably impressed by the immaculate white stonework of this huge building. A few words had been mumbled that morning between Jo and myself but little else. This particular derailing of relations was going to take some time to correct.

Having left the outskirts of Kazan behind us, it took us thirty minutes to realise that the spare tyre had a slow puncture. The tyre the spare had replaced was now fastened to Max's nose and was as flat as a pancake, the result of a puncture back in Latvia that we'd never done anything about. Jo pulled into a fortuitously placed 'garage', which had no tyres and couldn't repair ours. But they pointed us in the direction of the nearest village, where we might be able to get some help, making no attempt to hide their hysterical laughter.

At the bottom of a steep hill we found a settlement of wooden *izbas*, traditional style cottages, and nothing that looked very much like a garage. We left Max and went in search of anything or anyone who could help.

'We must have been sent down here for a reason,' maintained Jo optimistically. The village was sleeping or deserted. The narrow dusty streets were empty, not a human in sight; maybe the multitude of dogs that roamed the streets had eaten them.

Eventually, we found a shop with a heavily sprung metal door, requiring both of us to force it open.

If the word 'MAGAZENE' hadn't been written above the door, there would have been no clues as to what we'd walked into. The shelves behind a wide hardboard counter were stocked with three packets of the Papirosi brand of Russian cigarette with more filter than tobacco, a bag of eggs, a litre bottle of Fanta and two packets of Choco Pies.

Jo turned to the stony-faced babushka, who was guarding her fare like a goalkeeper just before a penalty kick, and asked in her best Russian where we might find a garage. '*Machina kaput... kooda?*'

Her words were received with a blank expression. Not surprising, as she was saying, 'Car broken, where?'

'*Machina kaput... Kooda* for God's sake,' Jo repeated herself, this time louder, adding a little emphasis.

Still nothing from the babushka! I thought it was a good time to move in with some of my best Russian, and just found myself saying exactly the same thing, only with

more emphasis and patronisingly slowly, '*Maaachiiinaa....*
Karpooott....... Kooooda!'

We had found ourselves in backwardsville and we were
getting nowhere. At least they did have a supply, albeit
small, of Choco Pies. I had developed quite a taste for
Choco Pies since we'd been in Russia – they were a bit like
Wagon Wheels but shaped differently, and the presence
of tiny bubbles in the chocolate made them more fluffy. I
pointed furiously at the pies and the bottle of Fanta – in one
fell swoop her stock was halved. We left the shop.

'I hope she's expecting a delivery soon!' said Jo. But
looking around at the deserted streets, did she really need
one?

As we arrived back at Max licking our lips, a car skidded
to a halt directly in front of us, enveloping us in a cloud of
dust. From out of the haze like a pantomime villain emerged
the driver, a stocky man with a large round head which
somehow didn't seem to belong to his body. His mouth
eventually made the shape of a sneer, revealing a full set
of gold teeth. His dark blue uniform gave him an air of
authority. Soon, at a more sedate pace, another car pulled
up alongside the first, this one very clearly a *politzeiski* van.
The driver of this vehicle was much taller and European
looking, and wore the same uniform as the other man.
He greeted his colleague with a chummy handshake, and
spoke a few words, possibly along the lines of, 'Great to be
working with you.'

The uniforms worn by these two were initially a source of
relief, but it still hadn't sunk in that the police were the bad
guys in Russia. After our experience in Vologda, we were

still harbouring a view quite the contrary. I was just about to wave my arms about and ask for a garage, when the shorter man barked: 'Documents!'

His tone was disorientating. With that one word, it was obvious that these guys weren't about to tell us we were crazy, slap us on the backs and send us on our way.

Both men lit cigarettes as I rooted inside Max for our passports, hoping that Jo would be able to soften the situation with some incomprehensible banter – but it just wasn't happening. However charming we may or may not have looked, these guys really didn't like us. It was weird to think that, officially, we were still in Europe.

They scrutinised our documents, and something in our visas caught their attention. They mumbled some words to one another, before the smaller guy spat, 'Petersburg!' He pointed to the visa, quite agitated. 'Petersburg,' he repeated, and then in the universal fashion when trying to be understood by bloody foreigners, he shouted, 'Petersburg *ettarh* Kaazann!' the words were slow and pronounced as he pointed to the ground beneath his heavy leather boots, a glint in his eye as if he had succeeded in catching us out. My heart sank. It wasn't difficult to understand what he was getting at: our visas only officially allowed us to visit St Petersburg, and he wanted to make this a problem. Unlike the kindly cops of Vologda and all the other militia we had met thus far in Russia, these guys did things by the book. Our passports vanished into the Tartar's pocket before he climbed into his car and drove off, leaving us with his mate. There seemed no point in trying to ingratiate ourselves with him; all I could think about was the long drive back to St Petersburg.

The tyre still had air in it, but not much; yet getting it fixed now seemed irrelevant. I even thought it would make a reasonable excuse for not being able to get back west. Jo couldn't bring herself to look at me. The disappointment consumed us both. At that moment we were both aware of how important our flawed mission to get across to Vladivostok had become, job or no job. Whatever had been going on between me and Jo now seemed completely insignificant: in adversity Team Max was united once more – and we both knew it.

It hadn't even crossed our minds to list every town/city we planned to visit during the journey on our visa application forms as was officially required. We had only listed St Petersburg and now we were a long way away from where we should have been. After an hour the Tartar returned in another cloud of dust.

'Petersburg,' he said, pointing up the hill we'd driven down. '*Davai*.' Come on, let's go.

'Petersburg, *Davai*.'

So we climbed into the van, Jo muttering the consolatory words, 'You fucking twats.'

He returned our passports and we crawled back up the hill, the policeman's Volga Sedan close behind us. It looked like he was seriously going to escort us all the way back to St Petersburg. However, when he was satisfied that we were heading in the right direction, he overtook and accelerated out of sight.

After about 5 kilometres, allowing enough time for the police to come back if they were going to, I pulled over to the side of the road. Jo stared blankly straight ahead.

I climbed out, and looked around. Where were we, what were we doing?

'What is it?' Jo questioned, concerned I might have lost something.

'St Petersburg or Vladivostok?' I mused.

'What do you think?' A smile edged its way onto Jo's face, a cheeky glint in her eye.

I turned Max around and put my foot down.

A few kilometres along the road, we were able to put air into the tyre and continue on our way. We were a little flustered, more than a little edgy. I nervously followed the progress of any vehicle that appeared and began growing, like a spectre, in the wing mirror. There weren't many. We passed an old ZIL truck crawling along, sweetcorn piled high in its trailer. The lack of other road users added to a growing feeling of isolation. The sky was grey and threatening, patches of cloud hung in the distant valleys, like quivering bits of wool stuck onto the landscape. Black and brown long-haired cattle were grazing in the seemingly endless fields, peppered with stumps of gorse displaying purple blossom. We passed a ragged-looking pony pulling a rickety wooden cart laden with hay piloted by a gnarled old man, a cigarette hanging precariously from his lips as he bumped along the uneven road. He didn't seem to notice as we passed him by. There was a feeling of moving through a soundless bubble of time and space, a peculiar sense of being invisible. The scale of the scenery we passed through was unlike anything either of us had imagined, and as we drove we were undergoing an awakening, soaking up the sheer magnitude of the country and the task we'd given ourselves.

Unsettled as I still was after the incident with the police, I took the wrong road – not a major disaster, but still an unnecessary detour. Rather than cross over the Kama River at a narrow point using a bridge, we had to cross over at one of its widest points by ferry. The terminal was beyond a settlement of dilapidated cabins which gave it the feel of a frontier town, with freshly felled tree trunks by the roadside. The ferry master's pretty *izba* stood out amongst its neighbours in that it was well maintained, flowers sat in window boxes and in the foreground on a neat patch of grass a tethered pony grazed beside the syrupy-looking river.

The Kama was a tributary of the Volga, beginning in Udmurtia to the north and flowing east some 1,805 kilometres through Tartarstan. The car ferry ran once a day, not frequent enough to keep up with the volume of traffic that used the service. When we arrived at the river, we joined the end of a queue, some twenty cars back. This was good because we would get a place on the ferry. This was bad because it meant there would be a long wait for the ferry.

We had left the police back on the outskirts of Kazan and had really hoped to put some distance between them and us. Now we had to wait six hours on the wrong side of the river. It was jumpy but not all bad, as there was a constant stream of old women making their way along the growing line of waiting traffic, selling tasty cooked fish. We ate our fill, washed down with Fanta. The queue, six hours later, was two, maybe three hundred vehicles long.

Ten more vehicles followed us slowly onto the ferry before the ramp was raised and closed with a metallic thump; we

were certainly cutting it fine but we had made it. We noted
the cars left queuing on dry land with some sympathy – they
still had a long wait. However, we were glad to be on-board,
and doubted that any of them were on the run from the
local police... well, not many of them anyway.

BASHKORTOSTAN

The pretty village of Tuymazy on the eastern bank of the
river was our first taste of the Republic of Bashkortostan.
The drive beyond the village was enjoyable – not just
because we were away from Tartarstan, and not halfway
back to Tallinn, but also because we both felt a renewed
exhilaration for the trip, as if we'd been given a second
chance.

NOTE ON BASHKORTOSTAN

Up until the sixteenth century the territory of what
is now modern Bashkortostan was divided between
Kazan and Siberian Khanates. After Kazan had been
captured by Ivan the Terrible, a handful of Bashkir
tribes approached the tsar with a request to join
Muscovy, which duly happened – a pretty lily-livered
act motivated by self-preservation rather than any
genuine loyalty, but nonetheless a plan that was
to prove successful as it saw off any future threats
from the east, and the Bashkirs have seen increasing
autonomy from Moscow.

The road was exhilarating, climbing long hills then gliding down into deep valleys, cutting through lush pastures and arable land. It was harvest time and the labourers appeared as in a time-frozen tableau with obsolete equipment and no great urgency. We passed unnoticed through the farms and countryside, arriving in Ufa late on a Friday afternoon.

Ufa is a provincial town on the edge of the Belaya River, capital to the republic's population of four million, and as we discovered, not a bad location to spend some time. However, Max's deteriorating engine was our first concern. The coughing had begun way back in Nizhny, but was only evident in the lower gears; up in fourth Max ran like a dream. All the petrol filtering had successfully masked the real problem with the engine, that of the gradual destruction of the coil – a result of the blended and thus low quality fuel we had been using, which had no small amount of extras floating around in it. (I had already fished out from the spare can grit, dead insects, small stones and even a ring pull.) We had both developed the mentality that if we just ignored it, the problem would go away, not wanting to confront the reality that with the end of Max would come the end of the trip and our return to England. The roads to Ufa had been flat and straight – so bar the occasional teasing splutter the problem had apparently gone away. However, once we had hit the outskirts of Ufa, it became clear that it hadn't and would have to be addressed. Even the most gentle of slopes had become a struggle for Max to climb, without having built up considerable speed beforehand.

We headed straight for a garage on our arrival. The shining light of hope was temporarily dimmed by a cheery man, who was just bolting the gates of his establishment ready to go home for the weekend. To our attempts at conveying our need of help with furious gestures and use of a hastily put together pidgin language, his response was simple. '*Soobota Nyet, Voskresenya Nyet,*' he said, with a sympathetic raised-hands gesture that any self-respecting Frenchman would have been pleased with. Anyone who decides to break down in central Russia will understand this to mean 'You're not going anywhere till Monday.'

We quickly got the picture: the Bashkirs took their weekends seriously. Reluctantly, we accepted that we'd just have to wait. A rest was needed anyway. Beneath the man's grey wiry hair his burnished cheeks were smooth, sweeping down into heavy jowls, which made him look sympathetic to our predicament – even if he wasn't. After another furious exchange of gestures and improvised Russlish, we settled in for the night, believing that we had arranged to meet with Alexi the following morning. For what purpose we weren't sure, but we went to sleep glad to have a 'friend' in this unknown town.

True enough, the following morning, just as the muffled light signalled a new day, Alexi appeared outside the van. He made no attempt to communicate – simply smiled and ushered us into the back of his Lada. He was relaxed in a way that suggested words were unnecessary and that all would become clear without them. The further we drove, the thicker the crowds of people which filled the road became, prompting Alexi to discard the car. Something was going down, we thought as we emerged.

We were quickly overpowered by the colours, vibrations, smells, shouts and ringing exhortations of the town's weekly market. The scene that greeted us, so unexpected and welcome, overwhelmed our sleepy senses. The endless packed and overflowing stalls tumbling from the thoroughfares were like some crazy theme park designed by Dante. It was like we had just walked into a medina in North Africa. The sheer chaotic tumultuous energy of the place, combined with the sense of a thousand pairs of eyes locked onto our pale faces, made us feel a very long way from home, and quite a long way from any of the Russia we had recently passed through. We were immediately glad to be with Alexi, who sensed our disorientation and wound up his apparently permanent smile – probably relieved that further attempts at verbal communication were impossible due to the exotic pandemonium. The babbling market was its own gloriously uncompromising son et lumière of Bashkir street life, hungrier than ever to declare its identity after the colourless Soviet days.

There was a churning rainbow of furling and unfurling fabrics; a cacophonous tympani of clanking pots and screaming infants; an aromatic cocktail of incense, unguents and sweat; a liquid kaleidoscope of rolling fruits and unrolled rugs, and huge knives that flashed, chopped and sliced faster than the sirocco. Voices contended endlessly for the attention of the passing onlookers, by turns hectoring, cajoling, imploring and sometimes pleading as if life depended on a sale. The movement was frenetic and unceasing, the din raucous and equally constant, the overall effect was giddying, uncertain, perhaps even euphoric. The market was an affirmation of the entire Bashkir culture, and Alexi knew all he had to do was throw us into it and the spell would be cast.

The sea of staring faces grew thicker as we pushed our way deeper into the crowds. The shouts, screams, wails, animal noises and jangling percussion of pots and pans and sharpening knives, and the bantering cries of the maniacally industrious stall holders all jostled together like notes on the market's orchestral score. It now began to fuse into a wall of sound – like a speeded-up recording in which an already discordant melody is flung around so hard that the brain can no longer work fast enough to process the noises slamming into the eardrums. The effect was tending towards the hypnotic. Suddenly, the potent witchcraft was punctured and my front brain kicked back into gear when Jo nudged me and yelled: 'I really need a pee!'

As we looked around for a suitable facility we were pushed to one side of the street to make way for a mule laden with baskets being led by its owner in our direction. It was the overbearing size of the mule and its burden that was to cause the ensuing fracas. A solitary man, sitting on a low stool in front of a shop, was unintentionally barged from his seat by the mule as it passed. Shaken and understandably angry the man began to lunge at the muleteer, who gave as good as he got. Soon things heated up and ugly and awkward punches were thrown. My own sympathy was with the man who had been dumped from his stool; the muleteer, obviously leading without due care and attention, didn't even offer an apology. It was doubtful that any official by-law existed to determine who was in the right, but both parties were insisting the other was in the wrong. Alexi, partly in virtue of his close proximity to the incident, stepped in between the two protagonists and attempted to separate them and cool them down. The stool man retrieved his overturned seat and, muttering loudly, sat defiantly down in his original position. The muleteer likewise returned to his mule, and was about to head off into the crowd again when, taking a backward glance, the sight of his disputant, proudly upright on his stool again, sent him into another rage. He flung down the reins, marched back and with both hands pushed his opponent. Satisfied he had had the last shove the muleteer tugged his charge quickly away. Seemingly pleased with the fulfilment of his civic responsibilities, Alexi proudly returned his attentions to us, and Jo's now quite serious need for a bathroom. Alexi pointed towards an alleyway.

A few metres along we arrived at a thin doorway masked by a flowing curtain. We were ushered through the doorway and emerged in a high-ceilinged hall. It was refreshingly calm, quiet and cool after the incessant bustle of the street: it seemed unimaginable when squeezing along through the jammed market that such a large and secluded place could be hidden away close by. It felt faintly magical. Alexi led us through the hall and into another equally large room, and turned to us with his biggest warm smile yet, his body language inviting us to survey the very pleasant nature of the surroundings. The scene wouldn't have been out of place in a riad in Fez, but in a backstreet house in Ufa it appeared more than a little incongruous. Every wall of the vast room was hung with carpets long and short, the floor space covered with pile upon pile of them. It crossed my mind that Jo's request for a WC had been confused with an imminent need to get our hands on a carpet, until a skinny man with Mongol features appeared and, after a brief exchange with Alexi, took Jo by the hand and led her away.

By Monday morning Max's condition appeared to have declined. Even getting the engine started took a while. We managed to get him as far as the garage, where he quickly conked out in the middle of a queue of Ladas waiting to fill up with petrol. When the babushka operating the pumps realised that we weren't in fact deliberately obstructing her busy Monday morning forecourt, she helped us push Max through a set of tall, rusting gates, the iron-work drooping like dying flowers.

It could have been a sixteenth-century Spanish villa with the cast of a Zorro film waiting off set – a stone courtyard set within a two-storey barn with a balcony running all around at first-floor level. The barn – built of a deep chestnut-coloured wood, recently creosoted – was the perfect setting for a heavily choreographed sword fight.

One side of the courtyard was given to a three-high pile of rusting Lada shells, garnished with an assortment of engine parts, and a sprinkling of tyres.

A man wearing faded stonewashed jeans beckoned us over. He had a dark complexion and film star looks. I steered the van over to the far side of the courtyard and pulled up in front of the man, who tapped the flat spare wheel on Max's nose before jumping into the cab beside me and offering a greasy hand to shake. The man's good looks somehow conveyed the impression that he was a superior mechanic.

I found myself reciprocating his greeting with enthusiasm. The mechanic was called Yuri and, disengaging from the handshake, he made himself comfortable thumbing through our Haynes manual, as un-thumbed as the day it was bought. Yuri was very appreciative of the photographs – of which Haynes' manuals have many.

It wasn't long before a small crowd had gathered. With the help of the audience Max was guided into a sheltered bay, and debris was cleared to make space. The concern of the onlookers huddling around gave the atmosphere of a road traffic accident being attended by a skilled surgeon; in this case we were hoping that was Yuri. The next hour was spent waiting in hopeful anticipation, watching Yuri's legs for any twitch that might suggest the operation was completed and that he would surface from the innards of the van in to the fresh morning air with a look of success on his face.

We drank tea, drew pictures in the dust, and then drank some more until Yuri emerged. His spanner aloft, he was grinning from ear to ear. He nodded his head with the air of a man who had just solved the last conundrum of the universe. Yuri then lit a cigarette and began to explain his findings to Jo, with his free arm resting on my shoulder. The audience responded with interest; we were none the wiser. We were just relieved to be in the hands of someone who seemed to know what he was doing.

Yuri once more disappeared beneath Max, whilst we were led away by the crowd. Stepping over engine parts and wheels, our hosts picked up various crates and boxes, which were upturned and arranged as makeshift tables. Some of the men washed their hands at a sink, others decorated the tables with mugs, water jugs, bread, cheese and preserves of various kinds. A small bearded man opened an oily green bag and produced a bunch of bananas, which he added, somewhat reluctantly, to the other offerings.

We each took a seat at the table, about fifteen people in all, some perched astride old generators, the luckier ones resplendent on stacks of plump truck tyres. It was difficult to work out where everyone had appeared from, but they all seemed to work there. The thick coffee and the redcurrant juice were kicked into life with vodka, while the samovar bubbled away in the background. When the last of the coffee was drunk, cigarettes were handed around, and our hosts warmly encouraged us to follow them in checking on Max.

The sun was now high in the sky, and as before Yuri's legs were the only visible part of him, his torso swallowed as if by the jaws of a metallic crocodile. With the audience back in place he rose slowly up, as if he had been waiting for a full house. Yuri looked more pensive than he had previously, as he again rested his hand on my shoulder and spoke to Jo. His voice had the quiet measured care of a doctor explaining a complex procedure to the close relative of a patient. His intense monologue, punctuated by lip-pursing and sighs, eventually reached a conclusion. Here half the spectators vanished inside, while the other half appeared to lose interest and sat down on the ground. Yuri grabbed my hand and energetically pulled me to the gates of the courtyard, and Jo followed as we lurched onto the street like a couple of drunks, where we were guided into the back of an aging Lada.

Ladas, despite their deceiving exterior, are quite the family car on the inside. Yuri looked strange behind the wheel of such a humble car, like Al Pacino whizzing up the high street on a Honda Express moped. We fast got the gist – we were going in search of a necessary part. The Lada sped off into the barren countryside, leaving the town a dot in the distance. After some forty-five minutes of driving the landscape became greener with trees and thickening scrub.

Some 40 per cent of Bashkortostan is covered by forest – that's roughly 62,000 square kilometres. It is home to a spectacular range of old growth Siberian and European forests, where the most eastern reaches of European broad-leaved forests rich in oak, lime, conifers, birch and maple meet the Siberian species. In turn the forests are home to a rather exotic gathering of fauna such as maral and roe deer, wolf, lynx, golden eagle, osprey and peregrine falcons. However, where there's a natural resource there's business, and there were already as many as 140 timber companies operating in Bashkortostan, as well as a number of mines digging for mostly chromes and non-ferrous metals.

Eventually the trees cleared again and Yuri pointed to a grey stone mass appearing ahead of us. It resembled a fortress from a distance, but at closer proximity it was the brickwork of a small cluster of apartment blocks. The buildings were severely cracked, and washing danced on lines giving the place colour. Everywhere there was junk, and piles of rubble, as if the place had recently been bombed. Endless discarded odds and ends of broken furniture, utensils and electrical gear lined the track that led into the heart of the block.

We climbed out of the Lada crunching glass underfoot, and followed our benefactor up the stairwell to the fourth floor and into a flat. Yuri called out 'Mamma' and we walked through a cluttered hallway and into a kitchen, where a woman rose from a chair to greet us. She had grey hair and was plump, with pockmarked skin. Only the set of her forehead and the glimmer in her eye gave away that she was indeed Yuri's mother.

Mamma pointed in the direction of a tall kitchen cupboard. When opened it revealed a cornucopia of engine parts, which Yuri enthusiastically began rummaging through. Coils, fan belts, oil caps and much more were laid out on the floor. Whilst this was going on Mamma had found some plates, and ladled something onto them from a simmering pot resting on the stove. It was *yuryu*, a type of oaten gruel – not tasty but filling in the way that cement would be. Yuri found his part and then joined us for lunch, and our second meal in so many hours. Mamma was watching our every mouthful with an expression on her face suggesting 'Mamma makes the best *yuryu* in all Bashkortostan'. Yuri had dispatched his bowlful with the speed of a seasoned devotee and began pacing like a caged predator, displaying all signs of being in a hurry. The pressure was too much for me and the idea of offending Yuri – or even worse, the idea of offending Yuri's mother – went well beyond my instinctive desire for harmony in the world. I painfully spooned up the last of the lumpy porridge, detaching it from the bowl like glue, and forced a look of satisfaction onto my face. Jo had no such scruples and conceded with half a bowl remaining. Mamma appeared bewildered, perhaps even a little angry,

Jo appeared to have turned a shade of yellow and Yuri appeared to be halfway out the door. So with no time to digest the Bashkir regional dish or even try to explain to Mamma that her gruel was perhaps a little heavy for our untrained stomachs, we made our goodbyes and returned with Yuri to Ufa.

Back at the hacienda Yuri casually bid us both a farewell, as if we'd simply bought a pint of milk from him, showing a lack of sentiment we were going to have to get used to in Russia. We were then led in another direction to the more corporate-looking section of the establishment, up on the first floor, where people were busying themselves in front of computer screens or on the phone. A man sporting an even bigger smile than Yuri ushered us to wait whilst he filled out some official-looking form, which he then handed to me with a hopeful look. It was an invoice for the work on Max, which had taken the best part of seven hours. I examined the figures in front of me, somewhat baffled, before handing over a crisp note. The sum in roubles translated to just over six pounds sterling.

We left Ufa both smiling from ear to ear that Monday afternoon, uncertain whether the kindness we had been shown was down to the Bashkirs, or whether the garage was run by Carlsberg – probably the best garage in the world. Forever after I would be slightly envious of the Ufemites of Ufa, who had such a dynamic and generous mechanic should their Ladas ever have carburettor trouble.

We joined the M5 – the largest of all the roads that had bypassed the town – with Max purring like a cat, new coil in place, and our confidence restored. I even went to the trouble of charting our route with the compass we'd picked up in St Petersburg. The next few hours' driving were an absolute delight. Fields crammed with sunflowers, gently swaying in the light breeze like a crowd at a music festival, were punctuated by wooded glades with sun reflecting off the silver bark. The road was as smooth as if it had been laid with fresh tarmac the day before, unlikely as it was. It was as if Max had folded away his wheels and switched to hover cruise!

And then we passed a signpost for:

'CAMAPA'

It was only minutes after I'd passed it that it sunk in. It was of course in Cyrillic script, which normally we'd both ignore because it was incomprehensible to us. However, 'Camapa' translates into English as 'Samara', so I couldn't really ignore it. I pulled over and grunted and waved my arms at a man standing on the edge of a field. He confirmed that we had indeed joined the M5 west instead of east and were now fast on our way to the Caucasus. The compass was thrown out the window. In future we'd stick to what we knew – good old-fashioned intuition.

CHAPTER SEVEN

ACROSS THE URALS AND INTO SIBERIA

Back on route, the Ural Mountains grew up around us. The surrounding slopes were dense with tall, thin trees – their skinny appearance suited the rocky ground from which they sprouted, patterned with crumbling boulders, stones and sparse vegetation. Autumnal leaves gave what little colour there was. Pulling into a roadside bazaar, Max was quickly engulfed by a gaggle of sunburnt women, resplendent in batik headscarves, selling plastic bags full of juicy pink shrimps. Jo bought a bag, if only to clear some space to open the door.

The Urals had been home to five of the Soviet Union's 'secret cities' for weapons research and development, and before Chernobyl took the title, it was Chelyabinsk-65 that was the site of the world's worst nuclear disaster when a waste tank exploded.

As was the Soviet way, news of the accident was suppressed for decades, whilst whole villages that had been affected were systematically wiped out. The region looked like it was still reeling from the effects of radiation and, come to think of it, they were extremely big shrimps.

It seemed to rain heavily the whole time we were passing through the Urals. We stocked up at a kiosk which was offering as a special that day polythene bags full of spotted eggs. It seemed a good idea to buy some, but they all got broken before we had a chance to eat them.

Eventually, we broke from the forested mountain borders along a waterlogged road, into a flat naked landscape. Our first impression of Siberia was bleak and desolate, cold and intimidating – pretty much what you'd expect, really. So where and what is Siberia? For some, it's simply the huge area east of the Urals continuing to the Pacific seaboard. For others, it's an ominous, dark place at the back of the mind, a symbol of all things bad, not really a place at all but an enigma. For some it's the worst bit of Russia, where nobody wants to be. For others it's Russia's Texas, where everything is bigger, the roads longer, the forests bigger, the lakes deeper, with the biggest energy reserves, that one day the rest of the world will be crying out for.

Regardless of where Siberia actually starts and finishes or indeed what Siberia is, the general consensus is that the best bits are in its heartland – in the middle. You could travel for days being tortured by your surroundings before you start happening across little parcels of paradise and quickly forget all the bits that went before. The native Siberian writer Valentin Rasputin says: 'From whichever direction you approach it, Siberia is in no hurry to reveal itself.' He believes the region works gradually on you, no sudden surprises, but slowly drawing you in physically and emotionally until eventually 'binding you tightly'.

The rain persisted and got heavier as we pushed on towards the sulky, unrewarding Soviet town of Tyumen. We filled up with petrol and were glad to drive on through. The weather cleared as we travelled south-east for 180 kilometres until reaching Omsk, where we pulled up for the night on the edge of a corn field bordered by silver birch trees aligned in perfect single file. There was an unearthly silence; the air was so pure it cleansed our skin. We could have been the only people alive.

We woke up the next morning to our first frost. A bridge across the rusty Irtysh River took us in to the centre of Omsk. Through the suburbs we passed sprawling Soviet industrialisation; factories, petrochemical plants, refineries – all contributing to the patchwork of pollution. It wasn't long after reaching the centre that we became lodged bumper to bumper in a traffic jam. A haphazard line of vehicles stretched out of sight in both directions. The irony of being in Siberia – one of the least populated regions of the world – and in a traffic jam didn't evade us.

We passed a policeman who had leant his motorbike up and was smoking a cigarette, surveying the scene with an air of detachment which suggested all was quite normal. An old fourgon sat up ahead with its lights flashing and a siren wailing, going nowhere; the red cross on its side wasn't persuading anyone to let it through. I chuckled as I peeped between the gaps in Omsk's decrepit tower blocks and glimpsed the miles of desolate steppe that lay beyond.

The city was founded in 1717 as a fortress for the Cossacks trying to keep the nomads at bay. Later a prison was built which was to become Dostoyevsky's inspiration for *The House of the Dead*, where he was to spend four years in exile for his part in a revolutionary circle back in St Petersburg. Siberia's rich tradition of playing host to political exiles, petty criminals and anyone else who managed to upset the rulers of the day went back several centuries and wasn't restricted to antagonists of the human variety.

The first exile was the Uglich Bell in 1593. Uglich is a town on the Volga which was the home to Ivan the Terrible's ten-year-old son and heir, Dmitri. Dmitri was found dead with his throat cut, and it was the bell that rung the news of the death around Uglich. The death prompted a rebellion by the locals that was easily quashed. It also prompted the Time of Troubles, between the end of the Rurik dynasty – of which Dmitri was the last – and the beginning of the Romanov, fifteen years later. When the immediate fuss caused by the murder had quietened down, suspicion fell on Boris Godunov for the murder; the official investigators, however, concluded the death to be accidental. With a shortage of suspects, it was the bell that got the blame: it had its tongue removed and was sent to Tobolsk, where it would remain until 1892. The bell, like many other exiles, was treated well, and in 1860 even had a tower built for it, the inanimate object equivalent of a penthouse suite. It now holds the record for the longest exile of any such object – coming in at 300 years. In the nineteenth century the people of Uglich battled hard for the return of the bell and eventually they got their wish, but not before a copy had been made and a chapel built for it to hang in – as it does today. Or does it? The story goes that a seventeenth-century fire in Tobolsk had completely melted the bell, which would make the bell returned to Uglich a copy, and the bell now in Tobolsk a copy of the copy.

Looking at the dishevelled inhabitants of Omsk trudging by, reflecting their surroundings perfectly as we passed through, the threat of a long spell in the city would have been quite a deterrent from any criminal activities. Omsk seemed to be one large construction site: roads were being dug up, buildings were either half completed or half demolished, and it looked like the victim of heavy bombing from the air. I noticed a building to the side of the road that looked strangely familiar; with its statue of Lenin and the red, white and blue of the Russian flag, it was a sight we could have seen in any number of Russian towns, but I was convinced we'd seen it before. Then I realised we had, about two hours before. We were going round in circles. We were trying to find the M51 which was, according to the map, an attractively straight road linking Omsk with the Siberian capital, Novosibirsk. All we'd managed to find was the town hall... again.

After several hours of unexplained gridlock we eventually broke free of Omsk, onto an enticing open road and a clear horizon ahead. This lasted for a mile or two. Our liberation was short lived as we were brought to a standstill by a gathering of 4x4s and trucks blocking the road. The vehicles had evidently been stopped by a massive expanse of standing water into which the road ahead had disappeared. A nearby river had been swollen by several days of torrential rain. Judging by the assembled engine power it would be impossible to cross. This included:

- A couple of Nivas – the Siberian four-wheel drive version of the Fiat Panda, a nippy little runabout that can also handle a few thousand miles of steppe or mountain.

- A Japanese landcruiser – a vehicle favoured by the St Petersburg mafia. Since crossing the Urals, this was probably the commonest vehicle on the roads, pushing the Lada into second place.

- A seven-and-a-half-tonne truck.

- A couple of UAZ vans – the Soviet cousin of the VW Transporter, probably Max's closest relative in Russia.

The drivers were all gathered around a modified fuel canister which bellowed black smoke into the air. Shashlik, chunks of meat on a skewer, was being cooked on the makeshift stove and washed down by warming vodka. We were pretty much ignored as at least two separate conversations were under way, the men taking it in turns to prod the meat. I took a map and a dictionary from the van. After some moments we began to get noticed.

'Novosibirsk,' I uttered with my finest flat palm shoulder shrug.

The effect of my utterance was a heavy chorus of sighs, tuts and aahs. A bulky man with a canal network of thread veins embroidered on his face snatched the map from my hands and gave it a long disdainful look before passing it on to the next man. The map then circulated the group, and once inspected by all it found its way back into my hands. After some moments of silence the group looked at me intently before bursting into laughter. The laughter subsided into chatter, and I caught the eye of the first man, who nonchalantly waved his stick in the direction we had come from.

'Omsk?' I responded cautiously.

'Novosibirsk!' came the chorused reply, eyes now wide as if they were dealing with idiots. The man's stick continued to point unwaveringly. I followed its direction closely for the first time, and realised that it was not in fact pointing towards Omsk but to a hole in a hedge by the side of the road. Noting my realisation the group all nodded in agreement before turning their attention back to the sizzling shashlik.

Cautiously I guided Max through the hole, which led into a muddy field, but wheel ruts ahead suggested the advice was sound – the track appeared fairly well-beaten, if a little unlikely. The tyres gently spun as the wheels struggled to get a grip on the wet grass. We slowly followed the track when it was visible, and when it suddenly vanished we guessed a route.

We continued, increasingly aware that we were off the map in western Siberia. Every kilometre felt like a bonus. It really did feel like we were swimming, holding our breath and seeing how long we could stay under before we lost our nerve and broke for the surface. The truth was there was now no visible surface to break for. We saw cattle being herded by a man on horseback in the distance, but that was the only show of life we saw that day. When darkness finally approached we pulled up in the shadow of a hulking oak tree. Rain was again steadily falling and we took the opportunity to wash in the warm raindrops. Then we lay in the back of the van watching distant silver birches turning gradually black and listening to the rhythm of the rain falling on the plastic roof. Neither of us had a clue where we were, but we were both where we wanted to be, and slept well that night.

The following morning the sun was shining and lush grass glistened all around. We had been joined by a herd of long-haired cattle, their flat noses sniffing Max. Now that the cloak of rain had lifted everything seemed much bigger, the space around us more daunting. There was no way of knowing whether we were heading towards Novosibirsk, but the sun was able to confirm that we were heading east. After three hours of slow crawl along an increasingly faint trail petrol was getting low.

Just when we most needed some reassurance, up ahead in the far distance we deciphered the outline of a stationary jeep. As we drew closer it was possible to see a man pacing up and down next to it, apparently slamming his hand down repeatedly onto the bonnet. We pulled up behind, and with one final bang on the bonnet the man climbed into the jeep and shook his head at us, driving off in the direction we'd come.

We pushed forward a little way beyond, and fast realised why he'd decided to turn back. The trail disappeared downwards into an expanse of water, which stretched some 30 metres into the distance. Any frustration was compounded by what looked like a magnificently broad and solid road of Roman proportions emerging from beyond the watery obstacle, and stretching into the distance as far as the eye could see. No wonder he had been thumping his bonnet. We slumped into our seats and imagined the pleasure of driving along the road that was so tantalisingly close – but yet so far. We continued to sit in silence, hoping that we would suddenly be spirited across the newly formed lake.

'We'll have to wait,' Jo broke the silence.

'Wait for what?' I snapped.

'For the ground to dry out,' she barked back. 'Or we could go back to Omsk – and wait there.'

Neither waiting nor returning to Omsk were bearable options; however, they were the only options, a fact that gradually and painfully sunk in as we sat and stared at the water, wishing it to not look as deep as it increasingly did.

Just as I had resigned to the second option, and the not-so-straight-forward task of navigating the way back to Omsk, I was distracted by a flicker in the wing mirror.

The claustrophobic silence was broken by the sound of an engine edging in behind us. A hatchback about the size of a Ford Fiesta covered from top to bottom in mud had joined us to admire the view.

Under closer observation, smoke drifted from the passenger window, on the sill of which rested a pair of old trainers, feet crossed. A rough crackle of radio interference came from within the vehicle, which made me jump to the conclusion that the Kazanian police had caught up with us. They'd taken their time. The vehicle crawled past and inched to the water's edge, like a dog seeking its bowl. The car then stopped and the engine died, restoring the great Siberian silence for several moments. We watched intently, curious to see the occupants. The long thin head of the driver appeared first, followed by his body of about six foot in length, which he stretched out in the manner of someone who had been cramped behind the wheel for some time.

The man proffered an ear-to-ear smile, revealing a full set of gold ware and a relaxed attitude to the obstacle ahead compared with our gloomy resignation. I tried to return the smile, which ended up more of a grimace – still, he was unperturbed and bounded over to the van, presenting a large leathery hand to shake. Next to clamber from the vehicle was the owner of the trainers; a large smile lit his face too, which was shaded by a huge bushy moustache and a mop of dishevelled hair. Cigarette in hand he greeted us both with equal enthusiasm to that of his friend.

Finally, the third amigo emerged from the car, not through the door but through the window, a man dressed in a worn old black suit; the jacket's buttons were all fastened and the trousers didn't fit. A cigarette rested in his mouth, and in his hand was a bottle of beer.

'*Atkooda?*' asked the tall man. We were always being asked this (it means 'where are you from?') and it was always nice to offer some initial hope that we might be able to hold a conversation by replying, '*Anglia.*' This brief glimmer of hope was generally fast extinguished by our blank faces when anything else was said. This time was no exception, but rather than meet our looks of confusion with 'Russian for foreigners' (the same thing repeated over and over with increasing volume), our lack of understanding was met by a look of sheepish embarrassment by the three men.

They were from Chechnya, a point revealed to us by the tall man gesturing to his friends and then himself and saying 'Chechna', and, assuming us to be Russian speakers, they believed our lack of comprehension was down to their poor Russian. A lot of people we met in Russia thought we must be Estonians, being of fair complexion and fat in the face. When they actually realised we were a lot further from home than they, they visibly relaxed. In a comical exchange, which to be honest could have been about anything, we discovered that they were headed to Novosibirsk for a boys' weekend away. They appeared completely unfazed by the water that still taunted us not 5 metres away. The guy in the suit looked over at the obstacle and, sensing our concerns, laughed loudly, choking on his cigarette, before saying:

'Nyet problem. Voda nyet problem.'

It felt good to hear his optimism, and in order to enjoy the temporary warm feeling of hope, I tried to prolong our conversation by conveying where we were going. To assist I produced our trusty map and traced my finger over the relevant bits. For some reason this sparked the same raucous hilarity as it had with the truckers back on the edge of Omsk. These guys were on their knees with laughter. It was clearly the map that was the source of the humour. The tall man went over to his car and returned with one of their maps, which he opened out in front of us. I couldn't recognise anything at first, but then it dawned on me – the map was of the area we were in, and was infinitely smaller in scale, with just about every tree and hedgerow indicated. We had been trying to navigate complex terrain with a map showing not much more than a single red line.

There was a bigger joke to come. The tall guy pointed to the M51 – a fat red line on our map – then walked us to the edge of the water and pointed ahead.

Stretching into the distance was indeed the M51 as on our map, but that's where the similarity to a road, as indicated by a cartographical symbol, ended. The M51 wasn't actually yet a road. There was just one long slush trail disappearing out of sight. How wrong our earlier evaluation of what lay ahead had been. The M51 was a work in progress. Substantial mounds of clay rose about a metre above the surrounding terrain, which, if the weather had been kinder, would have been just fine. However, several weeks of rainfall had sent the builders home and turned the unfinished concourse into a paddy field. Water-filled ditches ran either side and sections of piping that had been laid end to end attested to the surrender to the elements. Our companions looked on as we surveyed the scene that represented our bold red line; there was no more laughter and their expressions were sympathetic.

Bottles of beer were passed around, for which we were grateful. It helped to diffuse our anxiety and turn an altogether disastrous situation into nothing more than a small hitch.

The Chechens finished their beers and then jumped back into their small car and began crawling cautiously in the direction of the water. They made it to the other side, the water in fact not rising above the top of their hubcaps, and progressed painfully along the clay. Wheel spins and fish-tailing took them frighteningly close to the gaping drainage ravines on either side, but after a hundred metres or so the driver managed to keep the car pretty central. This gave us the confidence to follow.

We took the plunge. Max's body sat much lower than that of the hatchback, so it was still with much trepidation that we proceeded, watching the dirty puddle engulf Max's tyres and stop rising uncomfortably short of the exhaust. After just one stall and a few nervous splutters, with fingers tightly crossed we emerged onto the clay, but the difference in the two vehicles now became immediately clear. Max was that much heavier, sinking into the clay, and the rear-wheel drive of the camper certainly didn't help, as steering was near impossible. I was having to thrash the engine simply to move a few feet, and it felt like it was only a matter of time before we lurched off into a gorge.

The Chechens were doing well, and putting some distance between us. It wasn't long before the wheels on the van locked and we slid with a slow motion inevitability into one of the trenches.

There was a brief moment of pause before we lurched again and, spinning and gathering speed, we hit the side of the ravine and flew over the edge in reverse. We braced ourselves for a drop – but it never came. The involuntary speed induced by the wet clay had launched us not into the ditch but halfway across it. Max was bridged across the banks, the front and back wheels firmly lodged into the soft walls. There was no traction and the rear bumper had bitten into the offside bank. We were stuck. But not for long, as even more worryingly we were still moving. The van's weight was cutting slowly into the oozing clay walls of the ravine, and it seemed certain that it was only a matter of time before we would topple in.

We both sat still, not daring to move. Every tiny creak crunched our nerves, as the fresh breeze blew in through the window off the wet clay. We tentatively explored the van's precarious state of balance. Never had the contours of the van's mustard yellow leather upholstery seemed so intricate in texture. Each movement of arm or leg produced a groan and a slight shifting of position on the clay.

We were just beginning to consider evacuation when the Chechens came back into view, at first small, but with every second their car grew in size until it was parked up in front of Max. Nobody said very much as they clambered out of the car, but with military efficiency the guy in the suit attached a thick rope to the van's free bumper, before disappearing underneath the van into the ditch. One bone-rattling shunt later and we were all back on terra firma.

For the next 16 kilometres the Chechens hauled, steered, pushed and guided us onto more solid ground. We limped along the embryonic motorway, spinning and sliding, breaking fan belts and showering in clay, until eventually and with much relief arriving at a hard surface of crunchy gravel. The road was evidently being built from east to west.

The worst of the M51 having been successfully navigated, we joined our new friends for a roadside picnic of tomatoes and rye bread, and never had either tasted so good. The fresh air hardened the clay that covered us all, as we pondered what lay ahead. Pictures of families and home towns were brought out, and addresses exchanged, despite the unlikelihood we'd ever see these people again. The tall man, whose name was Dmitri, even put forward an invitation for us to visit him and his family: 'Home you come.'

I didn't know much about Chechnya, but I knew that there was a brutal war going on, and that Western hostages were lucky to leave with their heads attached to their shoulders. He laughed when I declined the offer to visit Chechnya, and was quick to tell me, 'Home is Omsk.'

Later that evening, something quite strange occurred. Probably because we'd been held up for so long on the M51, we broke a golden rule and carried on driving well after night had fallen; even more stupid, because we were so exhausted from the previous day. Driving in the dark was compounded by torrential rain, making Max's already weak headlights close to useless. We crossed some rail tracks on the outskirts of a town, and I was just building up speed, having slowed for the tracks, when out of the corner of my eye I caught sight of a man darting into the road. I had seen him too late, and with a heart stopping thud, ploughed straight into him. I broke sharply. I hadn't built up too much speed yet, but I'd still hit him.

We both just sat there, hypnotised by the rain battering against the windscreen, for what felt like a lot longer than the few moments that it must have been. Eventually, I climbed out, already settling down to life in a Russian prison, all manner of scenarios flying around my head, but there was no sign of him. The spare wheel stored on the front of the van had taken the force of the blow, but there was no damage, or any evidence that the man had hit it. We scoured the area around Max, but there was still no sign of him. Dazed and bewildered, we drove on into the town, and parked up for a night of unsettled sleep.

I once drove into a sheep in Wales, climbed out of the car expecting the worst, and sure enough the sheep lay lifeless. I carried it to a nearby field, and rested it down. Just as I had turned to leave, it jumped to its feet and, baa-ing, merrily ran off.

Perhaps in those few short moments we had frozen, the stunned man had got to his feet and run off into the night.

CHAPTER EIGHT
HEARTLANDS

'Space, in the end, may be all you remember of Novosibirsk.'

COLIN THUBRON

The morning after our arrival in Novosibirsk we headed for breakfast in an institutional Soviet-style canteen, a large characterless hall with faux stained glass windows and dusty chandeliers. Sleepily I approached the cafe's confusing breakfast counter. A particularly happy serving lady caught me contemplating the strange mixture of food on offer: 'Do you know this kind of breakfast?' she quizzed, as if her particular breakfast was somehow unique.

It was a type of breakfast I had indeed never previously come across: quite unique! Rice with cold frankfurters, heavily smothered in ketchup. This final touch was the sole responsibility of an irrationally enthusiastic man. Nothing about the breakfast that stared up at me seemed right at 7.30 in the morning, and my stomach was defiantly in league with my reason. I was bemused that in the six years I'd been away from Russia so little had changed that the average Russian was prepared to put up with such an early morning abuse on the taste buds. It reminded me of a warning I had received somewhere, to at all costs avoid the shashlik – which is regularly blamed for kidney infection. For shashlik it was too late – I had already acquired a taste for them – but it was not too late for this 'breakfast'. I would not be taking any chances, and if it meant missing out on a unique experience, so be it. Despite the lack of breakfast we were refreshed after a heavy sleep, and made up our minds not to rush out of town, but to try to enjoy it with some sightseeing. Or at least I fancied a bit of culture... Jo didn't, she opted to take the opportunity to write some letters and spend some quality time with Max.

I decided to visit the Novosibirsk State Art Museum in search of some Rerikh, the darling of the Siberian art scene. Nikolay Rerikh had lived from 1874 until 1947 and was both a painter (best known for his scenery for ballets) and a spiritual teacher. He was attracted by mountainous regions of Central Asia, finally settling in the Himalayas. He believed that 'Shambhala', a Buddhist paradise, could be found (and founded) in the Altai – a mountainous region south of Novosibirsk that has a foot in not only Russia but also China, Mongolia and Kazakhstan, sometimes referred to as 'the navel of the world' due to its similarity to a navel when illustrated on a map. Having connected with the region on a spiritual level, Rerikh set his sights on the creation of nirvana in the middle of Siberia. For one reason and another, this was never achieved, yet contemporary

Russians still travel to the Altai to soak up the region that had so inspired Rerikh.

A one-time traffic policeman from Moscow woke up one day in the early nineties and decided he was the Messiah; he soon had over four thousand followers and a not insignificant mountain retreat just up the road in Tuva. Vissarion, as he called himself, could claim (and probably did) to be following the traditions established by Rerikh of Shambhala, and its physical manifestation deep in the heartlands of Siberia – just another in a long line of Russians able to see the heavenly potential of the region. Either that or just another Russian who had finally been pushed round the bend. The line is a fine one.

RERIKH FACTS

- He was born in St Petersburg.

- He designed scenery for Sergey Pavlovich Diaghilev's ballets.

- His work includes *The Messenger* and *The Golden Fleece*.

- In 1921 he and his wife founded Agni Yoga, their own occult tradition. Agni Yoga endures to this day, predominantly in parts of the USA.

When I got to the museum I discovered the Rerikh section was closed for renovations and all the other artefacts on display – pots and busts – were in good need of repair. The pictures I saw I found confusing and inaccessible, and I fast concluded it wasn't worth the extortionate entrance fee (I had stupidly paid the equivalent of ten English pounds for this particular injection of culture). The women of a certain age huddled together in clusters whispering on every corner, their eyes fixed on me, also made it an incredibly uncomfortable experience.

'Enjoy your museum then?' Jo asked with a smile when we met back at the canteen at lunchtime, a location chosen for convenience and certainly not the food.

'No,' I replied honestly. 'I can't wait to get going again.'

'Yeah, about that…' Jo's voice took on an ominous tone.

'What?'

'There's no real hurry is there, why don't we slow down a bit?'

'What do you mean?'

'Well, go off and do some exploring. This is a big country and what are we seeing of it?' I had actually thought we were seeing quite a lot of it – but I took Jo's point and, thinking about it, perhaps she was right. As exciting as it had become, maybe we had started to miss the point. We were travelling, not breaking records. It had become a mad dash for Vladivostok – and work that was far from guaranteed. I hadn't as yet had any confirmation from Uncle Tony, so we were hurrying across Russia to nothing more than a name and address on a piece of scrappy paper.

'I'm tired – really tired – and if we're not careful there'll be no Russia left to drive across.' That wasn't strictly true, as a small church in Novosibirsk marks the geographical centre of Russia, so if I was going to be pedantic we still had the other half to drive across.

'So what's the plan?' I asked somewhat apprehensively, as I was now more than a little concerned at where Jo was heading. It was with considerable relief to me when she replied, 'I say we just jump on a train, bus, in any direction and just go for a few days.'

'What about Max?'

'We just lock up and leave him, he'll be OK.'

Only a little while ago we wouldn't have thought of leaving Max, but Siberia felt completely unthreatening. Whether it was the climate or that everyone was just content with their Siberian status, the mood was positively laid-back.

'OK, let's do it!'

We hurtled south from Novosibirsk in a shiny white Volga Sedan, the heavily tinted windows deflecting the glare of the strong Siberian sun in September. Our travelling companions for the four-hour journey through lush pastures, arable land and sporadic clusters of woodland comprised:

- Victor – a well-dressed, dapper man of business from Moscow, who smugly enjoyed the space and thus comfort afforded him by having claimed the front seat. He spent the entire journey clinging to a burning cigarette and pretending he was important.

- Two stocky Siberian men, Ali and Jona. Cheeks the colour of claret, they also spent the entire journey clinging on – to bottles of beer.

I was squashed into the back seat sandwiched between Jo and the window. The more passengers that are crammed into a taxi, the cheaper the fare. In Siberia you're not paying for the privilege but the benzene. Jo clung onto a half-full packet of wet wipes. I clung onto the hope of a safe conclusion to the journey.

Victor took any opportunity he had to speak with us in stammering English about the growing tourist economy in the nearby Altai region. He also took any opportunity to suggest that we eat a lot of bananas and drink a lot of water, neither of which anybody had – otherwise, sound advice.

Our sunburnt driver was an angry man, who took his aggression out on the road. The tyres of his pristine Soviet icon were earning their rubber. Anything in our way was fair game: not happy with a clean overtake he would often bully the slower car to the side of the road, slow down, sound his horn some more and only then accelerate. An overturned truck and the resulting log spill that blocked the road vexed our driver to such an extent he began repeatedly beating his bald head with clenched fists, his burnt face becoming even redder. Once his tantrum was over he grumbled that the time would be made up. It most certainly was – and we arrived at the bus station in Barnaul some forty-five minutes short of the recommended four hours.

It was a blisteringly hot day in Barnaul. We got some feeling back in our legs and arms whilst passing food sellers and taxi ranks, the drivers touting aggressively for business along the road around the station, and soon arrived at the war memorial. Tinny military band music pumped from speakers hung in the warm air. The memorial seemed to be ignored by all but a motley collection of the elderly and beggars, all giving colour to the collection of concrete benches provided.

SOME FACTS ABOUT RUSSIA'S WORLD WAR TWO

- In June 1941 the Germans invaded Russia, despite the Molotov–Ribbentrop Pact of 1939, catching the Soviets by surprise.

- In 1942, having captured most of Western Russia, the Nazis attempted to capture Stalingrad, a city on the Volga, vital for the Caucasus' oil fields.

- By 1944 the Germans had been driven right back to Poland.

- The Soviet Union emerged from the war much stronger; despite having lost over twenty million people it had gained much territory and became, alongside the United States, a world superpower, which it remained until its collapse in 1991.

On reaching the summer colours and the bustle of Lenina Street, the memory of our taxi journey had faded with our aching limbs. A leafy tree-lined avenue full of life and not short at 8 kilometres, it was the city's tarmac backbone. We followed the gently sloping central walkway. Groups of young men congregated intermittently, chatting and drinking. People carried plastic cups and bottles as they lined up for kvass – a light, thirst-quenching drink made from black bread and yeast, possessing a very strong odour. It was being served from bright yellow barrels positioned along the roadside, manned by plump women in frilly aprons disguised under heavy make-up. As well as kvass, everywhere I turned ice cream was available, as it is all year round, all over Russia. The Russians love their ice cream (a nice strawberry cornet washed down with a large shot of vodka). By the time we arrived at Hotel Altai we had warmed to Barnaul, both of us glad our decision to travel south had been quickly vindicated.

THREE REASONS TO VISIT BARNAUL

- Its location lends itself to exploration of the Altai Mountains to the south, where Kazakhstan, China and Mongolia all meet at a single point.

- Not far from the station there is a shop selling the largest selection of thermal underwear I've ever seen.

- It is very difficult to get lost in Barnaul.

TWO REASONS NOT TO VISIT BARNAUL

- Flies and mosquitoes in the summer.

- It rains a lot.

The next morning – after a restful evening enjoyed in the hackneyed environs of the hotel, with its early Stalinist splendour, followed by a deep and dreamy sleep in very comfortable beds – the cheery, sunny picture of the previous day had been replaced. Not helped by overcast skies, Barnaul appeared a little drab, and not surprisingly the joyful people of the previous day had become distant and glum. Determined to keep our spirits high, I left Jo to change some dollars and went in search of somebody who could take us down to the mountains and guide us in our search for our very own Altai Shambhala.

I walked up Lenina Street past a statue of Lenin, cut across to Prospekt Socialitiskaya, through side streets cluttered with badly parked cars. The second floor of number 87 was home to the Sputnik/Altai Travel Agency. They would be very interested to meet me, I had been told when I called the number given me by the hotel receptionist. I had spoken to Ivan, who had been quick to introduce himself as the 'company manager – a man of reason and diligent in making holiday happiness'.

Ivan greeted me with a suspicious look. 'Please sit down,' he said, ushering me to a seat in the corner of the mahogany office.

He continued thumbing through some papers, whilst discreetly checking me out. Ivan wasn't doing small talk. Jana, his assistant, had left the room to make coffee, so it was not the place for those crippled by silence. Ivan's efficiency made him appear awkward, almost clumsy.

'Please wait. It is Thom, yes? You want to go to the mountains?' He was playing it cool, but he knew the answer. Jana returned with coffee, and a smile suggesting I was the most attractive man she'd ever met and that she would like to spend the rest of her life with me.

'Thank you,' I said, more for the smile than the coffee.

'I go...' she giggled self-consciously. 'To live....' she giggled again. 'Moscow.' She sat down, relieved the English speaking ordeal was over, and the silence returned.

'Oh, OK, why's that?' I reluctantly quizzed, not wanting to see her struggle again. As Jana was building up to an answer, Ivan interrupted, 'She is moving to Moscow to work, start a new life.' I sensed this wouldn't be such a great loss for Sputnik, but wherever she went I'm sure her smile would be enjoyed. Something I couldn't say for her coffee.

In time Ivan pulled up a chair next to mine and presented me with some papers he'd obviously been preparing for me.

'This is some itineraries for you, for your trip to the Altai.' His eyes were fixed on me as I began to read. Blimey, I thought, all very thorough; in fact, far too thorough. I'd only called him twenty minutes ago, but then he had said he was diligent. The first three-day excursion had been organised down to the nearest minute. Example:

18.00	Leave horses for the night.
18.05	Go to *banya*.
18.15	Towel down, replace clothes.
18.17	Scratch your arse.

'I think the six-day is the best for you, it is our most popular.' Yeah right, like anyone had ever been on one of these trips. That said, the six-day did look like a lot of fun, with two days' horse trekking to Lake Teletskoye, a beautiful expanse of unspoilt water deep into the mountains, followed by three days of rafting down the Katun River – with a day of 'relaxation' sandwiched in the middle.

'With all the trips you will stay at our Sputnik's camping complex.' With this he showed me a picture of two men in matching red shell suits standing to attention, waving to the camera with forced smiles.

'These are the instructors.' I didn't dare ask for what.

'You can pay for the six-day tour now.'

I looked up, half expecting to see a gun pointing at me, for a moment forgetting that Ivan was a self-confessed man of reason. There was no gun, but Jana took my sudden movement to mean I wanted more coffee. Ivan's aftershave was beginning to leave me nauseous.

'This looks great,' I said unconvincingly, 'but we really just want a guide, someone to travel with and tell us about the area.'

'OK, perhaps you want three-day tour, this will be very interesting for you.'

Jana handed me another coffee, reiterating, 'Three-day this very good, for you!' The three-day tour was a shorter version of the six-day – one day of trekking, one day of rafting, with a day of 'relaxation' in the middle, and I couldn't really argue that I wouldn't indeed find it very interesting, it just wasn't what I was asking for. They weren't getting it – we just wanted to drift about, maybe take a few snaps, spend a few nights under the stars. I didn't want to be ferried out to a Soviet Butlin's and told to comb my hair at seven o'clock each morning.

I had simply wanted a guide – someone to talk to and get to know as a local of the region. Ivan's 'reason' clearly didn't extend to providing the customer with what they wanted, or perhaps so convinced was he of his own tours' ability to provide unequalled 'holiday happiness' that he simply wasn't prepared to compromise his proven formula, for anything or anyone. Either way, I was getting nowhere and it was time to beat a hasty retreat.

'OK, I'll take these and give it some thought.' I stood up. Ivan, sensing the prey was getting away, stood between me and the door.

'OK, you want bus tickets, train tickets, hotel accommodation.'

'I know where you are,' I offered. More alarming was that he knew where I was, something he reminded me of as I weaved past him to the door.

'Altai – this is a good hotel.'

'Yes, I like it.'

'I will meet you later, show you around,' was Ivan's passing shot.

I reciprocated Jana's rushed farewell, and hurried out onto the street guideless, with only the memory of her smile as compensation.

By evening the day had cooled, so we heated up again in a *banya*, relaxing by ourselves in a space big enough for a banquet. With mirrored panels on the ceiling it was an altogether more luxurious affair than Bathhouse No. 9 in St Petersburg. The key holder, a warm hearty lady from Azerbaijan, took much delight in our enjoyment of her well-managed *banya*. Or perhaps it was just our money, as one hour in the sauna cost more than a night at the Altai, this being a particularly expensive private *banya* that due to its location had a monopoly on residents of the hotel. We didn't stay long – it didn't matter how luxurious it might have been, we decided that a *banya* just wasn't the same without plenty of people dancing about beating each other with birch.

The moment I stepped back into my room the phone rang. I picked up the receiver warily. It was reception.

'Thomas?'

'Yes.'

'You have missed three calls from Ivan Utrobovich, from Sputnik Travel Agency. Please call on...'

'I know the number.'

I decided, against my better judgement, to call Ivan. He was a salesman and I wasn't interested in what he was selling; however, if he wanted to show us around his town we had no better offers and besides, I'd told Jo about my interlude at the travel agency and she was intrigued to meet him. We concluded the worst thing that could happen would be learning some more about the town.

'OK Thom, we meet in thirty minutes at Nikolovsky Church, you know?'

'No.'

'This is on Lenina Street, on the right side. Very beautiful church.'

He met us promptly at the church, a spectacular Russian Orthodox edifice whose recent renovation made it all the more impressive amongst the surrounding buildings. Ivan seemed oblivious to the cluster of beggars on the steps of the church, blistered and battered by climate and vodka, taking the shine away from the church's new spire somewhat, as he inelegantly scrambled past them to greet us. Such was the enthusiasm of his greeting he ended up shaking us both furiously by the hand at the same time. He had changed his clothes, ditching a shapeless suit for chinos, a pressed shirt and some shiny shoes. With the new outfit apparently came a new Ivan; gone was the diligent holiday salesman, replaced by an altogether more affable host. Or so I thought.

Having drawn our attention to the Nikolovsky Church Ivan had very little to say about it, and soon gestured to the imposing Stalinist building to the side.

'And this is our famous technology university.' The groups of young adults sporting colourful daypacks and trainers peopling the courtyard at its fore corroborated Ivan's words. He led us north along Lenina Street, dropping in snippets of information as we walked past plastic tables and chairs thrown carelessly onto the side of the street. The above became increasingly tantalising, not least with their suggestion of a nice cold beer as the early evening sun crept out from behind the clouds. Also, despite Ivan's newly apparent zeal, it was fast becoming clear that he probably hadn't saved the best for last, and that we had indeed seen it first. This was confirmed as we rounded the corner onto Stroiteley Street, where Ivan caught sight of the central post office on the opposite side of the road – a rather unassuming grey stone building – and proceeded to proffer its history since the 1917 revolution.

On reaching Pobedy Square and the war memorial near to the station, Ivan read the mood and suggested a drink at the Cafe Red, which after a not inconsiderable amount of Soviet history from our guide seemed quite appropriate. Once myself and Jo were seated Ivan skipped off towards the bar, giving Jo a chance to offer her appraisal.

'Oh, he's lovely! And he really knows his Barnaul history.'

She was right, Ivan did seem to be rather a pleasant man when unleashed from the confines of his office, and yes, he certainly knew a thing or two about Soviet stamps. So why wasn't I feeling entirely comfortable with him? Why was he spending time he clearly saw as valuable with us? Then, as Ivan returned to our table with a tray of Baltika beers, it all became clear.

The penny began its slow and painful descent as I watched Ivan weaving his way past the cafe's other evening drinkers, guiding the loaded tray with the care and precision of a soldier negotiating a minefield. Despite the vigilance he gave the task he still managed to knock against a lady slumped back in her chair, causing her to spill some coffee from her cup. Nobody actually seemed that bothered, least of all Ivan, whose priority was very much keeping his own glasses full to the brim. However, it was at this juncture that I noticed the tobacco brown satchel that hung from Ivan's shoulder – for it was this that had hit the coffee drinker. Usually pretty observant, I was surprised that this had gone under my radar for so long, although it wasn't so much that I hadn't noticed it sooner that caused me dismay as what it represented. Ivan might have appeared casual, but this leather bag had formal crying out from its sparkling buckles. Now what was in the satchel?

Having sat himself down and presented both of us with a beer, Ivan slumped back into his chair and for the first time a warm smile arrived on his face. After a couple of sips from his glass, he unbuckled his carrier and plunged his hand inside. He pulled out a great bundle of papers and placed them in front of me, before telling us with much excitement, 'I've made some changes to the six-day itinerary, this I think you will like.' Ivan scored highly for perseverance. An image came into my head of him popping up unexpectedly for the rest of our journey, each time with a newly modified tour on offer. He caught us by surprise – I really hadn't expected him to be still peddling his trips. Furthermore, he had us well and truly cornered.

Heavy storms left the streets of Barnaul waterlogged. The bus was due to leave at eight o'clock. The driver waited until mid afternoon, allowing the water level to drop. The girl sitting next to me on the crowded bus was leaving town (something was in the air) to work in Ust-Sema, a small village on the Katun River and an up-and-coming holiday destination for Russians. It certainly wasn't Moscow but she was sure that Ust-Sema was the place to find work. The words of Victor from the taxi about the growing tourist industry came to mind and increasingly made sense as the mountains rose up around us and – as mountains do the world over – transported the crowded bus into an enchanting world where man is powerless and insignificant.

From the regional capital Gorno-Altaisk along the several hundred kilometres to Chemal, the banks of the river were alive with the sounds of hammers and drills, cabins sprouting up wherever you looked, reluctant builders deliberating over half-built constructions. Russians loaded up with baggage disembarked sporadically along the route, many starting their holidays at institutional campsites (*turbazas*) like the Sputnik complex. As Victor had said, and I had now seen for myself, tourism was the region's new boom, offering welcome support to the traditional economy of cattle, yak and sheep breeding.

Despite Ivan's somewhat uncompromising approach to sales – the truth was that after a few more beers he could probably have sold us a tour around his kitchen – we had managed to negotiate a deal on his modified itinerary, which included total avoidance of the Sputnik camping complex. Instead, Ivan had given us the opportunity to stay with a 'friend' of his who just happened to run a hotel.

Hotel Chemal was in fact a work in progress, not having yet progressed much beyond being a two-bedroom cabin. The patron showed us the outside WC with a blush; the place was very obviously not yet operating as a hotel. Despite having to share the room of her ten-year-old son, she kept up the facade of being a hotel until we left. The son was a very tidy boy, insisting on lining our boots up every time they were taken off. The 'hotel' was perched on the edge of a steep bank looking down on the mighty Katun River.

In Altaic language, Katun means 'mistress'. The story goes that she battled with her master Bija to be the first to reach Mount Babyrgan. Bija won and they merged to form the Ob River, flowing as master and mistress ever since. The Katun's quarrelsome nature resulted in the taiga (the swampy coniferous forest of this region) and the mountains putting many obstacles in her path; she has 7,000 tributaries.

The town of Chemal was undeniably beautiful with flowing rapids and alpine backdrop, forests of cedar, pine and fir, meadows lush with edelweiss, globe flower, pulsatilla and poppy. Musk deer and wild ram roamed the hills, Siberian stag grazed on the slopes. It had all the romantic ingredients necessary for the most magical of fairytales.

As part of the modified itinerary we acquired the services of another 'friend' of Ivan's as our guide, who not long after our arrival at the hotel came to meet us. Yuri was the business; heavy-duty boots, worn battle fatigues, shotgun strapped to his back, battered cloth cap with a feather hanging down, a face that told the story of many a Siberian winter. He had horses, knew a man who had a raft, and knew the mountains like the back of his hand, having spent his whole life there. He was available all year round, and would even elicit the services of a cook should one be required. We agreed to leave with Yuri the following morning, after one more night at Hotel Chemal.

We arranged to meet Yuri by a small paddock where the edge of the village met the mountains, grassy slopes rising invitingly into the distance. Our guide arrived looking just as prepared (for absolutely anything) as he had the previous day, only now his rousing appearance had been augmented by a large hunting knife strapped to a thick leather belt on his waist. Faced by this battle-ready adventurer, I felt a little underprepared for our jaunt into the mountains. Yuri had the strange effect of bestowing huge confidence – by nature of being a walking arsenal – whilst at the same time leaving one slightly anxious and pondering why we were actually being taken somewhere that may require such defences. Some of Yuri's testosterone was diffused with the arrival of Andriy. In stark contrast to Yuri, Andriy's soft, unblemished face suggested he had never before been beyond the comfort of his apartment – let alone into the mountains. He had a gentle, easy smile which offered the impression that even if it was his first time, nothing would really be a problem for him. Rather than weaponry decorating his person, he had three saucepans dangling from a strap across his back, which clanked together with every step he made. Andriy was the cook and, I think much to everyone's relief, as a fluent English speaker, the interpreter as well.

Human introductions out of the way, it was time to meet our equine companions, one of which had made its way over to the fence of the paddock and begun butting the wooden rail in way of anticipation for the adventure ahead, I presumed.

'He's got spirit this one,' Andriy said, directing his words over to the speckled grey horse whose huge yellow teeth were now taking chunks out of the wooden rail. He reached out a hand in an attempt to stroke it and discourage the destruction of what appeared to be a fairly new piece of fencing; however, he thought better of it as in slow motion the horse's gaping mouth tried to take his hand off. 'This is Genghis.' Who else, I thought, whilst making a mental note to avoid having to ride him at all costs. Genghis had now been joined by an altogether more agreeable-looking nag, a pretty liver chestnut with a blaze running the length of her nose. I immediately felt a connection with Cleo as she came over and nuzzled my ear. The quartet of horses was made up by a weary-looking skewbald called Peter and a fiery black beauty called Pushkin.

Yuri greeted Pushkin like a long lost friend with a seemingly never-ending hug of his long, muscular neck – clearly indicating that they were 'together'. That left the three others, and by the way Yuri began sizing us all up the decision as to who I would be astride for the next few days would be his. We planned to be out for one night, and the route we had agreed on would involve the best part of one and a half days' riding, totalling about ten hours in the saddle. Now, to grace anyone's back and squeeze their belly for dear life for that amount of time requires more than a little mutual respect and understanding; a resolute and enduring bond has to be put in place early on, and nurtured with care and devotion. Yuri's imminent pairing was to be pivotal in the success of the whole mission. I had already made my mind up that Cleo was the only horse for me; what did Yuri have planned?

I actually thought Andriy the cook and Peter the skewbald made the perfect match. First impressions suggested them both to be slow and steady; just how slow and steady we were yet to discover. Despite Peter obviously being advanced in years, he was strong and more than capable of handling the extra supplies he was required to carry due to Andriy being the cook. If I'd given it any balanced consideration, I would have probably also believed Jo to be a pretty good match with Cleo. However, I didn't, as I was quickly flooded by a range of emotions that included both annoyance and fear on hearing Yuri's final proclamation via Andriy: 'And finally, Thom, you'll be riding Genghis.'

We both stared at each other, during which time Genghis bared his teeth. I quickly gathered that whatever feelings I might have had were mutual.

That first morning's ride took us through sweet-smelling cedar forests, as we gently climbed, in single file, away from the village. Yuri took the lead on Pushkin, who seemed to be prancing along on the tips of his hooves with the alertness of a meerkat. Andriy and Peter followed up the rear, Peter almost dragging his plump body along the ground. Only a few hours in and Andriy had wrapped his arms around Peter's neck and slouched forward, apparently catching up on his sleep. Jo seemed quite at one with Cleo nestled in behind Pushkin, whilst Genghis kept one all-seeing eye suspiciously on me and the other glued to Cleo's rump. With the exception of our leader, a bedraggled band we must have appeared.

By lunchtime we had broken from the forests into a clearing, and on reaching a subtle plateau Yuri came to a halt and made the very welcome proclamation, 'We'll rest here for a while.' Well, that's possibly what he said as he flung himself from Pushkin's back with a scissor kick that Zorro would have been proud of – there was no way of being certain, however, as our interpreter and chef was only just appearing from the shadows of the forest, some distance back. As he drew closer his heavy yawns and stretching suggested he had just woken from a deep sleep, and on coming to a standstill Peter quickly entered one. Yuri was quick to instruct Andriy, who responded by distributing carrots to each horse in turn and then followed this by presenting Jo and myself with a Snickers bar each – something of an anticlimax, I must admit, having hoped to have been feeding on berries and insects. Perhaps that came later. The thought crossed my mind that we would be feasting on chocolate for the next couple of days, and that Andriy's selection of pots and pans was mere window dressing. Yuri, squatting down and with one hand on his rifle, began to speak in a way that suggested he was revealing the greatest secrets of the universe.

'Many different peoples are united as Altaics... making the region very ethnically... and linguistically... diverse.' Andriy's translation began falteringly, punctuated by the occasional yawn, but he soon got his flow, prompted by the importance Yuri seemed to set by his words.

'However, a divide can be made between the North Altaics and the South Altaics. Those from the south belong to an Asiatic or south Siberian type of Mongoloid, whilst those to the north belong to a Uralic race, more European in appearance.'

Yuri paused to smell the light breeze – he clearly enjoyed an audience. Jo, who was now lying on her back with her legs above her head, vigorously massaging her saddle-sore buttocks, took the opportunity to interrupt, directing her query at nobody in particular, 'What about the deer, will we see some deer?' Yuri raised a hand as if to say 'all in good time' before continuing his train of thought.

'In 1756 Altaics from the south had joined the Russians of their own free will to avoid almost certain extermination through onslaughts by Kyrgyz people from the Yenisey, and Mongol descendants of Genghis Khan himself. The Russians had explored and been interested in the Altai well before the Soviet era. In 1633 Cossacks had reached as far south as Lake Teletskoye. It was good for their farming; animals enjoyed the mountains and so did crops. Survival was easier than on the steppe lands to the north. The rural economy depends on sheep, goats, yaks and maral deer, which are bred for their aphrodisiac antlers.'

At that point our leader, not convinced he had everybody's full attention, leapt to his feet and, with even more acrobatic prowess than his dismount, elevated himself onto Pushkin, who with the arrival of his master seemed to proffer a smile.

What we had seen so far of the Altai was undeniably beautiful, yet somehow tame, safe and controlled in a way it was difficult to put your finger on. It almost felt like we were passing through the New Forest rather than a distant corner of Siberia. We had left Andriy behind and followed Yuri a few hundred metres, coming to a halt next to a wire mesh fence some ten metres tall. Yuri beckoned for us to dismount with a finger over his lips. Genghis butted me with his head as I flailed around with one foot in the stirrup, making Yuri's request for silence impossible. Once on terra firma I joined Jo and Yuri peering through the oval gaps in the mesh to an area of thick grass and the occasional cluster of silver fir trees.

We were clearly looking into some kind of sanctuary but for what was not so clear. However, we continued to humour Yuri, the silence punctuated by a fairly regular finger-over-lip signal from Yuri accompanied with a gentle 'ssshh'. After ten minutes like this, uncertain how indeed we could have been any quieter without actually being dead and even more uncertain as to what we were looking at, I offered Yuri my most convincing 'And...?' hand and face gesture. To this he responded by making horns with his hands against his head – we were either searching for an elusive devil, or more likely peering into the sanctuary of a particularly shy deer. An hour passed in this way with only the occasional 'ssshh' from Yuri to break the boredom. We were confident Yuri knew what he was doing and we certainly didn't want to appear ungrateful as we were obviously only pressing our noses up against the cold wire in response to Jo's earlier enquiry about the deer in the Altai. But after an hour of not even seeing a blade of grass move and, as a result of Yuri's strict policing, not hearing anything, let alone the sound of a stag galloping across the grass, my senses felt suffocated... enough was enough, so as loudly as possible I fell over backwards. Yuri, ever sensitive to the attention deficit of others, took this correctly to mean it was time to move on and reluctantly lead us back to Andriy, who was flat out snoring like a wild boar back at the plateau.

The rest of the afternoon we rode through forests, a vibrant fusion of birch, cedar and pine, crossing sparkling streams that meandered aimlessly along, from a distance appearing like slithering snakes. As the sun lowered and the rich colours lost their strength, we came to rest at a hunter's cabin deep in the forest, where Andriy set to work preparing dinner and Yuri saw to feeding the horses before lighting a fire and telling us some more about the region.

'There are seventy-one thousand ethnic Altais who make up twenty-eight per cent of the Altai Republic. There are also Turkish speaking people, who until the eighteenth century were ruled by the Oirats of western Mongolia. One fifth of the population are ethnic Kazakhs who can be still seen living like nomads in their traditional yurts. Camels are wild in some parts. Perhaps we see some tomorrow.'

He paused, probably aware that after the deer spotting non-event we wouldn't be holding our breath to see any camels!

'The landscape of the Altai is much varied, from steppe to taiga, glaciers to semi-desert, waterfalls, rivers and many lakes. Perhaps the most beautiful lake is Teletskoye. This was originally a glacier. It is seventy-seven kilometres long and has seventy rivers flowing into it. The Baya River flows out. The Katun River finally merges with the Baya to form the world's fifth largest, the Ob River.'

Yuri certainly knew his stuff, and we were getting just the experience we had been looking for. Yuri was a gentle, good-humoured, easy-going man and we were both warming to him. However, despite this growing fondness, given the choice I wouldn't have shared a bed with him. The cabin consisted of a wood burner with a substantial pile of logs left – as is the etiquette – by the previous tenant, a stocky wooden table and a bare wooden slat single bunk. On seeing our quarters a look of confusion appeared on Jo's face as she indignantly eyed up her sleeping companions. For me, the situation was quickly clear. Despite being lined up with no room for a cigarette paper between us, lying on our backs like sardines about to begin the luge event at the winter Olympics, sleep came quickly. The burner provided a sauna-like warmth and I woke after a deep sleep with the first light of day, Yuri's head nestled into my chest with an expression of post-coital satisfaction displayed on his sleeping face. Soon after Jo began to stir, but any movement was made near impossible by one of Andriy's legs wrapped tightly around her waist. It must have looked like we had all fallen asleep during a game of Twister. Once Yuri was up and booted, I soon discovered that movement for me too was far from easy, for no other reason than that I was as stiff as the slats I had been sleeping on… it was to be a long day ahead.

The first obstacle was getting back onto Genghis.

Altai is a Mongolian word meaning 'land of gold'. It is also often referred to as the land of mountains, being home to Siberia's highest peak, Mount Belukha, which stands at 4,605 metres above sea level. The territory of Altai Krai is located in the southern reaches of western Siberia and borders Kazakhstan, China and Mongolia. The Altai's aesthetic and environmental appeal was recognised by UNESCO naming the area a World Heritage Site in 1998, not least because of its huge number of kurgans, or burial mounds; lumps of rocks, sometimes coloured with paint, that adorned the landscape. They were higher in number in the clearings away from the wooded areas, but the occasional one appeared in the forests too. I'm not sure how much they added to the artistry of the place but they certainly gave it a spiritual edge, something of which Nikolay Rerikh had been very aware.

In the Tibetan Buddhist tradition Shambhala is a mythical kingdom hidden somewhere in inner Asia, and is mentioned in many ancient texts. Generally, Shambhala is believed to be a place of peace and happiness; however, as with several Buddhist concepts, Shambhala is said to have both 'inner' and 'outer' meanings. The inner is the more subtle personal understanding, whereas the outer understands it to exist as an actual place, and there are various ideas as to where it is located. It is often placed in Central Asia, north-west of Tibet. Mongolians identify Shambhala in certain valleys of southern Siberia, and in line with the Mongolians Rerikh believed the Altai to be home to paradise on earth.

I'm not sure that Genghis would have considered himself to have been in paradise, but he seemed to have woken up and shrugged off the attitude. Perhaps it was because he knew he was heading home, but he danced along, head upright and stretched. He had even, as I had struggled to mount, given me a gentle nudge with his soft muzzle, in place of the previous day's headbutt. With permanent separation from my mount now within reach, I couldn't say I would be sorry to say goodbye. On the contrary, the previous day's riding followed by a night in the cabin had left me walking like John Wayne and feeling like nails were being repeatedly hammered into my thighs and buttocks. But I needed more time in the mountains – we had only just dipped a foot in, and we both agreed it would be nice to have a swim.

The bus chugged its way up to Gorno-Altaisk, giving us time to reflect on Rerikh's Shambhala theory, and we concluded that, pre-Soviet Union, he was probably onto something. The part of the region we had seen was truly awe-inspiring, and despite my limited experience when it came to creating nirvanas on earth and developing communities based on ancient principles of love and spiritual cleansing, I had certainly seen the potential that lay within the emphatic mountains of the Altai. I left feeling I'd found a calm and serenely beautiful part of the world, to which I certainly wished to return someday.

With no more than four passengers on-board at a time we passed through the settlements we had travelled through on the way down, there being only one obvious route back to Barnaul. Groups of young men collected at the bus stops, undistinguishable with shaven heads and style-less clothes; they drank beer, some squatted on their haunches, all were intimidating. Folk walked along the side of the road aimlessly. The driver seemed the most enthusiastic about the role that life had given him. For him, at least, the road went somewhere – and up to three times daily.

I bought a shashlik from a reluctant Altai on arrival at the bus station in Gorno-Altaisk. The meat was tasty and filling. Street dogs brushed past my legs. The guidebook's suggested base for exploration of the Altai, Gorno-Altaisk looked no more than a collection of rundown apartment blocks, despairing silently in their forgotten poverty. This place made Barnaul look like a holiday resort par excellence.

A stout, thick-necked Russian man approached me as we chewed on our lunch and tried to blend in. We had failed, as the exaggerated price he offered for a taxi back to Barnaul reflected. However, we decided to take it – the four-hour wait for a bus had rapidly felt like a hardship we would sooner forego.

Mikhail drove fast, faster than his rattling Volga would be able to sustain for very much longer. What had been an eight-hour bus ride Mikhail reduced to two and a half hours. He was disappointed that benzene prices had recently risen from 28 roubles per litre to 145 roubles per litre. So were we, not because we found Russian petrol prices anything but dirt cheap relative to Western European prices, but because Mikhail was obviously warming up to an even further inflated taxi fare. Such was his chagrin, he told me several times during our journey. He loved the Altai and he had grandchildren who made him happy. The summer made him happy, with all the lovely animals. Everything seemed to make Mikhail happy, except for the price of petrol, which he even wrote down for me on reaching Barnaul, in case there was the slightest chance that I hadn't gotten the picture.

Back in Barnaul, Jo went kiosk-hopping in search of some shampoo. Meanwhile, I settled on some steps, not far from the relative security of the station building, and was regarded by all who passed by.

'I love my town, but it very criminal.' The source of the spluttering English was a young man with a leather flat cap perched on his head, his face a silhouette against the sun's backdrop. A gold tooth sparkled, the vanguard for a sinister smile.

'*Americanski?*'

'No, English.'

I'm not sure what difference this correction made to my status, yet it made me feel more at ease.

'What crime?' I asked.

I thought I should feed the man's sense of mischief. He was joined by a companion, who equalled if not surmounted his air of aggression. His smile broadened.

'Narcotic, weapons, many, many weapons.'

He paused, obviously believing that he'd saved the best until last.

'And morder.'

He had! I'm not sure if he expected me to simply run towards the station. We all just looked round at each other for some time, saying nothing. Finally, the stand-off was interrupted by the arrival of Jo, equipped with two boxes of cotton buds, much moisturising lotion and a bottle of Head & Shoulders.

'I'll say one thing, it's cheap.' Jo looked at my two friends and scowled, before marching towards the station. 'Come on then.' I obediently followed, quite glad that we would soon be back within the safe confines of our bubble that was Max.

CHAPTER NINE
TOMSK

The first night back in Novosibirsk Jo came down with something. She spent a sleepless night, feverish and sick. The following day she was weak and we decided it was best to stay put a little longer. We had a long drive ahead of us to Krasnoyarsk and as we'd had nearly a week off already, we thought it better to wait until Jo was 100 per cent. Playing the martyr she suggested I travel north alone on the train to Tomsk. 'I'll be fine, don't worry.' I think she just wanted to recover in peace. I certainly wasn't the most sympathetic of nurses.

I was secretly glad: a bit of time out from each other and the journey was what was needed, and during our detour to the Altai I'd acquired a taste for exploring Siberia off route. We were already off our particular beaten track but now I just wanted to consume every last part of the country.

Hotel Sibir was a Soviet style hotel 'under repair' in the centre of Tomsk (Soviet style, adj.: grim, grey, characterless, overpriced, limited facilities, from Soviet period). I had stumbled into the building site reception of the first hotel that the taxi driver had come to from the train station.

A man appeared from behind a corrugated pillar; he looked malevolent, as if he had been sitting in wait for me. To my surprise, in near perfect English he gently suggested, 'The hotel might be full.' However, if I didn't mind waiting...? Eevan made no secret of wanting to practise his English, and to this end he put the kettle on. I wasn't sure if I would be waiting for somebody to leave or for him to find out if the hotel was full – but I just went with it.

Eevan was an Uzbek. He had been in the city for fourteen years, and as well as working on reception at the Hotel Sibir he was an English teacher at the university. He earned $300 a month and was quick to tell me that he could get one thousand in Moscow, but didn't have the necessary registration. I was tired after the early morning train journey from Novosibirsk and needed to sleep, and Eevan spoke a lot; much drifted straight over me. I think he would have continued talking if I'd laid down on the floor and started to snore.

I did, however, register the mention of a closed town, a few kilometres away, where the Americans wanted to dump nuclear waste. He also mentioned that he was learning Spanish, which after English seemed to be the language of choice for young Russian linguists. I was only the second Englishman he had ever met in Tomsk, which explained his flood of conversation. The first one had danced through the hotel reception in the early hours with a bottle of Stolichnaya in hand, wearing just his underpants.

Eevan offered to meet me the next day to show me around the university, an offer I was a little sceptical about accepting after 'Ivan Tours' down in Barnaul. However, a tour around the Tomsk public library would surely be less cynical than Ivan's effort. After a third cup of tea, Eevan paused for breath, and as if receiving the information telepathically, confirmed: 'Yes, there is a room for you.' This left me thinking I had just undergone some kind of interview to establish my suitability for staying at the hotel. Pleased that he had apparently deemed me to be a worthy candidate, I climbed the stairs to the third floor, the corridor protected by a dozing babushka. After a snooze in a very narrow, wooden bed, I ate breakfast in the dining room, exchanging a chit for an omelette and a slice of bread, whilst eavesdropping on a group of American businessmen talking with Russian counterparts.

'There is much space and empty buildings,' I overheard, unable to think about anything but nuclear dumping now that Eevan had sown the seed.

'Now's the time to use it. Leave it any later and it'll be too late.'

Too late for what?

Seversk is 15 kilometres north-west of Tomsk, and until 1993 had been known as Tomsk 7 – a post office box number. It is one of Russia's closed cities, which means there is no access to unauthorised personnel due to the risk of secrets being leaked. It has a buffer zone of 192 square kilometres, surrounded by triple barbed wire fences. Both of the roads that lead to the city are guarded by military checkpoints and there are six gates that must be passed through – this is only possible with a special passport, thus Tomsk 7 was never going to be a good option for a day trip. The town is visible from the Tom River, a tributary of the Ob River, which flows through Tomsk. This information I gleaned from Eevan, who could have been exaggerating to increase the enigma – it wouldn't have been unheard of in Russia – but he had no need to do that.

A report in *The Guardian* dated 3 November 2000 read: 'Radioactive contamination of rivers around a top-secret Russian nuclear weapons complex in Siberia has reached "staggering" levels, the worst ever monitored, and is out of "rational control".' During a monitoring expedition, a Russian/American nuclear watchdog had discovered alarming levels of radioactivity in tributaries of the Ob River. The levels found in the rivers Tom and Romashka grossly exceeded safety levels. As well as sources of radioactivity that could have dated back some forty years, there was evidence of phosphorous-32, which decays in only two weeks, meaning the deposit must have been very recent. A Greenpeace spokesman stated that radioactivity was leaking due to the way that waste was stored – in liquid form.

I went back to my room and switched the TV on – it was functional rather than just decorative, as is so often the case in Soviet style hotels. An old, stained fridge hummed into life in the corner, on which sat a porcelain tea set blanketed by a heavy layer of dust. This was certainly a luxury room: TV, finest bone china and even a trickle of cold water in the bathroom! I became quickly engrossed by a concert on the telly (not having watched any television for some months it was something of a novelty), a confusing mix of pop songs sung to an adoring audience of young fans, adorned in black tie and frocks suitable for a ball. Their heroes moved huge egos around the stage. Western pop done Russian style – lots of tight clothing and plenty of cheesy smiles.

I flicked through the channels. Next we had four Russian celebrities including actor Sergei Popov hamming up well-known songs, whilst being judged by an unbelievably glamorous panel of 'ordinary people'. On another channel a badly dubbed version of *Jaws* was showing, but within moments it cut to an advert break. Advertising is long and plentiful on Russian TV, and often reminders will run across the bottom of the screen continuously during a programme. The breaks come with rapid regularity and are considerably longer than the segment of the programme you are watching, and there is no warning before a commercial break. It is not a relaxing experience – in fact, it's impossible to concentrate on what you are watching. Ultimately, the need to escape the TV overpowers the original urge to use the TV to escape the world. If there are indeed telly addicts in Russia my heart goes out to them.

Tomsk has the greatest display of wooden lace architecture (the name given to the carved windows on old timber houses which are left unpainted to highlight the patterns created by the use of different types of wood) in its Zaitochye District; both mansions and bungalows still flaunt this eye-catching craft. These houses, hidden behind tree-lined streets, were an unexpected leap back in time. I was enjoying the cultural treat and probably the purest air I'd ever inhaled five minutes from a city centre, when in the blink of an eye a sunny morning gave in to torrential rain. It wasn't long before the raindrops graduated into hailstones, which didn't stop growing until they'd reached a size capable of doing some damage. I sought refuge beneath a large birch tree, of which there were many. But it wasn't long before I had the painful realisation that the hailstones were actually coming down at an angle. I spent the next hour with my back squeezed against the tree, as if avoiding sniper fire, before I looked for a more substantial retreat.

The unassuming ochre and white Atashev Palace had a couple of T-34 tanks abandoned in its courtyard, and the west wing had been turned into a museum. The aging receptionist seemed unsure what exactly they were exhibiting. When Anya the curator was called in, she said she was able to make three exhibitions available; however, none, she assured me, would be of any interest. She then proceeded to try to sell me CDs of Siberian history that were prominently on display in glass cabinets which were heavily locked, though I couldn't help wondering why. After some persuasion Anya, a librarian type with spectacles sitting on the tip of her nose and the distant confidence of an academic, reluctantly took me to the exhibition that she conceded would most suit me.

We entered a small room, where behind a cordon there was a table and four chairs, and five pictures on the wall. One picture was of Ivan Atashev, who had lived from 1794 to 1869 and been responsible for the building of the palace. He had made his money during the Siberian gold rush – which had come some years earlier than its American counterpart – which is how he had afforded to bring furniture from St Petersburg, the remnants of which made up the exhibition. Another of the pictures was of his wife. Anya giggled a little self-consciously as she told me all this, perhaps due to what she believed to be the inadequacy of the display. I was sympathetic and would have liked to ask about more recent history but I held back, so as not to make her uncomfortable. The chairs were nice, but I wanted her to fill in the gaps between the imperial splendour of Atashev's grand home and this dingy back room with a few chairs and a table. I put Anya out of her misery and left.

A narrow road lead down to the banks of the Ob River. As I followed the murky water along, I noticed a myriad of promenading couples walking past. All were glowing, visibly excited, I imagined, by the future and their world. There was something a little zombie-like about this glowing exhibition of happiness. I had witnessed this scene in Russia several times before. Young couples in love, oblivious to the reality of the world outside their bubble; determined, more likely, to enjoy every last minute before the onset of the long and harsh Siberian winter.

I ate shashlik at Beloye Lake with its pedaloes and bouncy castles. A drunk man stumbled after me screaming, 'Rich, Rich, give me roubles!' I was wearing jeans that had begun to rip at the knees, a pair of worn boots and a T-shirt that clung on to my under-nourished frame – in Russia I could be starving and helpless, yet I was a European, and that meant rich. I passed a girl standing outside a cafe dressed as a bottle of beer. The passers-by seemed unimpressed with the humour, mostly ignoring her completely. Perhaps your average Tomskian was still a little uncomfortable with advertising or maybe they had already sampled the beer being promoted.

Back at Hotel Sibir I stopped in the restaurant for a beer. The same waitress that had taken my chit at breakfast was working a split shift. The American group soon started to arrive in dribs and drabs for dinner. They were defiantly unprepared to help the waitress with pronunciation of the clumsily put together 'English menu' and instead helped themselves from the fridge, which was very obviously off limits. Their colonial arrogance and mock anglicisation of the foreign language made them look foolish and ugly, and made me cringe. She had worked all day for what individually they had spent on a couple of drinks. Yet, I concluded that nothing separated me in her mind from them: only in my own mind was I different, and perhaps that was no more than a self-contrived illusion. Feeling all too aware that to Russians we westerners were all the same, I had to leave.

After a day in Tomsk, time began to drag and I was ready to get back to Max and Jo in Novosibirsk. However, I was reluctant to let Eevan down, as he was friendly and I'd got the feeling spending some time with me would mean a lot to him. As I waited for our three o'clock meeting, I decided to take in some nearby attractions, firstly the Oppression Museum, the austere red-brick building once home to a KGB prison, now part sombre museum and part home to an arts academy. A thin wall separated young men and women singing and dancing from ghosts being beaten and tortured. As it happened, the museum was closed and the man I approached for information had never known it to be open.

Thinking on my feet, I meandered down the charmingly cobbled Bakunin Street, a narrow lane with artists at their easels at intervals along its winding way. It quickly conveyed me back a few centuries to a Russia of Tolstoy novels. The light at the end of this pleasant tunnel was the Voznesenskaya Church, an awe-inspiring gothic cathedral overlooking the city, pleasingly in a state of mid restoration in preparation for the city's 400-year centenary. Despite its size it had an air of delicacy, like Russia itself, its five sparkling spires reaching into the sky. I headed around to the entrance. I had no real desire to go inside – it was the exterior of holy buildings that left me humbled, man's achievements and all that, and going inside made me feel like a voyeur. That said, it's nice to have the option, something the heavily insulated babushka guarding the doorway wasn't going to give me. I wasn't about to argue with her; perhaps she had been quick to divine my undeserving intentions.

With the warming sun, the earlier storm forgotten, Tomsk began to show off her best side. Around the least suspecting corner she offered up more and more architectural gems, from the lace buildings to the splendour of churches such as the Petropavlovskaya Cathedral, whose state of mild dilapidation and location in the midst of a battered Soviet style estate didn't steal from its dignified grandeur. Its authenticity was helped by an orthodox priest holding audience with a group of beggars outside the grand entrance. Perhaps he was explaining, in subtler terms than the babushka had to me, why they couldn't enter.

Eevan was at the hotel reception at three o'clock prompt, having come straight from a class. He looked incongruous in a new pair of trainers and a utility vest, which part disguised a paunch that quite became him. His narrow, heavy eyes were kind, yet revealed the uncertainty of an outsider, as if he was never quite sure of how his differences would translate into the reactions of others. It was like the look of a man with a birthmark covering his face. His eyes leapt about, never holding mine for very long – not shady or untrustworthy, just uncertain.

We walked along the now busy Lenina Street (every town should have one! – and they have), the sun having brought everyone onto the streets. We passed the main university building, a well-maintained classical house, where students preened themselves in the gardens. Eevan excused himself for not knowing anything about this building, having been a pedagogical student for five years and frequenting another part of the campus.

He had come to Tomsk to study after leaving school in Uzbekistan, and he gave the impression of having been very studious.

'To tell the truth, I had to learn English – it was economic necessity. With English I am able to earn money. Many people are interested in English now in this city.'

He made it sound so much more than just another language, and I felt slightly guilty for taking my birth right so much for granted.

We walked up to the botanical park. Eevan was sure we wouldn't be allowed in, and sure enough a ferocious babushka stared at us from behind a dirty pane of glass as we looked longingly beyond the gates. Eevan tried gesticulating for her to open the gates, at which point she turned away and ignored us completely.

He quickly justified her rudeness, saying, 'To me she pays no attention, but it is good that the park is closed – there is no litter and the plants are protected.' I wasn't sure from exactly what.

Eevan was eager to please, yet didn't know quite how. This seemed common in Siberia, where people were very obviously desperate to ask not so much 'What would you like to see?' but 'Why would you like to see it?' Of course, they couldn't really ask this question. I fast gathered that I had to be decisive. I suggested we have a beer, and on this occasion the idea was warmly received and we found a terrace cafe.

Eevan was a Muslim – but not a serious one. 'There are no serious Muslims in Tomsk,' he clarified. 'As long as someone is a good person, this is all that matters,' Eevan concluded, whilst padding the sweat from his brow.

Sporadic drops of rain brought more people into the cafe from the street. Supermodel waitresses served ice cream and beer, whilst Neanderthal men couldn't have shown more indifference to the girls. Eevan's theory on the macho male of Siberia was simple: insecurity. It was a mere show put on by those who were, underneath the surface, very obviously without much confidence. In the same way, the Siberian girls put on an outward appearance – by no means unpleasant for the male eye. However, in the West the way they presented themselves would bridge a fine line between making the best of oneself and looking like a prostitute.

The sullen waitress ditched our bottles of beer on the table. With a quick glance Eevan thanked her, and insisted on paying. I was uncomfortable at this gesture of generosity as his salary had been brought up very early on. I had no need to worry, he said – his family was involved with the Uzbek coal industry and not doing badly at all, having helped Eevan with the $17,000 needed to buy his Tomsk apartment. With a monthly earning of $300 he was doing all right.

It appeared that along with home owners the world over, he was waiting for prices to rise sufficiently before moving into a larger place. If he was living in London, he would probably be a tycoon by now. Fortunately for me he was in Tomsk, and with that survival vest looked just the part.

'So do you get many tourists in Tomsk?'

Eevan paused and looked at me, as if I'd asked him to commit murder. 'No.'

'What, none at all?'

'Well, some, but only Russians. No, mostly businessmen come here.'

I had never linked Siberia with oil barons, but from now on it will probably be synonymous more and more. Mikhail Khodorkovsky, possibly the most infamous of the oligarchs, presently languishing in a Moscow gaol, owned many of the oil wells in the Tomsk region. Just before his dawn arrest by armed security forces, Khodorkovsky was putting the final touches to a deal set to bank him something in the region of $6 billion. Roman Abramovich, the owner of Chelsea Football Club, was another well-known Siberian. However, the growing need for Siberian oil and gas around the world could only bode badly for the average Siberian, with all prices being artificially inflated. Cities in the middle of Siberia with average prices higher than in London or Paris will never attract much interest unrelated to oil.

'So you don't get many tourists from, say, Europe?'

Eevan just nodded whilst swigging his beer, then completely changed the subject.

'Yes, Tomsk has all the drawbacks of any modern city. We have drunks, drug heads – everything.'

'But you get a lot of tourists from Moscow, yes?' I persisted.

'My future is English, I'm learning Spanish. Eventually I will get a job in a hotel in the West. Small countries will always be under the control of bigger ones.'

I'd lost him there.

The longer we were at the cafe, the more the speed of Eevan's consumption increased. He left me behind after the second bottle. Gone were Eevan's polite dealings with the waitress – he began yelling his demand for more beer the length of the cafe. On receipt of maybe his sixth or seventh beer, rather than paying the girl who had brought it to our table he shooed her away, slapping her hard on the buttock as she went. Aware of the increasing attention we were getting from others in the cafe, I thought it probably a good time to make my farewells. Leaving Eevan slumped in his chair gripping a bottle of beer, I caught the train back down to Novosibirsk.

Jo was itching to go, having fully recovered and stocked up on chocolate and Fanta.

CHAPTER TEN
KRASNOYARSK

East of Novosibirsk the road cut through tall, dark, imposing forests, which gave way to lush grasslands, where shaggy ponies grazed against a backdrop of pure blue sky. It was a gently winding wilderness of sloped elevations fretted with breathtaking panoramic horizons. Occasionally we passed through straggling and colourful settlements, where children played in the dusty streets, babushkas filled up at water pumps and logs were being sliced ready for winter. The break from driving had been good for us. Jo was fully fit again and we now felt we were really seeing and feeling Siberia, and not just being conveyed through it in a metal capsule. The outskirts of Krasnoyarsk arrived with a comforting evening – rundown industrial buildings were crudely fused with ramshackle *izbas*, 'sunk to their window frames in the earth' (Valentin Rasputin).

We pulled up on the bank of the Yenisey River, a natural divide between western and eastern Siberia, and watched lovers promenading beside its clear waters, sharing ice creams as the sun went down. Anton Chekhov crossed Siberia in a horse-drawn carriage during his well-documented journey to Sakhalin:

Cold plains, crooked birch trees, puddles, lakes here and there, snow in May, and the dreary uninhabited banks of the tributaries of the river Ob – that's all my memory manages to retain out of the first two thousand verst.

This all changed, however, when he reached the Yenisey River. 'Never in my life have I seen a river more magnificent than the Yenisey.'

Chekhov was quite taken by the Yenisey, and from then on during his trip everything around him came alive, even mile upon mile of hypnotically dull taiga seemed to get him excited. We fell asleep by the river feeling pretty good too.

Probably Krasnoyarsk's most famous son is the painter Vasily Surikov, whose work is on permanent display in the Russian Museum in St Petersburg. His pictures are on the big side; large-scale historical representations of the lives of ordinary people. Most significantly he painted *The Conquest of Siberia by Yermak*, a huge picture, depicting the Cossacks scrapping it out with Kuchum and his Tartars. The conquerors of Siberia were the Cossacks, led by Yermak Timofeyevich in the sixteenth century. Who? His true name isn't really known; most information about him has been handed down in the form of folk songs. Was he simply an opportunist brigand who, having spent most of his life travelling up and down the Volga and Don rivers plundering wealthy merchants, decided to try his luck east of the Urals? Or was he part of a more organised expedition supported and financed by said wealthy merchants? It is believed by certain Russian historians that he was on the payroll of the Stroganov family, merchants operating in the Ural region. Nobody will ever know for sure the part played by Yermak; however, he is certainly the people's favourite to be the conqueror of Siberia. He is the embodiment of the Russians' freedom-loving aspirations.

Aspirations they never seem to achieve.

Surikov was born into a family of Siberian Cossacks – his ancestors having fought alongside Yermak – and he said that Siberia gave him 'spirit, strength and health'. He married the granddaughter of Svistunov, one of the Decembrists (more of whom later), settled in Moscow in 1877 and now spends all his time at the Vagankovskoye Cemetery in the capital.

Surikov was also a keen traveller, and after the collector Pavel Tretyakov bought most of his work he travelled Europe on the proceeds, joining the Society for Travelling Art Exhibitions. Another one of his big canvasses depicts the Cossacks returning victorious, having defeated the Persians somewhere – it's called *Stepan Razin* and is now better known for the popular Russian beer named after it.

After only a few hours' sleep, we were woken by a fist thumping on the window. The noise was accompanied by the blinding light of a torch refracting through the glass and a voice.

'You! You!'

I was followed by the light beam as I clambered towards the interior light switch.

'Documents!' was the next staccato command. Here we go again!

Outside, in the chill night air, we were met by three young militia. They got the obligatory frisking out of the way, before lighting cigarettes. The torch guy's curiosity got the better of him, as he proceeded to examine the van inside and out.

They studied our passports, studied us with bemusement and, when they realised we understood very little of what they said, visibly lost interest in us. Finishing their cigarettes, they handed back our passports, and almost as an afterthought one of them mentioned 'Visa finish… twenty-four hours, *zavtra*' before they drove off into the night.

With all the distractions we had completely forgotten the time restraint on our visas. I think, subconsciously, because we had managed to venture so far beyond the paperwork's official jurisdiction, i.e. further than St Petersburg, with few members of the militia even batting an eyelid, we simply hadn't been that bothered, carrying the notion that if we did reach Vladivostok with out-of-date paperwork, we would be grateful for any help we might get with leaving the country. This timely reminder got the better of our consciences.

The financial implications of upsetting the immigration people were the biggest concern. On the matter of the area that the visa actually covered, lines were a bit blurred, whereas a date was fairly clear, and feeling legal in the country gave us confidence – this, we needed. Driving around in the belief that we might one day arrive at Vladivostok alive was one thing, but doing it whilst blatantly messing with Russian laws was another, however weird and corrupt they might be. Thus the following morning, having found a hotel to freshen up in, we headed across town to see what all the fuss regarding the OVIR was all about.

Krasnoyarsk is an undeniably attractive and prosperous city – an administrative centre for the region and popular destination for industry. The streets were lined with expensive-looking shops, cars were new, and the inhabitants seemed well dressed.

The air was chaste and invigorating, there was a certain civic pride about the place, a hopefulness that had been vacant in other parts of Siberia, and people spoke English – well, they wanted to give it a try, rather than listen to us destroying their language.

The OVIR office was an unassuming wooden building a couple of kilometres from the town's centre, located in a leafy suburb. A scene of colourful chaos greeted us the other side of a delicately laced front door. Whole families appeared to be camped out, mainly dark-skinned Kazakhs from the south. Children scrambled over seats whilst parents jostled for the attention of a sullen official protected by a heavy shield of glass. It was an assault of richly coloured exotic clothing and equally rich smells. If there was any kind of queue, it was one that would take a while to decipher. We stood dazed, pondering our next move.

After an hour had passed we had managed little more than finding a free window sill on which to perch, so, remembering the actions of a man at an equally disorganised consulate in Latvia, going against my natural instincts I pushed my way through the near frantic crowd and arrived at the official's window.

'*Angliski, Angliski!*' I bellowed shamefully, expecting this to propel me into a light of some significance.

The official considered me for several moments and then offered the reassuring words, 'One moment.'

With the whole weight of Kazakhstan pinning me against the glass, I waited expectantly.

Meanwhile, on the other side of the room Jo had been enveloped by a babushka, who appeared to have tears in her eyes. The embrace seemed to last an age, and all I could make out were cries of '*Izviniteah*'. I hadn't noticed my official doing anything; however, moments later a suited Russian man appeared from an inside door and beckoned us both to follow him. Once we had escaped the crush, I asked Jo, 'What was that all about?'

'I don't know – I think she said some thing about Princess Diana being killed!'

'Oh right...'

The OVIR official was going to do all he could to extend our visas for another month, a process that would take three days. Time to explore Krasnoyarsk.

THREE REASONS TO VISIT KRASNOYARSK

- You might be lucky enough to happen across some gold – first discovered here in the seventeenth century.

- The city is home to five museums and one hundred public libraries.

- The territory of Krasnoyarsk is rich in raw materials, producing synthetic rubber and aluminium.

TWO REASONS NOT TO VISIT KRASNOYARSK

- Chances of finding any gold now are fairly slim.

- Due to its natural riches, the town is a large centre for organised crime.

Our first stop was the long distance telephone bureau. A call to Uncle Tony was well overdue, if only to alert him to the fact that there was now a strong possibility we would reach Vladivostok. Whichever map you were looking at we were over halfway. Of course, the journey itself was taking on a life of its own, completely overshadowing any job that may or may not exist at the end of the road. Looking back on the ground we covered and the land mass that is Russia, it was fairly naive to think it could have been any different. How could anything be of more import than driving the breadth of Russia? It was fast becoming all about the moment, the future a long way from our minds. Yet with every kilometre, taking up employment in the Far East became more of a reality. It would have certainly been nice to have someone/thing to receive us on our arrival – a city is always made more welcoming by a local's name or telephone number.

The telephone bureau was full of the youthful smiling faces of Indian medical students, who certainly didn't do anything to reduce the disorder that prevails over such places Russia-wide. But they did do something to diffuse the air of aggression created by Russians bristling with the anticipation of conversing with loved ones far away in Moscow or St Petersburg. On first inspection the students had made the venue their social centre. Groups huddled together, laughing and chatting. We slipped in relatively unnoticed – which made a pleasant change from the intense staring we usually received on entering a public building. There was no answer from Uncle Tony.

Our wanderings took us along streets lined with attractive wooden mansions, and also streets lined with unattractive sombre grey Soviet blocks. Washing hung out to dry on the balconies coloured their drabness. Gradually the lush grass of distant pastures came to dominate our view, until only thirty minutes from the airy centre to the north, we had broken free of the city. We climbed the steep Karaulnaya hill to the Chasoviya Chapel, a pretty little structure overlooking Krasnoyarsk and much of the surrounding emptiness. The light breeze was refreshing, the last of the day's sun warming, as by the side of the chapel, ignored by the populace of the town, we dozed away the rest of the daylight.

The following day, whilst out searching for some sausages in batter – not healthy, but tasty – I was approached by two smartly dressed young men with briefcases. Both wore black suits and black ties, and shiny black shoes. I was walking towards them when they caught my gaze, and both proffered alarmingly large smiles. For the first time in Russia, I actually thought somebody else looked more out of place than I did.

I was right. Seth and Josh were out of place, on a year's placement from the United States. They weren't students, and the only thing they had to sell was impossible to put a price on – hope. They were Mormons.

Seth and Josh were in a unique position, and so was I, for that matter – and I don't mean being in the middle of Siberia, although that wasn't so run-of-the-mill for any of us.

No, it was unique in that there was no door for me to shut in their faces, and for them, no door to be shut in their faces! In fact, there was nowhere to run. When Jehovah's Witnesses and the like turn up at home, it's a quick 'Not today', and no more is said on the matter as they move on up the street to the next door. On this occasion, even if there had been a door, the last thing I wanted to do was shut it. These two guys, as odd as they might have looked, were probably the warmest, most open people we'd met in Russia. Bombs could have been dropping all around, and their serene faces would have remained unaltered, their complete belief in their faith keeping the repose. Of course, this was only the vanguard to a more complex agenda – but I had only just met them.

And I, from the minute we left Tallinn, or England really, was open to suggestion as a traveller. Even if you don't choose to be open to new people and ideas, circumstances force this state of mind upon you. A friendly face, a common language and hope by the bucketload is a potent cocktail for anyone a long way from home. So when Seth ventured 'Shall we sit down for a coffee?' my affirmative response was only natural.

Josh brought the lukewarm coffees in plastic cups over to the table. Seth had already begun sizing me up.

'So what brings you to Krasnoyarsk?' I asked.

'We're missionaries,' Seth replied, in a tone that suggested he thought this was obvious.

'How long will you stay here?'

'Our replacements arrive next month.'

'How's it been?'

'It's been a lot of fun,' Josh mused.

I couldn't for a second believe the average Russian had given them the time of day, it not being easy to take seriously a faith whose spiritual figurehead had fifty-two wives.

'What do you actually do here?' I asked.

Josh had picked up on my cynicism by now, and was defensive.

'We represent the Church of Latter-Day Saints.' They both looked hard for a reaction; I didn't give them one. Their church isn't registered as a church in Russia, but as a 'religious association', which greatly reduces their status and any kudos they might have. Basically, the Russians will put up with the likes of Seth and Josh, as long as they're getting something from them, for example handouts, English teaching, etc. However, if my two companions suddenly combusted into flames, it's questionable whether anyone would actually pee on them. Reverend Vsevolod, a chaplain of the Russian Orthodox Church is reported as saying: 'We don't approve of the LDS Church's missionary effort among the orthodox believers… Our advice to them is, concentrate more on your own country. There are lots of problems in the United States to keep you busy.'

My initial enthusiasm at meeting two friendly strangers had all but fizzled out the second I'd noticed that Seth's briefcase was in fact attached to his wrist by a metal chain. Just as I was about to slam my imaginary door in their faces, I remembered Jo, battered sausages and a genuine excuse to leave: 'I really must collect my visa.'

CHAPTER ELEVEN
LAKE BAIKAL

The winding and gently twisting road to Irkutsk led us through wooden settlements, some brightly coloured in the old believers' style, others with no style at all. The first town of note was Kansk. The wide street that cut the town down the middle was dusty, and most of the buildings were Soviet and grey. Despite its Soviet credentials it had the atmosphere of a frontier town of the Wild West, and you expected somebody to stumble through the doors of a saloon any minute, to see tumbleweed bounce down the street and to hear the echo of coffins being hammered together. Clint Eastwood wasn't in town but a collective of local 'yoof' was fast to gather around Max as we bought provisions from a kiosk close to the central timber church.

Beyond Kansk it really felt like we were gliding downhill, caught on the wind dancing in from the steppe. The steppe was more barren, but the stark vastness imbued the smallest blots of shrubs or boulders with an intensity they couldn't have possessed in any other landscape. Faced with unending

217

inclines I slipped Max out of gear and we took it in turns hanging out the windows, like members of a display team, wing walkers strapped to a bi-plane.

The display came to an end when we joined the Angara River at Angarsk, the first indication of modernity since leaving Krasnoyarsk. Founded in 1948 as an industrial community, three years later it gained city status. Angarsk boasts the largest industrial zone in all Asia, which includes such Soviet industrial giants as the Angarsk Petrochemical Complex and the Angarsk Electrolysis Chemical Complex. For a little more culture, the city is home to a Museum of Clocks and Watches.

We parked up on the bank of the Angara River, downwind of the smell of bread being baked in a nearby factory. Fishermen passed by, returning home with the day's catch. Behind us were two churches protectively positioned on either side of the road into Irkutsk. I met Ivor whilst buying some cheese at a nearby shop. He was a giant of a man, hirsute, with thick-lens spectacles tinted just enough to make it difficult to see his eyes. He recommended a variety of cheese from Bratsk – a place he'd once lived north-west of Lake Baikal, more notable for its dam than its cheese. Having seen where the van was parked up he promised to pop round that evening with some proper Irish stout – Ivor was half Irish.

Just after dark, as good as his word, Ivor appeared tapping on the window, several dark brown bottles under his arm. It was a tight fit for him but he quickly warmed us all up and set about discussing a variety of conspiracy theories regarding the death of Diana a week earlier. He had a talent for yarn-spinning, weaving speculative and generalised pictures of people and situations.

'The Russians,' he was keen to detach himself, and his intact Irish accent helped, 'do much of their own business at night, well, not so much business but scheming. They love to scheme, not so much for financial reward, but more for the enjoyment of the process. Money isn't real to them, merely something to play with. It comes and goes in much the same way as their ideas do; usually very quickly.'

It was strange, the three of us squashed in to the back of the van, chatting as if we'd been friends for years.

'Anyone who's doing well in Irkutsk is leading the life of a vampire. Sleeping by day and getting their hands on the life blood by night. You'll never see the true schemers.'

I don't really think we knew what he was on about, but that didn't matter. With a mischievous tone in his voice, Ivor posed the question, 'So what about Diana?'

'We don't know anything about it really,' I replied honestly.

'The Egyptian secret service – they did it.'

You couldn't really argue with that, but Ivor paused, giving us both the chance to do so.

'Al-Fayed, he didn't need the hassle from MI5. Diana was pregnant, it was all going to get messy.'

'Maybe it was MI5,' I suggested.

'Yah, could be, they would have had orders from above. There was no way the royal family wanted an Arab baby in the picture. Or perhaps the IRA – payback time. With a worldwide smokescreen they'd never get blamed – just by us three in this van in Siberia... we know the truth.'

After several hours had passed, Ivor disappeared into the night, and we soon realised that we had learned very little about the man himself. We had discovered that pretty much anyone the world over could have killed Diana, yet who was Ivor? The thought did cross our mind that Ivor had in fact killed Diana, and was now in hiding. He wasn't going to get caught in Irkutsk, unless he kept talking about it.

The next morning we went to the town square to find the communication bureau in the town hall. Jo needed to put in a call home this time, and I was keen to get some idea of what was waiting for us a couple of thousand kilometres down the line in Vladivostok. These places were nearly as dispiriting as the OVIR offices. When you had eventually conveyed all your information to the telephonist – no mean feat – you sat and waited for a cubicle to become free. When it did the number of the booth was announced, at which point the call was connected. It was then necessary to get to the phone as quickly as possible to save what was left of the call time. Often this was very little time as the bureaus were generally packed with people, and some had up to fifty cubicles, and if you happened to find yourself at the wrong end of the hall from your cubicle... The chances of even getting the chance to run for your cubicle of course depended on whether you'd understood what was being announced over the loudspeaker. Despite the considerable annoyance factor, there was something just a little romantic about long-distance telephone call centres, in the way of a platform at a train station, in the days before email and mobile phones fried our brains and put our emotions on warp drive.

Outside the town hall there was a ramshackle collection of kiosks and a littering of plastic tables and chairs. Music blared out over the scene as folk passed their time drinking beer. Jo made her call – all ten seconds of it, due to not being a particularly good sprinter. I fared a little better by rather spookily predicting the number of my cubicle; this bought me nearly twice as much time on the phone with Tony.

'How the devil are you, those Russkies treating you well? And where the devil are you?' Tony roared.

'Irkutsk, we've just arrived in Irkutsk close to Lake Baikal,' I blurted out, aware of the clock ticking.

'Lake what? Which lake's that... this line is shite!'

'Look, any word from Nikolai? I haven't got much time,' I interrupted.

'Is that Lake Baikal – have you bloody well made it to Lake Baikal?'

'Yeah, we're near Lake Baikal.'

'Well, bugger me and call me Simon.'

'I haven't got much time, Tony – any word from Nikolai in Vladivostok?'

'Olkhon Island!' Tony yelled, ignoring my question. 'Svetlana! Guesthouse! Old friend of mine – send her my best!' The line went dead.

Well, that was a success – and how the hell did Tony have a friend in the middle of Lake Baikal?

Weathered by history and life, Irkutsk now stands calm and wise, knowing its own value, moderately famous for its glory, past and present, cultured since olden times and traditionally hospitable.

I can't disagree with the words of the writer John Foster Fraser, although the fare for the taxi that took us the short distance into town suggested the taxi driver might be somewhat deluded with regards to his own value.

> *There is a special hour when Irkutsk easily responds to your feelings for it. This hour comes at the early part of a summer dawn, before the sun rises, then kindles and washes away, like a hot wave, the smells emanating from the nocturnal depths that linger all night, until pedestrians hurrying by disperse them, and before the rumble of traffic, destroys the rare, brief stillness.*

We had just missed this special hour, but got the gist of what Fraser was saying. The city is located close to the south shore of Lake Baikal, where it has been for the last three hundred or so years, starting life as a fort – the winter quarters of Ivan Pokhabov, a base for the collection of a fur tax from the indigenous Buryats.

In the distance, on the river's edge, I could see the Znamenskya Monastery. Its turquoise paintwork was clashing with the clear blue of the Angara, the morning sun catching its golden cupolas, adding to the serene beauty of one of the few picture postcard images I'd acknowledged. I felt elated. I had a feeling that I was going to like Irkutsk, and so far so good.

Despite Irkutsk's growth with Russia's expansion east, by the end of the seventeenth century only one thousand people lived there. It was in the nineteenth century that it really hit the big time, by coincidence of being in the middle of Russia's gold region. It was the centre for the Russian gold rush. John Foster Fraser, who recounts his travels in Siberia almost a century ago in his book *The Real Siberia*, said Irkutsk was 'Like a restless, bustling Western American town near the region of gold diggings. There is one street two miles long, and all the others are at right angles.' Karla Marxa Street must have been that street, and the rest of the centre runs from it.

Fraser goes on to write about the many people that became gold millionaires. By law all the gold mined in eastern Siberia had to go through the government laboratory, which was located in Irkutsk. However, the laboratory only ever saw half the gold being mined. At the time Fraser was writing, the Irkutsk gold was guarded by two old men, the Russian authorities reasoning that they were less likely to run off with the gold, as had previously happened when the responsibility had been given to a troop of Cossacks. As Fraser points out, the two men of course were never likely to be 'hit on the head some night with a mallet'. Most of the gold that wasn't reaching the lab in Irkutsk was simply being squandered on the high life. Some of it would be bought by Chinamen masquerading as tea dealers. In order to get the gold out of Russia and back to China, they would employ the services of dead Chinamen. Fraser writes:

Peeping through a keyhole at an embalming operation not long ago, the Irkutsk police saw gold dust blown through a tube up the nostrils into an empty skull. So they discovered why the Chinese were so anxious to give the soul of their dead brother peace by burial at home.

*His head was to serve as a carrier of gold till he reached
the flowery land, and then the dust was to be extracted.*

We had acquired the assistance of a dapper taxi driver and
his very smart Nissan saloon car to transport us to Khuzhir,
the main town on Olkhon Island. This was something of
a detour to say the least, but amongst other things my
curiosity had got the better of me. I was all too aware that
Uncle Tony knew or liked to think he knew everyone, but a
friend on Olkhon Island in the middle of Lake Baikal – that
was a result even for him.

Jo had pointed out the driver's similarity to Richard Gere
– he was Richard from then on. He drove very fast along
the recently gravelled road, and my head hit the cushioned
roof – annoying at first, then, once I'd resigned myself to it,
the sensation was enjoyable. Some twenty minutes outside
the city the woodland thinned out, and gentle undulating
steppe took over as the backdrop. Richard said very little,
occasionally fiddling with the radio tuner, jumping from
fizzy high-energy Russian pop to distorted violins as he tried
to figure out what actually suited his mood. Whilst I tried
to sleep, Jo waited with great anticipation for the lake to
appear beyond the next mountain, promising to wake me
as soon as it broke its cover. There was no need; I wouldn't
be getting any sleep.

Lake Baikal accounts for one sixth of the world's fresh
water, and some 1,200 of the creatures that live in the lake
are unique to it. The Russians tend to speak of the lake as a
person – with a godlike reverence. It's hard to imagine the
personification of Old Man Baikal not to have a long white

beard, and a hooded cloak down to his feet. Eventually, after peak after teasing peak, there in the distance appeared the azure waters, captivating and mystical. On a certain level it was easy to share the Russian consensus. I was hypnotised by the picture ahead...

We arrived at the small port just as the ferry was loading up an eclectic array of vehicles for the twenty-minute crossing. We shared the trip with a couple of fourgons both bursting with passengers; a large truck loaded down with barrels, two rosy-cheeked men sitting in the cab with damp expressions suggesting it wasn't the first time they'd made the crossing, more likely the tenth that day; and a couple of bicycles. That was all the ferry could accommodate. And apparently it wasn't designed for smart Japanese saloons with low suspensions – Richard, having great difficulty climbing the ramp, had to be helped by two local Buryats and a timber plank. We all clambered out in order to lighten the load. Richard seemed most put out as we stood looking on, gazing at the fourgons and their wilderness suspension with admiration. In order to make up for the hitch whilst boarding the ferry, Richard felt the need (as did all Siberian taxi drivers) to put his foot down for the final leg of the journey to Khuzhir. I had been quoted 'two hours from ferry to the island's main town', but we were crawling the dusty backstreets of Khuzhir searching for the guest house in less than thirty minutes.

We finally came to rest outside Guesthouse Svetlana. A tatty board displaying the name swung in the breeze outside a wooden bungalow painted bright green. Svetlana was a warm bulky babushka, with a large crop of peroxide hair and bright red lipstick to help disguise her aging skin. Having met Svetlana, I wasn't sure it was in fact a good idea to mention Tony; the risk of unearthing knowledge about him – the actual nature of his relationship with this woman – was quite undesirable. I kept my curiosity at bay as she showed us to our rooms and got the heating going, as it was now considerably colder than it had been in the city. She then insisted that we eat.

Svetlana's guesthouse was a work in progress, as was much of Khuzhir. Local Buryat carpenters were at work in her backyard, knocking scrupulously designed, intricately carved sheds together. It was the first time I'd heard the Buryat language spoken. It was like music with soft and flowing rhythms, like birds singing sweetly to one another. These sounds married well with the Buryats' serenely soft features, by far the most attractive of the indigenous people we'd come across so far.

The fare laid out on the dining room table included the local speciality omul, a type of fish from the salmon family often served raw or as a soup. Svetlana, fortunately, guessing our Western stomachs to be less courageous than those of the locals, had smoked the omul on this occasion. Local Buryat shamans used to ask the sea god Dianda to stop the sarma – a wind that blows from the north-west for about one hundred days of the year, at 80 miles an hour – and to drive the omul closer to the shore.

Svetlana made light conversation with us, which always came back to the offer of an excursion to Cape Khoboi on the island's north shore. After some time she left us to it. The fish was delicious, which is more than can be said for dessert. Svetlana returned, cleared the table, and presented us with a bowl of cold semolina each.

'Way to Russia' say of Olkhon Island in their online guide to the region: 'Olkhon is a beautiful nude land that seems to have emerged from the fresh waters of Baikal... It is a great place to get away from civilisation.'

The guide goes on to say that there are no power lines or telephone wires. I would disagree. Perhaps the biggest eyesore – which we had followed all the way from Irkutsk – were the huge metal towers that blighted the horizon in all directions. The pylons held the island captive, like aliens from a seventies science fiction movie.

Despite this particular ugliness, the island is one of the most powerful symbols in the Buryat world, and the centre for Buryat shamanism. The story goes that shamans have used the island as a sanctuary from persecution for many, many years, and due to other religions not having reached the island, the shamanism to be found there is still of the purest form, having preserved the most ancient of shamanic beliefs. Whether this is the case or not, with the summer months comes the annual pilgrimage to the island of indigenous shamans, New Agers, tour groups and archaeologists. And most of them ended up at Nikita's Guesthouse, on the other side of the wide central boulevard that dissected the town.

The season was winding down; however, there were still a few tourists on the island, and it was Nikita who seemed to have the monopoly on independent travellers who visited. A short, plump bespectacled girl was manning the Nikita tourist information kiosk on the edge of the quickly expanding Nikita tourist complex. Slabs of timber were being cut and erected at the same pace as they had been over at Svetlana's: they either both had inside info about the speed of the growing tourist industry, or they were preparing themselves for the following season before the weather prevented such work. The girl, who had introduced herself as Olga, seemed quite bewildered that my friend and I were staying over the way at Svetlana's and not at Nikita's. She as good as said, 'Why are you not staying here, this is where all the Western travellers stay!'

I enjoyed her mild dismay. I had upset the balance of the way things should be, and the fact that she was annoyed gave me a deviant pleasure.

To one side of the kiosk was a chalk board, listing excursions and events. Olga, seeing me reading about the first trip on the board, was quick to offer: 'The minibus leaves for Cape Khoboi at ten o'clock – would you like to come?'

'Oh, I don't know, perhaps,' I replied, not having given the question too much thought.

'Why not?' she barked.

I assumed she was joking – but she wasn't.

'I just don't know what my friend and I are doing – that's all,' I rather timidly added.

'So you and you're friend will be here at ten o'clock.'

This definitely sounded like an instruction – from the mouth of the white witch, not from a native of the most spiritual place in Russia. I said goodbye and walked off.

First Svetlana, and then with considerably more ferocity Olga – why the great push to get people to Cape Khoboi?

I really didn't want to go there at all now.

So many superlatives are always used when talking about the lake. The biggest (though it's actually only the second biggest), the deepest, the oldest lake in the world. Having climbed the hill to a vantage point above Khuzhir – Olga for some reason had told me not to – I was now offered a spectacular view out onto Baikal, beyond the much photographed Shaman Rocks. It was difficult not to be impressed. It really did feel a million miles from Russia. I've never been there, but the atmosphere was the same as the one I get from programmes about Nova Scotia. Tranquil... yes... spectacular... yes. But also fairly sinister.

Olkhon's shape closely resembles that of Baikal itself, as if cut to size and then dropped into place at the deepest part where the lake reaches down to 1,637 metres.

There is controversy over the exact meaning of Olkhon – some say it means 'sparsely forested', others 'dry'. Both apply to the island – there is forest around Khuzhir but the majority of the scenery is made up of bleak steppe. Rainfall seldom exceeds 200 millimetres per year. I read this in the island's tourist information pamphlet, which I had picked up at Olga's kiosk. It went on to tell me that the population of the island is less than 1,500, the majority of whom are living in Khuzhir, which was founded in 1939. The native inhabitants are Buryats whose main activities are fishing and sheep herding... and on it went, reflecting the true Russian obsession with making a potentially interesting subject very dull indeed.

I followed the cliff top around, for the first time noticing the sarma, not yet 'furious' as it had been described in the pamphlet, but nevertheless strong. Olkhon has an unusual climate, hotter than the rest of the region in summer and much colder in winter. Autumn sees the arrival of the heavy north-westerly winds that batter the island and cause havoc for the fishermen.

Popping my head through the door of the town's only church, which was mid restoration, I saw a couple of icon painters hard at work. I continued to Khuzhir's little port on the southern shore of the town. Tethered to a decrepit pontoon was a fleet of ten fishing boats, all grey and identical in style, all in need of some TLC. Broken bottles and rubbish littered the small stretch of beach that ran up to a burnt-out boathouse – a long time abandoned. I wandered back through the town's dusty streets, the occasional motorbike accelerating past me. By the time I had reached Svetlana's place, I had a mangy pack of wild dogs in tow.

Jo was reclining on a wooden bench in the courtyard. She caught sight of me.

'There's something bloody weird going on here,' she exclaimed.

I think I knew exactly what she meant, but asked anyway.

'What do you mean?'

'Well, I went for a walk up into the forest, and there were just piles of bones everywhere – some old, some recently dead carcasses.'

'Dogs?' I offered.

'Yeah, there are lots of dead dogs, and plenty of living dead dogs.' She was referring to the packs of under-nourished and under-loved dogs that roamed the streets of the town. 'But lots of other larger animals as well,' she continued. 'I'm not being funny but is this place radioactive or something?' Jo had her extremely serious face on.

The pamphlet I had acquired from lovely Olga had boasted of over 155 different species of birds and animals on the island, including lynx, red fox, black grouse and woodpecker. Thinking about it, I hadn't seen any birds or animals – but then I hadn't really left the town.

'I didn't see one single bird.' She looked at me, disturbed. Pulling herself upright, she cleared her throat and said, 'No, strangely there was absolutely no sign of life.'

My mind leapt back to the Altai. Whilst there I had heard no singing birds, or seen any wild animals either. I had simply buried thoughts of Siberia's nuclear heritage. But again it was there, staring me in the face.

'I swear there were human bones as well.' Jo was trying not to laugh, but the fact did remain that Siberia had very few animals other than manky starving street dogs.

Jo, never scared to ruffle a few feathers, put this to Svetlana when we all came together for dinner. The two of us silently acknowledged that what had been served up was the food we had left from the previous dinner, only on this occasion the fish was cold, and smelt a little worse, not unlike the bag I was collecting my dirty socks in until a chance came to wash them.

Svetlana, it appeared, was in complete denial. 'Bear, lynx, small red dog, many birds – all live on Olkhon,' she reeled off, like some mantra she had been forced to digest and repeat to tourists.

Perhaps they were simply shy, and particularly wary of tourists brandishing cameras or rifles. Perhaps the wildlife of Buryatia had learnt from the tigers of Primorsky Krai to the east, and in an act of self-preservation gone into permanent hiding. Perhaps they'd all made their way up to Cape Khoboi!

The following day I suggested a hike down to the next village, the home of the Olkhon shaman. I'm sure most of the island's inhabitants were shamans if you wanted them to be… for a reasonable fee. However, it was this particular village, and this particular shaman, that Nikita and his people had chosen for another tour heavily touted by Olga – a visit to the shaman for an 'authentic shamanic experience'. Photos had revealed Western faces, some bewildered, some barely holding back fits of laughter, none able to disguise the farce as they stood in traditional costume, no doubt chanting under the shaman's guidance.

We both agreed we would bypass the tour, but we were still curious to see what it was all about. So we followed the shore of the lake for a couple of kilometres to a village that appeared to have been deserted a long time ago. Dust whipped up by the wind added to the desolate scene. Wooden houses lined the track that ran through the middle, the floor of the theatre was covered in cow shit and the houses hadn't been lived in for a while, it seemed. Up ahead a couple of Buryat men were loading sacks onto a trailer. Maybe they would be able to direct us to the shaman.

THE BURYATS AND TENGERISM

The Buryats are the largest ethnic group in Siberia, and are mainly to be found living in the Republic of Buryatia, the region that runs from the eastern shore of Baikal east and south to Mongolia. They share many traits with their Mongolian cousins, including a nomadic style of living which involves the yurt – a Russian variation on the Mongolian ger. The faith most widely associated with Buryatia is Buddhism, which attracted the attention of Alexander III, who was particularly interested in certain medical practices involving herbs and acupuncture. Such was the tsar's interest he called one of the region's doctors, S. Badmayev, to court. The practices that Badmayev took to St Petersburg amazed the government, and it didn't take long for the humble man from Baikal to achieve celebrity status – opening his own clinic and pharmacy he became rich, and shone a bright light on Buryatia, a region that had largely been regarded as an uncivilised corner of Siberia. He did for Buryatia what Rasputin failed to do for Tobolsk.

With the fall of the Soviet Union, Buddhism underwent something of a renaissance, and now many in Buryatia follow the word of the Buddha. However, in the strange pocket of Siberia that is Olkhon Island, it is shamanism that is the faith of choice, or more accurately, Tengerism. Tengerism means a reverence for the spirits, while shamanism means a reverence towards the shamans. Shamans are not worshipped, but are respected as high priests of Tengerism.

Tengerism believes that the natural world is alive: plants, rocks, animals and water all possess spirits, which need to be protected and respected. Personal responsibility, responsibility for one's own actions, is of utmost importance in Tengerism – a philosophy shared by anarchists. Tengerists believe in a concept called buyan, which is similar to karma. In the West the shaman is generally labelled as a medicine man or witch doctor. However, Siberian beliefs run much deeper than this. There are many kinds of healers, all specialising in their own particular field, for example:

- Otoshi – general practitioners
- Barashi – bone-setters
- Bariyachi – midwives

The shaman is the true master of the spirit world; chosen at birth, an extra spirit – the udha – enters them, and they must gather other spiritual helpers to protect them. The shaman's main role is to maintain balance within a community, which is achieved by conducting blessings, hunting magic and divination. During Communist times, shamans were persecuted, often imprisoned or executed, but nowadays they are free to follow their ancient beliefs once more.

I asked one of the men where I could find the shaman. He looked at me, and slowly shook his head, with an expression that suggested it wasn't the first time the question had been asked.

'He's not here today, or he's never here?'

The man, who had returned to his loading, paused before simply saying, 'No shaman.'

I had been told by Jack Sherementoff, a local guide and hostel owner I'd met whilst procuring the services of Richard Gere in Irkutsk, who apparently led the vanguard for tourism on Olkhon Island, that a visit to the shaman wasn't such a good idea, as the Olkhon shaman was getting fed up with curious tourists and their cameras. As a result of persistent hassling he hadn't been seen for some time. I now concluded that Jack must be right, and that Olga's shaman must only be available for group bookings or special holidays.

We trudged back to Khuzhir, I think somewhat relieved that we hadn't found an ageing Buryat waiting for the phone to ring, dressed up in an elaborate traditional costume.

Irkutsk's Angara Hotel was a relatively deluxe establishment overlooking Kirova Square. All in all it proved that things had progressed for the better since John Foster Fraser's day – who had said in the nineteenth century about Irkutsk: 'There is a small fortune awaiting the man who will build a good hotel.'

He was probably right – the Angara's owner was making a small fortune with the prices the hotel charged. Not a problem for us, of course – we had the van and just used the hotel as a rather luxurious washing facility.

It was early morning as we zigzagged down roads lined with wooden homes, mansions built by exiles and merchants rich on gold. We emerged at the river, and followed it along Gagarina Boulevard, until reaching the landing point, used by cruisers in the summer months. Across the river sat the grand station building, trains vanishing into it, trains emerging somehow different the other side. A few metres back from the landing stage proudly rested a statue of Gagarin, a local hero who had found his way into space before anyone else.

Following Karla Marxa Road north out of the centre, we found two modestly graceful houses. Though not particularly grand in stature, they were nevertheless of some consequence.

The first was the Trubetskoy House, which was closed, and looked like it had been for some time. Two streets away was the house of Prince Volkonsky – grey and white, charmingly simple – home to Irkutsk's cultural heart due to the efforts of Maria Volkonsky, the prince's wife, who came to personify 'romantic sacrifice'. As the wife of a Decembrist, she followed her husband to Siberia to share in his exile after just two years of marriage.

THE DECEMBRIST UPRISING

The Decembrist uprising was an attempt by a group of army officers to take power from the tsar on 14 December 1825. The revolt took place in Senate Square, St Petersburg, which to mark the event was renamed Decembrist Square.

Those responsible for the event and the thinking behind it were young aristocratic soldiers, who had been greatly affected by the war of 1812, and had developed relationships and solidarity with other classes of society. 'Relationships formed at the bivouac and on the battlefield in the sharing of

equal labors and perils,' Sergei Trubetskoy puts it.
These wars opened people's consciousness to what it
meant to be Russian, and after such an opening the
Decembrists were in agreement that serfdom would
have to go, being both immoral and now, after such
an awakening, dangerous.

During the wars the Decembrists had also had an
insight into the politics of other European countries,
and thus were able to see where Russia was lacking.
They returned wanting changes. Pushkin grew up
in this environment; never a Decembrist himself,
he wrote much poetry that celebrated their ideals,
and the female protagonist of *Eugene Onegin*,
Tatyana, is based on the wife of a Decembrist. The
majority of those believing in the Decembrist way
of thinking were fairly apolitical, content simply
to try to incorporate their ideas into day-to-day
life, enhancing the way they lived. However, there
were a relatively small number who were political,
and prepared to use violence. It was this lot who
made a complete cock-up of taking power in 1825.
Rather than making life better in Russia, they were
probably responsible for making it a lot worse, as
now the tsars would see the Decembrists' ideas such
as civil liberty and rule of law as hostile, and so react
against them.

The next day's driving took us through spacious timber
settlements, which came and went like folk tale villages. We
stopped in one village on the lake's east bank at a street

market that was ablaze with colour – silk and other finery from the south, local farm produce and the town's toy maker showing off hand-carved dolls and model fishing boats. The clippety-clop of horse-drawn carts had replaced the hum of engines, leaving a hollow space of sound that was filled by the tones of idle conversation washed around on the breeze. Loaded with provisions we broke away from the wooded protection of the lake's forests and plunged into the vacuum of the steppe – a sparse and dusty wilderness carrying the distant echoes of Genghis Khan and his hordes – and began the long haul to Chita.

We arrived in darkness that same night at a small settlement of *izbas* and yurts, somewhere in the middle of the steppe not far from Ulan-Ude. Badly needing to fill up with water, I approached one of the yurts. The purple mountains in the distance had been shaded by the dark glare of the night. We were greeted with a bowl of soup and a warm yurt, logs roaring in the burner in the centre of the tent. We got the idea that we'd happened across some kind of yurt camp for paying guests, a sort of Travel Yurt stopover, and far too exotic for us to pass up. We'd wanted to stay in a traditional yurt whilst on Olkhon Island but settled for Svetlana's place instead, and now the opportunity had unexpectedly cropped up – we didn't have to be asked twice!

Due to the autumnal season there was nobody else staying at the camp, except for Robert, who occupied the neighbouring yurt. I happened across him whilst stumbling through the dark in search of a loo. He stood no more than a silhouette against the solemn backdrop, arms crossed and apparently naked. I stood still, and a few moments passed before he offered: 'G'day!'

With daylight, the full spectacle of what we'd happened upon was revealed. The yurt camp was positioned by the edge of a pristine and very beautiful lake. It was like a miniature Baikal, the Baikal you'd find on Lilliput.

The next few days we passed by the side of the lake. Jo fell in love with a couple of stray dogs. Chita, a rather misleading name for a dog, was named after the town we were driving towards, but his 'girlfriend' was more consistently named 'Girlfriend'.

The three of them were inseparable for the extent of our stay, and much to the chagrin of our hosts, the dogs enjoyed both the warmth of our yurt and much of the food Jo was unable to eat. The camp was run by five brothers, including Stephan, the man Friday, who more than anybody else seemed to understand the love Jo gave the dogs; he kept the fire burning, stealing into the yurt in the early hours with fresh wood. Due to some confusion in an early 'conversation' we had convinced Stephan that I was in the market for a new Mongolian style 'del' – an ornate and colourful over-garment. To this end, for the length of our stay he was forever confronting me with pieces of paper covered by scribbled designs in the belief that he had a commission in the bag. The huddle of women – wife, sister, sister's daughter, etc – he kept back at his yurt were keen to knock something together. I felt like some princely khan waving away my obedient courtier every time I saw him.

Robert was a sarcastic Australian. He was on a time-out from working in Beijing, was never wrong about anything, and carried a sizeable chip on his shoulder, but I rather liked him. He was blunt and to the point; that is, when it was possible to wade through the depth of his constant sarcasm. He lived in a parallel ironic universe, where it was impossible to function without a negative angle. He seemed to like nobody so I suppose he was in the right place, miles from anywhere in an isolated outreach of Siberia. Robert especially reaped satisfaction from spitting bile at the Chinese. It was never long before he dragged the Chinese kicking and screaming into the conversation in order to give them a good verbal kicking himself. I'm sure if we hadn't been there, he would have had a special place on the end of his boot reserved for the English.

He was from a tough suburb of Melbourne. Lack of funding had brought a 'promising career in academia' to an end and left him drowning in self-pity whilst collecting state benefits. His two children were now living with their mother, 'an anorexic psycho bitch', and her 'conservative asshole English boyfriend' of five years. He apparently had quite happily left Oz and his current girlfriend, with whom he shared a common interest in Bollywood films.

Robert was no different to a hundred and one other disillusioned thirty-somethings you find travelling around the globe, in search of some minute trace of meaning in a life that hasn't quite met the expectations that had been laid down. Throughout your twenties you're bursting in readiness to springboard into a life that meets those dreams at least some of the way, yet the springboard simply doesn't spring. He didn't like us because we were still bursting in readiness, and probably because we'd disturbed his peace.

So Robert was nothing unique; however, he was interesting because Jo took an instant dislike to him, which made the time we spent with him quite amusing. With every moment they were together I could feel the atmosphere closing in – it was only a matter of time before they came to blows. Jo was convinced that the underlying reason for Robert's attitude was simple: 'He obviously hates women.' I thought there was more to it. We had discovered Robert alone in a yurt in an isolated settlement in eastern Siberia, in late autumn, with winter and the prospect of being stranded just around the corner. I thought this a little extreme as reactions go, even for a sensitive soul like Robert, just because he had an issue with women. I think it was secretly love at first sight for Jo.

The three of us took some ponies up into the gentle mountains by the lake; trees covered the slopes like stubble, making narrow pathways. Mongol ponies equal short necks and small steps, dead mouths, and on the whole a strong reluctance to move forward. I imagine that in the right hands they could be the mighty steeds that all Mongols profess; in ours they were closer to donkeys. The hard wooden Kazakh-style saddles added little to the experience. Our guide was a Buryat-speaking local herder called Munkbaatar, and dressed in the traditional del he looked nothing less than the great Mongol horseman. He, like many of his countrymen, had first been put in the saddle at the age of four, and had spent considerably more time there during his life than on his own feet, which his John Wayne gait confirmed. He also had a perfectly formed pair of fangs, which suggested he shouldn't have been out at all during daylight.

Robert, much to our amusement, didn't share our problem of a nag that wouldn't budge – on the contrary, there was simply no stopping it… and no way of steering it. From the moment we set off, Robert could be seen, arms flailing, as his pony zigzagged at speed through trees and shrubs.

We followed the shore of the lake, before stopping at a small hut on the lakeside. Munkbaatar seemed to know the bulging lady who greeted us, as if welcoming us into the Mustang Ranch in Nevada rather than a shabby fisherman's hut. A white fox skin adorned the door we passed through into her hovel. There was a pan full of boiling water on the stove and she was quick to offer us tea, salty and heavy. We all squashed up onto the only bed, beside which was a copy, in Russian, of a Sidney Sheldon story.

'So yous have ridden a lot,' Robert seemed to address the question to the fox skin, 'Ay?'

'No, not for a while, but I suppose it's like riding a bike,' I replied, holding back the giggles.

'Well, it's not really is it, coz you're in control of riding a bike.'

Jo couldn't contain herself, and before long we were both in fits of laughter. Robert looked on stony-faced. Jo's was simply spiteful laughter; however, at that moment I felt a mild degree of pity. How was it possible for someone to find themselves so far removed from their comfort zone? Surely all he could do was laugh at the situation.

We hadn't been there long when a stocky, dark-skinned man pushed the door open and dropped a canvas wrap full of fish onto the floor of the hut. Big smelly fish. Jo nearly retched. The fish were awash with bloody entrails and smelt a long time dead.

The man's cheeks appeared to get redder the longer he remained – he seemed not to like the attention, he was different to the usually brazen Russian male. He looked bizarre in a smart tweed jacket with the sleeves pulled up above his elbows, as if auditioning for a New Romantic comeback band.

Despite her enthusiastic opening, so far the lady had done little other than stare at the three of us, but now the fish had arrived she stretched to the extent of her English. 'One thousand roubles,' she said, pointing to the pile of fish.

Our hosts had lost the attention of Jo, who was staring out of the window, looking out over the shimmering lake. The idea of eating the cooked fish back at the yurt was appealing, but at that moment I couldn't see beyond what lay at our feet. However, Robert, as if sensing the general consensus, spoke up, 'Yee all right eyell av one – yer go on then.'

And within seconds his jacket was off, sleeves were rolled up, and he was mixing up the selection of herbs that had been proffered for marinating. Garlic and more garlic, pretty much. His reason may have been suspect, but in that short time Robert came into his own, and the light which until that moment had failed to shine started to glimmer. Cooking the fish, he seemed almost to be enjoying himself, animated, as if he'd come alive. Somehow, during that moment, maybe he'd realised life was all right, and however bad it looks there is always something there to warrant your participation.

The fish tasted delicious, although Jo will never know quite how delicious!

CHAPTER TWELVE
CHITA

All roads came to a halt at Chita, a town basking in the steppe some thousand or so kilometres east of Irkutsk, according to our map. The main artery east came to an abrupt end whilst a few smaller veins trickled on a little further before fizzling out, and that was it for all roads until Blagoveshchensk, a town perched on the Chinese border, where lines of varying thickness re-emerged. This left thousands of kilometres apparently impassable. Fortunately our map was wrong, but we did have the small problem of several hundred kilometres of wasteland to get across.

As Chita was a major railway junction – gateway to the Chinese Eastern Railway – and a key stop on the Trans-Siberian, we thought that the rail office would be the place to glean the best information. When we tracked it down we were told to come back the day after tomorrow, as there was a public holiday in progress. However, we were kindly given directions to a hotel in town which we might want to use as it was, we were enthusiastically told, run by an

Englishman. Intrigued as to what or whom had brought a countryman to this particular part of Siberia we went in search of man and hotel.

The Panama City Motel was in a suburb north of the centre, part of a block decorated with washing hanging from balconies. We felt particularly conspicuous as we counted off the numbers marked on each door, until we came to the number written on the directions we'd been given. We were quietly excited about meeting someone from Britain – we were a long way from home, and it had been a while. It always takes some effort to get on with your countrymen back home, but for some strange reason, travel several thousand miles away from Britain and you're guaranteed to get on like a house on fire. Like the Chinese we come together like magnets when abroad, usually to complain about the natives.

Unfortunately, it was not to be. When we arrived at the hotel, the patron, who looked more Mongolian than English, told us he was from Madrid. The brief conversation went a bit like this:

Jo – So what brings you out here?

Pat – I, I, I, I no ondastand... slowly *spasibah*.

Jo – Why do you live here in Siberia, Russia?

Pat – Yes, yes I from Madrid.

Jo – So you're not English?

Pat – Yes, yes I know... you eat?

Jo – Yeah, go on then, I could eat a horse, so to speak, I'm a vegetarian. VEG-ET-AR-IAN!

Our host watched with interest as we battled with some noodle soup through a thick fog of flies; with his pot belly bursting through his sweat-stained shirt, he began to muse in a sort of Russlish, completely incomprehensible. Jo simply ignored him as she continued to flick flies from her spoon, whilst I offered the occasional tortured smile, all the encouragement he needed.

It wasn't long before we'd been joined by his entire family. He carried on talking while his wife and two daughters stared at us. We eventually edged our way out of the hotel, bidding hearty farewells, swearing to avoid the English for the rest of the trip at all costs. Somewhere along the line, some wires had been crossed.

Jo bought some creamy cakes that looked delicious from a kiosk, to go with a plastic cup of coffee. Outside, the sun having fallen, the purple evening gave in to cold dark night, as we waited impatiently for Monday morning to arrive. Jo, deciding she had been deceived by the appearance of her cake after a mouthful, concluded 'This is inedible', and passed it on to a young child playing near to the bench on which we sat. She smiled broadly and managed to disguise it as a present. The kid also smiled broadly, overjoyed, as his mother looked on unmoved.

Whilst watching the kid feasting on Jo's cast-off, I became aware of a heavily built lady repeatedly walking past our bench. Each time she passed, she had a good old stare, making no attempt to conceal her curiosity. After passing by enough times to have worn through the soles of her leather boots, she timidly approached. Tiptoeing the few feet to the bench, her foundation-splattered face soon came to rest inches from Jo's.

'Heeeellow,' glided from her mouth.

Jo acknowledged her greeting with a look that said: 'Here we go, another Mickey Mouse conversation!'

'I am Mona,' she whispered. Jo looked at her, pretty sure she was dealing with a nutter, but still the tiniest room for doubt forced her to be civil.

'I'm Jo,' she said and offered a hand. We were tired, and granted, everything seemed to be happening in slow motion, but the ensuing shaking of hands felt like it went on for light years.

'And this is Thom,' Jo nodded towards me, still shaking, trying to share some of the attention that so far had been only on her. However, I got not so much as a glance.

Mona only had eyes for Jo. I was intrigued; this was going to be one of those baffling interactions with a local, but one I would be able to sit back and enjoy.

'You are veery beaytiful.' The shake had finished, but Jo's hand was now being stroked. Jo reached for her cup of now cold coffee.

'You have beaytiful skeeen.' Judging by the quantity of foundation covering Mona's skin this was not something they had in common.

'Your heer is sow smoooth.' Mona reached out and Jo pulled her head back instinctively, and then allowed her to touch it. At this point Jo announced that she needed to powder her nose. Don't be long, I heard myself mutter. A silent stand-off followed over the bench, Mona sneaking the occasional look at me. I couldn't find anything to say to her. After several very long minutes Jo returned and, obviously having given the matter some thought whilst away, was quick to ask Mona: 'So what brings you here?'

'I live jost theeah.' Mona pointed in the direction of a ramshackle block. 'I just return from my class in Ulan-Ude,' Mona replied to Jo's enquiry, and quickly continued with the following offer: 'You come to my home to eat?'

We weren't exactly busy, so it was an offer we couldn't really refuse.

Standing forlornly outside the solid steel front door of Mona's block was a young boy.

'He has Russian lesson,' Mona barked, scowling down at him whilst rummaging through her bag for keys.

Mona was a language teacher. She had been away for some days, and reddened eyes suggested a lack of sleep. In fact, the uneven application of foundation suggested she might have slept in a coffin.

'I am very tired,' she confirmed. 'My flat very dirty – I must clean.' Without wasting a minute on entering her flat, she had filled up a bowl with water, and cloth in hand was down on her knees scrubbing the floor.

Perhaps her young student would have to wait a little longer for his lesson. I retreated out onto her cramped balcony, an upturned sofa taking up most of the space, overlooking the town. When I returned minutes later, Mona was still on all fours mopping the floor furiously, whilst at the same time bellowing instructions at her student, who sat in a state of bewilderment with his text book open.

'This is a bad student, I make him better,' she reassured Jo, who had found somewhere to sit in amongst the chaos.

The timid ten-year-old's confusion was compounded by the conversation Mona proceeded to have with Jo in English, whilst teaching him Russian.

'My emotions were high ten years ago, but now they are low,' she panted.

'I live here alone, with me there is no family now.' Her flat was two rooms, a bed and some indiscriminate broken furniture in one, cockroaches and rusty kitchen stuff in the other. In between bouts of frenzied cleaning she found a reflective surface – a dusty window – and rubbed cream onto her cheeks.

Mona had worked as a translator buying cars for people in Hong Kong, and she had spent some time in China. She didn't, unsurprisingly, like the Chinese.

'Seventy per cent don't like you unless they can get something from you.' I was interested to know how she could be so specific.

She was a trained graphic designer, but now taught English and Russian and studied part-time for a teaching qualification. Once the cleaning was complete, the lesson too came to an end, and the young boy was up and out the door before you could say *'Spasiba!'* (Thank you!).

She spoke openly to us – as if we were kindred spirits, unlike anybody else she had ever met. Now she had a chance to lift the repression, by talking to strangers who somehow seemed to understand. Mona was a romantic. However, I think her main repression was poverty, as the subject of us finding her an English gentleman to marry came up again and again. The food we ate was simple; we made light work of fried potatoes and rice, sharing Mona's one fork between the three of us. The arrival of another student seemed an appropriate juncture to take our leave from Mona. The student was a middle-aged man in uniform; his formal attire gave the impression that he would expect his teacher's full attention, so when Jo managed to pull herself away from a back-breaking hug, we skipped down the stairwell and out onto the street.

Back in the town square, it wasn't long before we were approached by two men, who looked like they were sleeping rough and on the beg, but on seeing our chessboard one of the men stopped rattling his tin cup about and challenged Jo to a game.

Jo was keen to take him up on the offer. Having never played before leaving England, she was now beating me every time, approaching each game with the focus of an athlete about to compete in a sprint.

Edvard and Sasha had been in the Soviet Army, of which there was a substantial base in Chita. Both men had done most of their service to the south in Afghanistan, we were able to deduce from Sasha, who repeatedly pointed to his stump – once a leg – mournfully muttering, 'Afghani. Afghani.'

In a conflict often referred to as Russia's Vietnam, the Soviets invaded Afghanistan in 1979 by way of support for the existing government, run by the Marxist People's Democratic Party of Afghanistan, against the Islamic fundamentalist Mujahadeen, insurgents fighting to overthrow the government. The rebels got their support from the likes of Pakistan and other Muslim countries, and ironically the United States. The Soviet troops were out of their depth fighting a guerrilla war in such mountainous terrain – a familiar story. After ten years of heavy casualties, massive economic costs and decreasing support from home, they were forced to withdraw. Total losses amounted to 14,453 soldiers. Edvard and Sasha had been the lucky ones, although you wouldn't think so looking at them.

Afghanistan had figured in Russian foreign policy since way back. The country was the focus of the Great Game of the nineteenth and early twentieth centuries, which is usually taken to refer to British and Russian interests in Afghanistan, but was actually played out over the passes and valleys all over Central Asia. I love the idea of the two biggest empires of the time employing trickery and subterfuge in order to secure the upper hand in the region, and managing not to actually go to war over it. I doubt events were as simple as British diplomats posing in kaftans and burkhas in order to gain strategic secrets, but the images of a *Carry On* film do make it all seem quite playful.

Edvard and Sasha were beating Jo on the chessboard – best of five – a great game nonetheless! Despite having to beg to stay alive, they seemed to accept their lot with some dignity. Sasha viewed the constant reminder that he was missing a leg more as a necessity of his job than with any deep-rooted self-pity. When we left them, Jo slipped some roubles into Sasha's cup, more for being a worthy opponent than for being at the butt end of an egotistical foreign policy.

We arrived at the rail office at eight o'clock sharp on the morning after the holiday. It was a hive of activity but we were quick to get the attention of a middle-aged lady doing a very good impression of a pantomime dame in caked-on make-up. We quickly gathered that there was going to be no recommended driving option, so went down the route of getting Max onto a train. We'd seen Japanese cars flooding into the region en masse, and assumed they weren't being airdropped in. The dame made call after call, accompanied by much rolling of eyes in exasperation. This filled us with some hope, whilst we were given coffee and a table in a quiet corner of the office from which to nervously watch her progress. Eventually, she glided over with a piece of paper, which she placed theatrically down on the table. On the paper was written a solitary figure:

$50,000

It was hard to contain a gasp. My immediate thought was 'sod it, we'll drive'. The Russians being reluctant to travel a few miles down the road to the next village, it was probably even possible to drive, just that nobody did. Our mentor, gauging our feelings, was quick to return to her phone. A while later she returned with a new figure of:

$25,000

At that point I thought I would save everybody some time, and taking the paper wrote our final and only offer:

$100

It was met with a resigned shrug of the shoulders. She didn't even look surprised and scuttled back to her phone – returning moments later with the news in her best English:

'The English specialist – he comes.'

She smiled, shaking her head furiously, whilst the rest of her body wobbled like a jelly. It looked like we might have a bargain.

After plenty more coffee, Dima arrived, a man with sloping shoulders and a floppy fringe that covered one eye, which he periodically swept aside with a single finger. His eyes had a look of wistful resignation permeated by the occasional glint of latent animation. On meeting us Dima shyly produced a large tape recorder and played us a recording of an American evangelist. Baffled for a few moments, we then realised that the tape was Dima's credentials as an English specialist. Rather than just flash his card, he went one step further and played his tape. He smiled inanely; Jo didn't. He smiled at me as if to suggest that I must convince Jo that he was the real deal.

It became apparent before long that Dima spoke no English at all, despite having the status of English specialist status amongst his colleagues. I couldn't help thinking that we would manage much better without him – we'd been all right this far – but we didn't want to get him into any trouble, so we put up with him. The panic on his face as he struggled with every word, which finally came out in Russian, was comic compensation for his jittery incompetence.

'*Tak Tak*', which roughly translates as 'now then', prefixed everything he did or didn't say – we were probably the first speakers of his chosen specialism he had ever met. Despite our blank faces he appeared to think that things were going fairly well. His buoyant attitude at least gave us some hope.

That hope was confirmed when I was asked to manoeuvre Max into a container which stood at the ready on the track. On completion of this task Dima was positively ecstatic, 'tak-taking' all the way back to the office to do the paperwork. Form after form had to be filled out, which Dima diligently guided me through, whilst Jo checked out Max's temporary new home, a 15 foot by 5 foot timber container, some 7 foot high, with a sliding door fastened on the outside by a padlock.

On completion of the paperwork, Dima repeatedly indicated his watch and the passing of time, whilst spluttering 'eight' in Russian. I guessed this was the departure time.

Everything concluded, and with a few hours spare, Dima took us back to his flat, stopping on the way to buy some vegetables from a market as well as some supplies for our journey. He cooked spaghetti and tomatoes in his tiny seventh-floor flat, and we ate, Dima constantly looking at his watch. It was the first time for several weeks that we had had to make a deadline – and we soon realised that we'd been completely thrown by all the time zones that we'd passed through. Our confusion wasn't helped by clocks showing Moscow time everywhere. I loved it – we were existing in a world of severe dyslexia and disorientation. For the benefit of the tape we were now seven hours in front of Moscow, some ten hours in front of the UK and some five hours behind Sydney, Australia.

When we returned to the track, Max's container had been linked up to many others, which ran as far as the eye could see along the track. There was some urgency now so we were helped up into the container by Dima and a signalman.

Moments after, a series of shunts happened, and then we began crawling along the track. Dima waved uncontrollably from the side, until we were out of sight. Meanwhile we were left to ponder our new surroundings, which were now dark and very cold.

The first few hours we spent listening to the creaks and groans of the track, occasional voices, the clunking beat of trains passing on other lines. This was broken up by a guard leading us up into his control tower for some hot fruity tea. It was cold in the container and this was just what we'd needed, so we stayed with the guard watching the trains coming and going, until it was time for him to clock off, when we returned to the container to try to sleep. A restless night followed. Much shunting made it impossible to sleep for very long, but all the movement did give us the impression that we were in fact going somewhere. It was quite a surprise waking up the next day all bleary-eyed and disorientated to find that we had travelled no more than a few metres further down the track. Despite twelve hours in the container we hadn't left Chita yet.

Opening the door to get the heat from the morning sun, it wasn't long before we were surrounded by curious brake men. We spent all day until evening with Dmitry, who seemed to be in charge, and his colourful crew. The time was spent deliberating long and hard over moves on the chessboard, and exchanging information. Occasionally a couple of the group would cross some track to release barriers or to shift a brake into place, but for most of the day we sat in Chita, and they used us as an excuse to avoid very much work and to sip from a bottle of vodka they stashed in the corner of our container. Dmitry strode about in a mid-length sheepskin coat, unbuttoned to reveal a thick leather holster, which harboured a pistol of some kind. On first meeting him, he had looked every bit the wild Siberian railroader, oozing frontier adventure; however, as the day progressed and he got more and more drunk, Dmitry and his pistol made us more and more anxious.

When the sun eventually gave way to a faint distant moon, we said our goodbyes once again and this time the train pulled away, leaving Chita and its brake men behind. That is, except for Dmitry, who came with us, hanging from the rail on the back of a carriage, in his drunkenness quite sinister, not unlike the character from the closing scene of *Live and Let Die*. We were both relieved when he stumbled away into the half-light at the first small settlement we came to.

For the next five days the train stammered along the route of the Trans-Siberian, stopping intermittently at settlements reached only by the railway, our home for that time the container. During daylight we opened the sliding door to be hypnotised by the panoramic view of thick taiga broken up by steppe passing slowly by, like a film reel. Often the thick tangled silver birches were close enough to touch. By night we did our best to keep the door shut and the freezing Siberian air at bay, and what sleep we did manage to get in the back of the van was disturbed by alien sounds and voices. Each morning, with much relief, we slid open the door to soak in the heat from the waking sun.

The Trans-Siberian is the name given to the three routes that run across Siberia. As well as the original, running to the port of Vladivostok in the Far East, there is the Trans-Mongolian and the Trans-Manchurian, both travelling to Beijing, but as the name suggests the Trans-Mongolian goes across Mongolia via Ulan Bator. It is the world's longest single service railway. It took twenty-six years to complete, built by exiles and convicts using only hand tools, amidst cholera, plague, bandits and tigers. Floods often swept away bridges and permafrost did its best to sabotage progress. Chugging slowly along only a fraction of it as we did, the scale of the achievement was certainly driven home – although I doubt many of those responsible would have been given the opportunity to sit back and appreciate their work.

The more time we spent in the container the more disorientated we became. We knew that we had roughly 500 kilometres to cover on the train, and that we would be leaving the container at a town called Skovorodino; however, how long this would take we had no idea, nor how we would know when we arrived at our destination, tucked up and out of sight in the container – when we had left Chita we were one in a chain of containers a mile in length. It didn't help that the guards insisted on the sliding door of the container being fastened from the outside whilst the train was moving, which left us completely at their mercy to open it. The first twenty-four hours this just didn't happen, so eventually we called upon much force to prise it open ourselves. Thus as time passed, and hours turned into days, the situation was completely out of our hands.

We had come to a noisy and shuddering halt many times over the five days, for perhaps several minutes or several hours at a time. During one such stop, after the third hour of no forward movement other than the odd shunt we were both fairly sure we had reached Skovorodino, just north of the northernmost part of China.

Greeted by an overcast morning, we were positioned bang in the middle of ten tracks, a fair distance from any visible sidings. Max would be going nowhere fast. This gave us plenty of time to join Abdul and Simma for breakfast in their wagon, located a short way down the track. Abdul had whistled my attention through the small gap in his container door whilst I had been searching for confirmation of our location.

They had been with us all the way from Chita, we just hadn't known it. They were originally from Azerbaijan – dark friendly faces with deep searching eyes – their wagon full to the ceiling with sacks of potatoes ready to sell at market. In the middle of all the spuds was a makeshift table and a mouth-watering spread of foods sat ready to be devoured. I couldn't help thinking how much more comfortable our few days would have been if we'd known about them earlier. However, we made up for it by spending a very hearty time with them until our container arrived alongside the platform. Planks of wood in place, Max's vacation was over.

It would be the last time that I doubted in any way the organisation or reliability of the Russian railways.

After a couple of hours' drive east from Skovorodino, we passed through the ominously named village of Never, a gathering of wooden *izbas* protected from the sky by towering evergreens. The most attractive road out of Never lead north to Tynda, which was a major stop on the Trans-Siberian's poor relative, the BAM railway, which passed through Siberia north of Lake Baikal. However, we were stuck travelling east on a heavily potholed gravel track, the taiga getting thicker with every kilometre. The densely tangled forest was mesmerising – for some, too much so, as the so-called taiga sickness has been known to mesmerise people into a state of madness. The solitude was intimidating yet it was impossible not to be captivated and to buzz off the latent energy that surrounded us. We were convinced the spirits that lurked within the taiga were benevolent.

CHAPTER THIRTEEN
THE FAR EAST

The third day out from Skovorodino we had not passed any indicators that we were still on a planet inhabited by other mammals. We were making heavy weather of the gravel road and not progressing particularly fast. Nights were now cold and even the sunlight we craved to warm us during the days seemed to have lost its heat. When the generator light on the dashboard began to glare bright red my first instinct was just to ignore it. I even put a cassette in front of it to mask the intrusion. However, the red light got inside my head – brighter and brighter, soon flashing like a beacon until I actually began to feel quite nauseous. Eventually, it was too much. I stopped the engine and searched through the manual for some clue as to what the ominous red light could mean. Jo was calm and started rooting clumsily around the engine. We both knew we would achieve nothing – it was a gesture of ability, a placebo, as if somehow over the past few months perhaps one of us had in fact acquired some mechanical knowledge to get us out of the pickle we would be in should the engine cease to function. Our investigation turned up nothing – other than discovering that the generator was pretty much the main physiognomy of the engine. Once we had concluded that there was nothing we would be able to do, we tried to cast the problem from our minds, and continued.

We got as far as a town called Svobodny (which translates as freedom) when at last our worst nightmare was realised. Max came wheezing and groaning to a standstill and as he did, so did our freedom. We were within sight of the gateway to an army barracks. After numerous doomed attempts to re-ignite any hope of getting beyond Svobodny, we began eyeing up the young soldier on guard duty outside his sentry box, who as yet hadn't so much as batted an eyelid at the arrival of an alien vehicle carrying two equally alien passengers. With a camp full of soldiers to hand, perhaps our luck was in. We both approached him with our most helpless expressions. However, despite our best attempts at explaining the predicament with flailing arms and grunts, the best response he could muster was *'nyet'* followed by *'nyet'* and a look that suggested he would appreciate it very much if we would kindly just go away.

So we did, but only as far as our dejected-looking campervan, where a cup of coffee was brewed and Plan B devised.

Sitting in a vehicle that has broken down in eastern Siberia, many, many miles from home with night drawing in, Plan B takes little if any thinking about and involves simply stopping anyone you might see for help – anyone not wearing a uniform, that is. It was a couple of hours before the first vehicle to come along dazzled me in Max's wing mirror. With the sight of headlights we both flung ourselves into the middle of the road, giving the driver of the Soviet-built UAZ jeep no option but to slow down to a halt.

Far from being at all put out, the large smartly dressed Siberian man who climbed from the vehicle didn't even wait long enough to witness Jo's frantic explanatory performance through to the end. He had the van hitched up to the back of his own solid rough terrain vehicle and before we could say 'Vladivostok here we come' we were gliding along behind the jeep, gushing buckets of silent relief. The sky was soon peppered with stars and a near full moon lit up an unpopulated landscape.

After several hours the jeep pulled in to a roadside service area with petrol pumps and a small cafe selling tea and sausages. Our benefactor gathered his rope, shook us both warmly by the hands and then drove off into the darkness. People were milling about, and they and the unfamiliar sounds were comforting – and it was as good a place as any to spend what was left of the night. The kindness already shown to us had the effect of making us feel safe. However, it wasn't to be long before the second instalment of Siberian benevolence pulled off the road.

Sometime after we'd locked Max up and settled in for the night a bright red Hiach family estate, or 'space wagon' as we were still calling them, parked up in front of us.

The driver, a stocky man with a weather-beaten face, jumped out from behind the wheel and immediately began investigating Max. The rest of his family – a wife and a herd of young children – seemed to be bouncing around in the back of his wagon, faces pressed against the windows. Such was his interest, and the apparent interest of the rest of his tribe, I wound the window down and uttered a somewhat weary salutation. Over a lukewarm cup of Nescafé, I explained in a much less emphatic manner than I'd previously been able to muster, that the subject of his interest was in fact 'not working', and that we were trying to get to Vladivostok. Ironically, now we were broken down and seemingly unable to complete our journey, I had developed a total belief that we would complete it. I could almost smell the fresh wood shavings that I planned to dive into on arriving at Nikolai's timber yard.

The man appeared to understand or at least get the gist of my ramblings and looked on without a hint of cynicism. Coffee break over, as with our previous guardian angel, we were hitched up to the back of the 'space wagon', and before we knew it were hurtling along pitch black roads, both myself and Jo praying that we weren't in fact fast asleep and sharing a particularly hopeful dream. We had been towed some 290 kilometres by the time we reached Blagoveshchensk.

Once we had arrived at our destination, the man introduced himself as Kostos, and then introduced his beautiful wife and their six children. He explained that they were all tired and needed to sleep, with an expression not unlike guilt, as if he hadn't done enough for us. So having said good night to the rest of his family, Kostos drove us a short distance to what appeared to be a hotel. He led us into the reception, where he left us in the hands of a babushka, who in turn led us to an empty dormitory. Ten beds took up most of the space with a samovar at one end. We washed with hot water, before having a very good night's sleep.

It was a migrant workers' hotel. For some reason there were no workers at that time, but usually the place would have been full of Chinese, who crossed the nearby border to fill the void of Russian workers in the region, or else traders travelling from China with their wares for sale – cheaply made shoes and other leather products. This was something that was greatly encouraged and helped by the declaration of a free trade zone between Blagoveshchensk and the Chinese town Heihe, no more than a kilometre across the Amur River. So close are the two towns that during the cultural revolution the Chinese blasted out twenty-four-hour propaganda from loudspeakers across the Amur.

The following morning we made our way down to the spot we'd left Max. Daylight revealed that we had left him outside the high galvanised gates of a yard, where he had been surrounded by a group of inquisitive men, all apparently waiting to start their day's work in the yard beyond the gates. After a few moments of inspection from the assembled group, Kostos appeared, his attire spotless in stark contrast to that of the other men, who, seeing him, fell silent. A few of the men stepped forward to shake his hand. Kostos was clearly the boss, and after handing out some instructions he unlocked the heavy padlock that secured the gates. The family man from the night before had become a very alert-looking businessman whose hands we were glad to be in.

Max was hooked up to a Soviet jeep and towed halfway across town to a workshop, located in the heart of a rundown housing estate. Sebastion had averred back in St Petersburg that the Russians can and will repair anything, and we had been witness to the truth of these words on numerous occasions across the country. However, now in a small workshop hidden away in the depths of Blagoveshchensk, the true spirit of the Russian 'never say die' character was to be seen.

The projects being worked on were moved out of the way, making room for Max to be heaved into position above the pit. Three serious-looking mechanics set to work. We hadn't even been asked what was wrong – either it didn't matter or they had quickly divined, we didn't know. Not for the first time, all we could do was look on with feelings of relief and respect. Kostos then took us back to his office in order to introduce us to Valya, his English-speaking assistant, and to share a hearty breakfast with us.

His assistant spoke shyly, calling upon a framed map of the world on the wall as a prop. With her help we were able to talk Kostos through our journey to date, and our (fingers crossed) intentions. Occasionally, he gently shook his head in respectful disbelief.

'Kostos thought you were Dutch,' Valya reported, her somewhat austere front dissolved by her softly spoken English. He had obviously understood very little of my explanation the previous night.

'He thinks your journey is... what you say... fantastic, and is surprised that you come so far.' She paused self-consciously. 'Russia is a dangerous country at this time.'

The dangers of Russia were still largely unknown to us; had we actually believed this we would probably never have left St Petersburg. Perhaps it was just our naivety, but on the whole we had felt ourselves to be in no danger for the majority of the trip. I had actually convinced myself that it was how Russians liked their country to be perceived, a country that presented a challenge only Russians themselves were capable of meeting. The only things that worried me about Russia were the militia, the hospitals and the women behind thick glass selling train tickets.

Kostos was also a New Russian, embracing the free market and all that entailed, and like Peter the Great before him he believed there was something to be learnt from the West. Not that he thought he could learn anything from Jo or me, but we were products of that democratic world he aspired to so much. What we were doing in our van was a by-product of the freedom of mind that went with his notions of democracy and the future that he wanted for his family. Cars were his thing – he had started off importing car batteries from the States, and in a short time he was importing anything and everything to do with cars. He now imported cars from Japan.

'He likes your antique, but wonders why you have this for your journey.'

Neither of us replied immediately, so Valya smiled. We thought Max looked cool – Max somehow suited our frame of mind – but there was no way we were going to offer Kostos such a weak response.

'Vans like this are very popular in England, there are a lot of them,' I said unconvincingly.

Kostos breathed through his nose with a chuckle. *'Angliski!'*

When the breakfast and talking was done, cool or not, we were reunited with a roaring Max. I didn't remember the engine running so well since leaving Ufa. Kostos' generosity was not over yet. He led us around to his car care centre, which appeared to sell anything from industrial-sized puncture repair kits to furry dice. We were loaded up with all sorts of useful bits and bobs, including a spare battery and a selection of Allen keys. Not content that there was very little room left in the van for anything more, his final offering was a selection of what proved to be inedible Chinese cakes. He then led us to the outskirts of the city, and pointed us in the right direction, before he careered back into town. Kostos, like other guardian angels in Russia, had no time for sentiment, but his kindness and the empty road ahead left us emotional.

Wide gravel tracks lined with mixed coniferous/deciduous forests accompanied us for the next couple of days as we travelled parallel to the border with China. The tracks were straight and undulating, the uneven gravel hard going. Settlements were few and far between.

VAGUELY INTERESTING IMMIGRATION FACTS

In an article written in 2003 by Vladimir Radyuhin, he comments on the growing Chinese population in Russian territory. Chinese is now the fourth largest ethnic group:

- Russians – 104.1 million
- Tartars – 7.2 million

- Ukrainians – 5.1 million
- Chinese – 3.26 million

These figures, he says, 'lend chilling reality to Russia's age old nightmare of a Chinese take over of the Asian part of Russia'. These words show a not unexpected note of Russia's longstanding xenophobia, but whatever way you look at it, the Chinese population in Siberia is on the up and will continue to grow. As eighteen million Russians stretch out into the open space of Siberia every day, they are faced by 250 million very cramped Chinese in China's northern provinces. When the Soviet Union collapsed, the 4,300 kilometres of border that we now followed was opened for bilateral trade. Chinese traders flooded into Russia to sell clothes, shoes and inedible cakes to the Russians, who were at this point deep in economic crisis. The Chinese returned across the border with timber, scrap metal, ginseng roots, frogs and jellyfish.

Some 70 per cent of the region's timber trade heads to China, where demand is high and the Chinese don't ask any sensitive environmental questions, just like the Japanese and Korean companies trading in the Far East. Many of the world's inexpensive wood products are manufactured close by in China from timber produced in the forests of the Amur-Heilong basin, which in turn provides an increasingly fragile home to the endangered Siberian tiger and Amur leopard. The American company Walmart buys some

84 per cent of its wood products from China – toilet seats, pictures frames, cots and candle holders. China is also IKEA's biggest supplier of solid wood furniture. Thanks to all this trade, glistening new towns have sprung up on the Chinese side of the border, whilst much of the Russian region remains stagnant. Russia needs the migrant workforce to keep the economy turning over.

Russians are generally concerned about anybody entering their country, but in the case of Chinese migration there may be cause for some actual concern. Various Chinese leaders have been noted for believing that certain Russian territory did indeed, by rights, belong to China. Mao Zedong once said he thought both Vladivostok and Khabarovsk should belong to China. In 1997, Russia and China signed a border demarcation accord, which settled all disputes that had occurred involving rivers and 'islands' in the rivers, except for three islands. In the meantime Chinese have been spotted trying to link these islands with their own territory by dropping rocks and sand into the water.

When we came to the next settlement, having parked up alongside a protective hedgerow in view of an orthodox church, I went to find some bread and chocolate. These had become our staple pretty much, along with cheese. Bread and cheese fried on the stove... delicious, followed by a couple of bars of chocolate, and washed down with some phony Fanta. This wasn't ever going to be a good long-term plan for our teeth, but then this wasn't going to be a long-term diet. These were not only the most readily available sources of sustenance, but pretty much all vegetarian Jo could eat, such was the prevalence of meat-based produce.

As I meandered down the main street of Arhara – the village's name, according to the map, which we knew meant we could have been anywhere within a 1,000-kilometre radius of Arhara – my attention was caught by a sign above a doorway:

PECTOPAH

The word glaring back at me was another of those Russian words made up of Cyrillic symbols that was easily translated, and one along with others such as bread, toilet, shop, police, petrol and milk that I had been quick to learn out of necessity. 'Restaurant' in provincial Russia could mean a hundred and one things, including:

- Food

- Food is available

- Food is available to purchase

- Food is visibly being eaten by other people

- Food is visibly being eaten by other people, how you too can eat it is anyone's guess

- Food can be eaten by you too, it just might take a little time

Not only was I standing in front of a restaurant; closer inspection revealed lights to be on and, having nudged the door open, I needed no more proof. It was open. For now the bread and chocolate would have to wait, for we would be feasting on finer foods. Well, I would be anyway! I swiftly returned to the van with the news.

The sheer frustration of not being understood must not be underestimated. I'm not talking about amusing little language faux pas whilst entertaining the waiter with your clumsy lingo. I'm talking not having the slightest clue what's going on. We were alone in the restaurant, with a sullen teenage waitress, smartly dressed in her black and whites. I didn't want or expect any special treatment – but just some acknowledgement that she didn't get tourists from England in her restaurant every day would have been nice. Maybe she got a steady stream, and maybe there was some point in her being so well presented in a small backwater in the middle of Siberia as to make us feel under dressed. But I doubt both the above.

After we'd had a cursory glance across the menu, the waitress arrived by the side of our table, pad and pen at the ready. The menu was comprehensive, running to several pages of mouth-watering delicacies. Or perhaps not, as we didn't have a clue what it was offering. Jo's face sunk with a look that said: 'This is why we never go out to restaurants!'

The waitress was getting impatient.

Another life-saving word I'd learnt was '*kartoshka*', a lovely-sounding Russian word meaning potato. Under closer scrutiny, *kartoshka* made several appearances on the menu – as you'd expect – probably available in many different tasty guises, which we'd never know, but seeing the word I was able to play my trump card. '*Kartoshka, kartoshka,*' I bellowed at the waitress, who simply looked at me vacantly. I'd learnt that the best way to deal with bolshy Russians working in the service sector was to shout at them. Jo looked relieved to have salvaged something from the unhealthy amounts of hope we'd managed to build up in such a short space of time. The waitress had reluctantly written something on her pad. Just as I was about to discard the menu and force a look of satisfaction onto my face, another word caught my attention. Once I'd seen it, I saw that it popped up all over the menu: '*myasso*'. Now what did that mean? I couldn't be sure, but I was convinced it was the word for meat, and it certainly made sense that it was. Sod it, even if it wasn't meat it had to be edible – didn't it? I pointed furiously, making sure that the waitress included the word on her pad. Twice. And off she went to get our Meat and Potatoes.

Now I was bursting over with anticipation, that is, until Jo asked, 'What is it?'

'What's what?'

'What else did you ask for?'

'Meat... I think. I think I asked for meat.'

'Oh, great.' Oh no, I had forgotten. When you're hungry, tired, in need of a good shower and hopeful, the smallest things escalate. Jo sat scowling at me, pissed off, I think more because there was a good chance I was going to get a decent meal, than because she had become a vegetarian before going to possibly the most carnivorous country in the world.

'Look,' I tried to appease her, 'it'll probably be inedible dog or cat or something, but you can't blame me for trying.'

'Well, it's not very sensitive is it?'

'You'll probably get a big portion of potatoes, they'll be really tasty, and you can have mine as well.'

'Yeah, all right, I will.' We sat in silent anticipation.

It wasn't long before nasty Nastia reappeared bearing a large tray. Two sizeable bowls of steaming, meaty stew – which in outer appearance at least had probably appeared in one of my food fantasies – were launched onto the table. Feeling slightly uncomfortable under the spotlight of Jo's glare, I tucked in. I didn't care whether it was a street dog or the family's aging cat that bubbled in front of me – it was delicious. Moments later the waitress, muttering something incomprehensible, landed two much smaller bowls onto the table. Closer inspection revealed two boiled potatoes in each bowl, roughly the size of genetically modified cherry tomatoes.

Jo's face turned red as a tomato as she rose to her feet.

'You can stick your goulash up your arse!' she shrieked, before storming out.

I felt terrible for a couple of seconds, before enjoying every mouthful of the stew, which was wonderfully complimented by the side order of boiled spuds. Siberia is no place to be caring about the inhumane treatment of our fellow mammals.

Some 200 kilometres west of Birobidzhan, going totally against type, we picked up a hitcher. Whether this was a subconscious reaction to the kindness shown us back in

Blagoveshchensk, I'm not sure. I think it was more a case that the recipient of our good deed was in fact standing bang in the middle of the road holding a shotgun to his chest. Maybe the army fatigues he wore and the fact that he looked like a cross between Fidel Castro and Rasputin came into the decision-making process, however fleetingly. Having said that, sharing a ride with Castro would probably be an experience worth having – Rasputin, maybe not.

Perhaps because of the distances involved in Siberia, and the low volume of traffic passing through, all niceties of hitching a ride are put to one side. We didn't have time to think this one through, because as soon as Max had come to a halt, the man with the gun was ensconced in the back. He didn't look very friendly, and after mumbling a few incomprehensible words, one of which I just made out to be 'Birobidzhan', spent the next few hours breathing vodka breath down my neck. It hadn't been easy keeping the van particularly clean, but there was an unspoken rule that the area south of the 'cockpit' was the sanitised zone, shoes off if possible and that sort of thing, so our guest covering our Millets four season sleeping bags, amongst other things, with mud from his soiled sized twelve para boots was a bad start. A closer look gave away that he was indeed half cut. He came to rest well within my personal space, which left me uncomfortable, the barrel of the gun pointing at Jo, which left her uncomfortable. How far to Birobidzhan?

Too far!

The next few kilometres our new guest swung in and out of consciousness. For anyone observing it would have looked like he was munching on my neck, as Jo nervously dodged the line of fire. About an hour in, with a van-shaking jerk, he sprung to alertness, and after soaking up his surroundings, began muttering in Russian. Intermittently, he paused as if waiting for a reply. We both just smiled like a couple of idiots, and unperturbed he carried on talking. Whatever he was saying, he found it quite funny. This one-sided banter continued for the next two hours.

He left us outside the post office in the centre of Birobidzhan, probably thinking that of all the people he could have got a lift with, he had to get a couple of Estonian retards, and leaving both Jo and myself still unaware as to whether the ride we'd given him had been compulsory or optional. I do know that it took quite some time to get rid of the smell he left wafting around the van. Not for the first time we muttered something about learning Russian.

Birobidzhan is the capital of the Jewish autonomous region of the federation, and the place was a dump, anyone with any sense probably having upped sticks and moved to Israel by now. The hitcher had unnerved us, so rather than the planned night's sleep, we carried on along the road to Khabarovsk. However, just in case anyone is interested:

A COUPLE OF THINGS YOU PROBABLY DIDN'T KNOW AND DIDN'T CARE TO KNOW ABOUT BIROBIDZHAN

1. The town has its own newspaper in Yiddish
2. Both Hebrew and Yiddish are taught in schools

When researching Birobidzhan, I turned up very little, but I did happen across a short article (courtesy of the Union of Councils for Jews in the Former Soviet Union) about how residents of the region celebrate Purim. Purim is a spring holiday, to celebrate the 'saving of Jews from destruction, as described in the Book of Esther'. Sounds like an excuse for a holiday to me. Either a dish called 'Haman's Ears' is prepared, or meat pies. Children take part in the 'Beating of the Haman', whilst adults, in accordance with the Talmud, are expected to drink themselves under the table.

Only 5 per cent of the region is populated by Jews, but the occasion apparently turns into a drinking contest between Jews and non-Jews. That's everybody.

As we approached Khabarovsk we came in increasing proximity to the Pacific. With every kilometre we seemed to relax a little more, the closer we got to the eastern edge of Russia. It was like running a marathon, and knowing that all the hills were behind you, although we still had quite a few miles to go beyond Khabarovsk and I've never run a marathon.

In 1639 Ivan Moskvitin was the first Russian to see the Pacific. He was a Cossack from Tomsk, originally Moscow – I'm guessing from his name – who became the first person on record to sail on the Sea of Okhotsk. The Russians' conquest of Siberia had been achieved at some pace, the Pacific being reached a mere fifty-eight years after Yermak first pillaged the Urals. Why the speed? Fur. Siberia was rich in sable pelt, the ultimate European status symbol. The demand in Europe was increasing rapidly and the Cossacks were making hay whilst the eastern sun was shining. In March 1642 the first Russian map of the Far East was drawn based on Moskvitin's account. And it wouldn't have surprised me to discover that was the map we'd been using.

We crossed the Amur River by ferry. We still had some 800 kilometres to drive in order to reach Vladivostok, but even if we had to stop now, it didn't seem to matter as much as it had for so many kilometres. Whatever happened over the next few days, we would be leaving Russia by way of the Pacific. A return to St Petersburg would be for another trip now.

Khabarovsk certainly helped this growing feeling of invincibility. Whether it was because we had been so starved of such civility or because the city was genuinely vibrant and attractive I won't really know unless I ever go back there. But on this occasion it was like we had arrived at a European seaside town, the atmosphere that of La Rochelle in July. (Probably an exaggeration, but then we had just come from Birobidzhan.) The people on the streets were upbeat, even cheerful. Many of them were from across the water in Japan, there having been a small invasion of Japanese cars and business.

The town's namesake and number three in the list of top ten exploring Cossacks was:

YEROFEY KHABAROV

By the middle of the seventeenth century the Russian empire, best known as Muscovy at the time, was probably the largest empire on earth. With Russia's acquisition of Siberia it had acquired a land rich in natural resources, but one diverse in its peoples, and one very disagreeable climate. Siberia was fast becoming no more than a massive dumping ground, as Tartarstan before, for anything Muscovy simply wanted to forget about.

With this region also came an increasingly large border in the south that needed to be defended, not least from the formidable Manchus. To the east the Pacific offered a natural border and defence. The lands of the Far East, however, were also fertile and offered a very agreeable climate, potentially a larder for Siberia. Furthermore, the potential trade routes to the east couldn't be ignored.

Under Khabarov a force of Cossacks captured the lands around the Amur basin and for a while were able to see off attacks from the disgruntled Chinese to the south.

Eventually, however, the region became impossible to defend, due to its distance from Europe. A treaty was negotiated with the Chinese – a treaty that was to stay in place for the next couple of centuries.

The streets of the city heaved with foreign vehicles, their metalwork glistening in the sun, contrasting with Max's mud-caked body. We'd passed many imports on our way across Siberia, but now we'd arrived at the chaotic nest, home to the buzz of the Mitsubishi and the hum of the Toyota. Any Ladas we saw were forgotten shells by the roadside, or else being used as storage space – we even noted one full of plants apparently in use as a greenhouse. The foreign influence was everywhere to be seen, Asian faces were predominant on the streets; Koreans, Chinese and Japanese. I followed the lead of the Khabarovskians and parked Max amongst other deserted cars in an area that was quite clearly a road (when in Rome...) and we headed for a Japanese noodle bar, well advertised by a sign in clear English: 'JAPANESE NOODLE BAR'. Understandably, Jo wasn't going to accept the truth of this tantalising declaration until she had thoroughly appraised the fare on offer. It was with much relief that Jo was able to confirm that moist, delicious smelling noodles were indeed available at this wooden, slightly dilapidated kiosk in Khabarovsk. We bought two boxes each from a very cheerful Japanese, and walked round to a nearby tree-lined park, where we basked in our relative proximity to the ocean and, sitting on the grass, ate noodles until we could eat no more.

CHAPTER FOURTEEN
VLADIVOSTOK!

Several weeks after leaving St Petersburg the end of the road was near. The peninsula of Primorsky Krai, bordered by sea on one side and China on the other, runs from Khabarovsk down to Vladivostok. The last 800 kilometres offered a couple of days of pleasant driving through bland landscapes; beaten flatlands, as if left by a retreating army, met the horizon in all directions. The region was best known for its near mythical tigers – now poised on the brink of extinction – and the Goldi (or Nani) tribesman Dersu Uzala. The latter was made famous by his friendship with the nineteenth-century Russian explorer Vladimir Arseniev, who mapped much of the region during a series of scientific expeditions between 1902 and 1930. An account of one of these trips documents his meeting with the nomad Uzala, who became his guide. The book *Dersu the Trapper* later became a film in Soviet times by Japanese director Akira Kurosawa, winning him an Oscar.

The cruising speed we had maintained most of the way slumped to something of a crawl by the time we reached the ramshackle outskirts of Vladivostok. The reason for our snail's pace for the last hundred or so kilometres was simple – we hadn't been able to get out of second gear. Our mechanical knowledge had improved enough during the journey for us to deduce that we had a problem with the engine again, and one that was deteriorating quickly. The humour of Max coughing, spluttering and back-firing violently, sounding like an old horse with wind as we reached Vladivostok, didn't pass either of us by. We added hysterical laughter to the troubled symphony of sounds that burst from the van as we passed into the city centre. The only thing on our minds as we pathetically climbed the hill was finding and securing the aid of a skilled mechanic.

Having reached the outer hub of the city's centre we parked up on an unassuming street. I had dug out the piece of paper upon which Tony had hastily scribbled Nikolai's name and the address of the timber yard back in Estonia. It glared defiantly at me from the dashboard – but it would have to wait. We left Max and walked the short distance to the nearest cafe, where we ordered a drink. With Max worn and now crippled and without the first idea where the timber yard might be found, we spent what was left of the day in peaceful reflection on the previous few months, both amazed and grateful that our 'old rust bucket' had done us proud.

With the hazy light of a new day, carried by a Pacific breeze we ventured down to the harbour and docks. We hadn't seen the sea since leaving St Petersburg, despite it being tantalisingly close ever since Khabarovsk, and the prospect of now seeing it induced a childish excitement. The decision had been made the previous night that we would go in search of a garage first thing. That and:

- Give something back to the people of Russia
- Never take anyone for granted ever again
- Live life to the full
- Help strangers
- Give something back to the people of Russia etc. etc. hic, hic!

We had also given some reluctant consideration to Plan B, not yet convinced about employment and a ready-made life in Vladivostok. Uncle Tony had given us the name of his contact and the hope of what could be waiting for us; however, he had also given us very little confidence that it would not simply be a repeat of Pärnu – no work to do and no wages. That said, Tony had given us something a lot more valuable, whether he knew it or not – an incredible adventure that it is doubtful we would have given any consideration to without him. Regarding a Plan B, there was no way we were driving back home across Russia, and we were under the delusion that the streets of Japan were paved with gold, a notion derived from the days travellers went to Japan and earned a lot of money teaching English and doing bar work. The need for money was imminent so we would cash in on Japan's generosity to the working foreigner and 'pop across' the Sea of Japan.

The scene that met us down by the docks was altogether quite moving. The centrepiece for probably the whole of the city must be the station, the final stop for, amongst other trains, the Rossiya, having completed the Trans-Siberian. It simply shouts finality, in that it is so physically obvious that the journey can not go on in the same form. The station in Vladivostok, the aquamarine imperial building – bustling, beautiful and animated, with the watery backdrop – makes a very powerful statement of 'The End'. The scene that greeted us had the lot: soldiers, sailors, sailors with wooden legs, drunken sailors, drunken soldiers, the Rossiya at rest with attendants in their red and blue seeing to the alighting passengers, who looked like they had come only a few miles down the track, not the more likely six-day marathon from Moscow. Babushki lined the walkways selling just about anything and everything, although there was a definite prevalence of battered sausage and piroshki (meat pies). Beyond the station, containers were being hoisted onto the big ships, and bodies crawled over the hulking mass of the *Mikhail Sholokhov*, which sat calmly in preparation for voyage. (Quick note on M. Sholokhov – a self-taught diehard Communist responsible for writing *And Quiet Flows the Don*, the heaviest novel I've ever come across. At over 13,000 pages long, I believe it even pips *War and Peace* to the title of longest novel in the world.)

Trams rattled up the hill past the station and out of sight towards the Amursky Gulf. In the other direction the rusty remains of the Russian Pacific Fleet hugged the Golden Horn Bay, grey and austere. The decline of the Pacific Fleet had been a marked one since the break up of the Soviet Union.

During Yeltsin's early administration, the decision was made to halt production of nuclear submarines. By 1996 only forty-six nuclear subs remained active in the Pacific, and by 1998 the figure was approximately twenty-six. The only remaining active duty SSBNs were the four Delta III subs, stationed in Kamchatka. The major concern of the fleet now was the dismantlement of the subs, as currently there were no facilities capable of the task. Despite the dismal picture that we witnessed, worryingly the Pacific Fleet was still operational, waiting on funding – as was the complete decommissioning.

During the Soviet period, Vladivostok had been a remote closed city, shrouded in mystery – if you had actually heard of it. It hadn't always been that way, however. Before the revolution of 1917, it had been a cosmopolitan city, home to merchants from around the world. The city had truly lived up to its moniker of 'Lord of the East', although that possibly suggested a glamour beyond what it actually offered, as with Irkutsk, the 'Paris of Siberia'. 'Lord of the Russian East' would have been more appropriate.

Stalin got rid of the Asians responsible for making the city glamorous, making up four fifths of the population. Gradually the life and soul was drained from the place until in 1958 Vladivostok was officially closed.

After a lot of procrastinating we got round to relocating Max on to Naberezhnaya Street, a quiet road not far from the docks and the centre of town, overlooking the Amursky Gulf. It was just around the corner from a garage which agreed to operate on Max – but only in three days' time. We decided to use this time for reluctant research into Plan B, along with some light coffee drinking... the latter proved to be a lot more rewarding.

Plan B was vague to say the least; however, a solid thread running through all its variations was that we needed to get ourselves and Max across to Japan.

We visited a handful of soul-crushing grey offices, and spoke with an equal number of Sovietly obstinate officials, probably the most uniquely unhelpful being those at the Far East Shipping Company, whose biggest concern seemed to be that we were roaming around the city with a free rein, off the official radar, despite our attempts to explain that we were trying our hardest to leave. Such was our frustration at the dead ends we ventured down, we started musing over alternative escape plans:

- Leave Max and fly to Japan – this was like leaving an old friend behind, heartbreaking and utterly unthinkable for more than the few seconds that we did.

- Leave me with Max, Jo flies to Japan – slightly less unthinkable than the above, but nonetheless a pretty bad idea.

- Forget about Japan, stay in Vladivostok – we had gone full circle very quickly and were back to Plan A.

Naberezhnaya Street, due to its location overlooking the ocean, was an understandably popular place for evening promenaders, folk whiling away the last of the summer days with a gentle stroll. I spent many a choice moment watching the strollers, watching me watching them. We met Vika as she was taking one such constitutional. She was a long awkward-looking lady, probably in her early thirties, yet looking much older. The length of her thin arms and her spindly legs gave her an insect quality. Her big round glasses magnified her big round eyes.

The evening we met her she was meandering along arm in arm with her husband, Andry, a man almost half her height. The first thing about Vika that got my attention was not her physicality but her wardrobe. She was dressed like a backing singer for Slade. I was trying to alert Jo to the psychedelic creation that was coming our way, when Vika and Andry came to a standstill alongside the van.

'Good evening, please come with us.'

Now, normally such a request would arouse just a little bit of suspicion, perhaps prompting a query as to where they wanted us to go: 'Are you a KGB tribute act?' Neither of us seemed to care, however, and the need for a diversion, anything to fill the time, outweighed any potential concerns. Plus the fact that the only thing threatening about Vika or Andry was Vika's dress sense, which was more of a threat to Jo, who had been known to look to the seventies for inspiration with her own shirts. In fact, such was our level of boredom, piddling a few hours away with someone looking like Vika could be nothing but a pleasure.

We followed obediently, as they led us a short distance, through a playground, down some steps into the basement of a large block and through two heavy steel doors, both of which Andry had to unlock then re-lock, and finally into an office. Still not a ripple of concern from either of us. Behind a desk that took up most of the space, in a large black leather chair sat another lady, an expectant look on her face. Vika, who hadn't spoken since the initial invitation/instruction/ order, was quick to introduce the lady: 'This is Sveta, sister of Andry.' She looked at her husband.

It was at this point, framed by a window, that I caught sight of Max – not too far away. They'd been watching us from this office. It was a set up – Vika and Andrey weren't just out for a stroll... We'd walked into Russia's real-life version of *Life on Mars*, the science fiction police drama set in the 1970s, and we were the bad guys. Well, maybe. Andry hadn't said anything yet, in English or Russian, and he wasn't going to. Sveta spoke in staccato bursts of Russian, which always climaxed with a giggle fit. Vika poured everyone a glass of Sovietskaya champagne, and then toasted us. Sveta stared at Jo, Jo stared at me. Andry, without Vika on his arm, looked like he'd lost the will to live. Jo's expression suggested she too had lost the will to live. I didn't really know what was going on.

Vika spoke: 'We have visitor from United States only two weeks before.'

'Really?' I responded, hoping to draw her in, and at least kill the uncomfortable atmosphere. But that was it. We finished our drinks and were released. Lots of head-nodding and hand-shaking. Christ, she might have dressed like she lived off a diet of psilocybin, but Vika certainly didn't know how to throw a party. We went back to Max, conscious that we would have a few more days of them staring at us through the window. I knew they were only being friendly, doing the right thing for guests in their country. Just a little bit too weird.

We met Dmitry and Pavel at the Eagle's Nest. I wouldn't call Dmitry and Pavel weird but I would call them obnoxious, in the way that Russians who have spent a period of time in the United States, developed a reasonable handle on 'twang' English and have the 'right' labels showing on their sporty leisurewear can be. They were just too enthusiastic, too excited and up for it, which doesn't really sit with being Russian. I'd learned to like my Russians morose and cynical. Both Pavel and Dmitry wanted to be American, or maybe just didn't want to be Russian, or maybe thought they could impress people like me with their Nike trainers and love of potato chips.

The Eagle's Nest was the name they gave to the location of a smart Japanese financed hotel, the toilets of which we visited each morning to freshen up during our stay in the city. We became particularly partial to the reams of tissue paper available, and a never-ending supply of liquid soap from a magic dispenser. They used the reception lounge as their office, which offered a great view of the gulf, hence the name Eagle's Nest. They introduced themselves as tour guides – mainly working with the wealthy Japanese visitors, although they apparently did a sideline in money exchange, judging by the constant flow of people sidling up to them who made no secret of landing large wads of cash on the table. Pavel surreptitiously slipped said bundles of notes into his pocket, replacing them with other bundles of notes – only a different colour. If they were there during our morning ablutions, we'd have a coffee and pass some time with them.

Pavel and Dmitry, like much of Russia, were playing the game of capitalism, having fun with the free market, making some money, losing some money, scheming – adopting Western ideas and ideals, looking to the West to guide them into the future. A big change was just around the corner. In 1998, less than a year later, the rouble would collapse, and people went from being millionaires to being on the street in a matter of hours. Chaos and financial crisis arrived; the bubble had burst. Up until 17 August 1998 the government had gradually been devaluing the rouble; on that date the then Prime Minister Kiriyenko and the Central Bank of Russia were forced to suspend the payment of all foreign debts, and the rouble went into free fall. As Russians frantically tried to buy dollars, massive queues were to be seen outside banks across Russia – many closed overnight, those in charge simply vanishing. Dmitry and Pavel's sideline would be no more, as Russia's free market bubble – built on corruption, false optimism and greed – well and truly burst. And so began a long drawn-out rejection of the West. Pavel and Dmitry would have been all right, they still had their Japanese businessmen to pay their bills – but many Russians didn't. In fact, many Russians were left with absolutely nothing. I wonder what they would have made of our trip a couple of years later. I was glad that Uncle Tony's entrepreneurial optimism had been used for something positive in the early nineties.

On our third morning we joined Pavel and Dmitry in their 'office' for coffee. During an earlier meeting I had mentioned that we would be spending some time formulating a Plan B, which would involve trying to organise shipment for Max. At the time I had believed my words to have been met with very little interest – however, Pavel was to prove me wrong.

'I have a friend. I think he can help you with your problem. He'll be here soon,' Pavel said in a low voice, adding to the already suspicious air, and as if Victor had been waiting for his cue, a few seconds passed before he made his entrance. Victor was a small hyperactive man, with a pair of flimsy spectacles perched on the end of his nose. He exuded great amounts of energy, which suggested he could indeed help with just about any problem we might have.

'Sure I can get you on a boat!' he boasted in a high-pitched voice.

There would be room for us on the last passage of the year. We were never actually sure who indeed Victor was, and still aren't, only that he had connections with one of the container ships that crossed to Niigata on the west coast of Japan, and was an old school friend of Pavel's. However, he seemed to know everyone who mattered, so it didn't seem so important who he was. Despite it being somewhat vague, it felt good to have something of a Plan B in place, so I went to sleep that night with a head full of pleasant thoughts which were followed by gentle dreams – except for one, that is.

I was sitting on a station platform when I was joined by a dark, leathery skinned man. He wore no shoes. He insisted on shaking my hand repeatedly as we watched an old lady washing her feet in a nearby puddle. The man assured me that he was very drunk. Drunk men particularly seem to enjoy my sober company – and there is no surer place to find them than at a Russian station. If you have time to kill there is no better place than a station – in particular stations in Russia, oozing bygone romance, with soldiers, sailors, beggars and thieves all adding their colour to the chaotic stage setting.

The station was Russia in micro. The round faces of the Far East, the sinister eyes of Tartarstan, the dark skin of the Caucasus – they were all represented, all woven together in a seemingly futile attempt to go somewhere. I was going somewhere, although I had no idea when. Then Jo appeared.

'It's all sorted, I've just been down to check in with Victor, we leave on Thursday.'

Yikes, I was overcome by a feeling of relief and apprehension. We had now been in Vladivostok for several weeks – that made it the closest place to home we'd had since leaving Tallinn. I liked it, I felt safe. That was all about to change.

The day arrived, and just after dawn we crawled down to the docks.

Victor was there to oversee the hoisting of Max onto the ship. We looked on as he was harnessed and then swung through the air, like an animal being air-lifted to safety. For the first time since leaving England Max appeared vulnerable, helpless even, and I realised just how important he had been. Not just because he'd been our home for so long, but also because he had been a good friend. Over the months he had taken on his own identity, many characteristics strangely human. There had been three of us on the trip. Seeing him flying through the air, I just wanted to tuck him up in a warm garage away from the elements. VW campervans are durable and much-loved icons, though probably not many people's first choice for crossing Siberia. We had put him through more than most vans would have to deal with in a lifetime.

Once he had disappeared into the depths of the ship, we joined the other passengers at the terminal, and began a document check marathon. Despite the presence of Victor – who I assume could simply have explained our situation to anyone who needed an explanation – everybody within a 5-mile radius of Vladivostok who happened to be wearing a uniform found it necessary to check our papers. That was a lot of checks. Eventually Victor gripped us both like long lost friends, before steering us onto the gangplank. Halfway along, the ship we were heading towards simply disappeared and we both tumbled over the edge into the water below. At this point I woke up with a start. I was now determined to find Nikolai and ensure that Plan B remained exactly that.

It was on a tightly packed tram no. 2 that we climbed the hill away from the docks, following the intelligence of an aging trapeze artist we had met at the central bus station when asking for directions – who as well as guiding us through a photographic history of his life with the Moscow State Circus had provided directions (in some detail) to the address of Nikolai's yard. Having reached the final stop we were to jump on a bus headed for the airport.

'Disembark four stops and thirty minutes after when the town has gone and the trees are many.' This we did, into what appeared to be the middle of a forest. By this stage we were allowing ourselves to get more than a little bit excited, as the location in a forest gave the address more than a little credibility as being home to a timber yard.

The closer we got the more nervous I became. I felt butterflies in my stomach as we stood amongst the towering pine trees, considering which way to go. Despite having completely resigned ourselves to the fact that there would not actually be anything for us in Vladivostok, there still seemed to be room for disappointment now we were so close. Over the previous weeks, Nikolai had germinated from merely a name on a piece of paper to a living being of gargantuan proportions in my head. I even had his appearance nailed – down to the neatly cultivated moustache and weather-beaten complexion. I had built him up into a Kurtz type character, a rogue timber trader running his operations incognito from a heavily fortified yard in Vladivostok – capital of the wild East.

In that tall, dense forest some distance from the city, there were very few signs of any fortified timber yards. Actually, the more time we spent anxiously assessing our surroundings the more we realised there was very little sign of anything at all, except for trees as far as the eye could see. No surprises there. Russia is one of the world's largest timber exporters, felling more than three and a half million cubic feet every year. The Vladivostok region alone accounts for a huge percentage of that figure. Thick logs of oak, ash, spruce and pine are shipped to Japan, China and South Korea amongst others – some of the world's largest timber importers. However, much of the industry in the region is illegal, damaging fragile ecosystems and killing off rare species. Greenpeace has shown that Primorsky Krai is responsible for over half of all the valuable species of trees illicitly cut down in Russia. In an area with high unemployment, the rich, seemingly endless forests and the timber they produced was a sure-fire way of making a living, and with very little if any state control the criminal organisations had moved in, managing the forests with the consideration and forethought you would expect from a 'get rich quick' culture.

As I considered the sheer scope of the forestation that surrounded us, I spotted the rapidly shrinking outline of an elderly woman who must have alighted the bus at the same time. I caught up with her and, too agitated to go through the motions of not being understood, I acted dumb and simply shoved the address in front of her. Either dumb herself or assuming I was Estonian and thus strange, she silently swung around and pointed to back where Jo was waiting. On closer inspection I was able to make out the rough outline of what would have once been a path. Seeing my mind working the old lady began nodding enthusiastically, and shooing me back towards Jo.

We waded along the overgrown path – now thick with brambles – which obviously hadn't been trodden for some time, and just as any hope of finding Nikolai or anybody at the end of it was all but vanquished, the trees began to thin and we stumbled out into a clearing to be met by something that on first sight looked like an abandoned tank. Closer inspection revealed a wood shredder whose condition suggested it had moved very little for three or four winters.

This particular green monster was more orange from rust now, but as with its relation in Pärnu it too was 'kaput'. The sight of the shredder produced a sinking feeling in my stomach. Our spirits were fast lifted, albeit briefly, by the scene a short distance beyond. Split trunks and piles of logs lined a track up to an open-fronted aircraft hangar. There were no planes, just abandoned escalators and conveyor belts, forgotten machinery and other timber industry paraphernalia that I couldn't help thinking would have been useful for Olavi back at his yard in Estonia. As we poked around it was like discovering a lost city – the population of which had left many years ago. A lost sawmill, anyway. Formidable weathered trunks some 20 metres in length provided the framework, while battered galvanised metal sheets furnished the sides and the roof – once durable and strong, it now appeared to have been moulded from tin cans. Nikolai's yard was very obviously not open for business. We both found a couple of logs to perch on whilst the discovery sunk in. We went through all the possible reasons for the yard's demise until, unable to make sense of all the contradictions, we simply gave up, hopeful that instead of bowing down to the demands of the criminal gangs and their brutal disregard for the environment, Nikolai too had simply given up. It was difficult not to consider more unsavoury conclusions.

Looking around, a smile came onto my face and I quickly realised that I wasn't really all that disappointed. We could have taken the train or flown to Vladivostok, and probably would have done if it had been about the end, but it hadn't been: it was about the means. Uncle Tony had known that when he pointed us in the right direction. It quickly dawned on us that Tony probably hadn't been in contact with Nikolai for years – or certainly not in recent years – probably unsure whether he was alive or dead.

VLADIVOSTOK!

It didn't matter – none of it mattered. We had already done what we came to Vladivostok to do – we had been doing it since leaving England.

A YEAR
IN THE
SCHEISSE

Getting to Know the

Germans

ROGER BOYES

A YEAR IN THE SCHEISSE

Getting to Know the Germans

Roger Boyes

ISBN: 978 1 84024 648 3   Paperback   £8.99

'I scheissed myself laughing. Herr Boyes has written a thigh-slapper of a book'

Henning Wehn

This is the story of an English journalist's absurd adventures living in Germany. Facing bankruptcy, Roger is advised by his accountant to make use of a legal loophole: in Germany married couples have their tax bill halved. So the search is on for a bride. Meanwhile his father, a former war hero, is also in financial trouble and is threatening to move to Germany and sponge off his son. The combination of crises sets in motion a hilarious romp during which we discover more than we really wanted to about German nudist beaches, the British media's obsession with Adolf Hitler and how to cheat at the Berlin marathon.

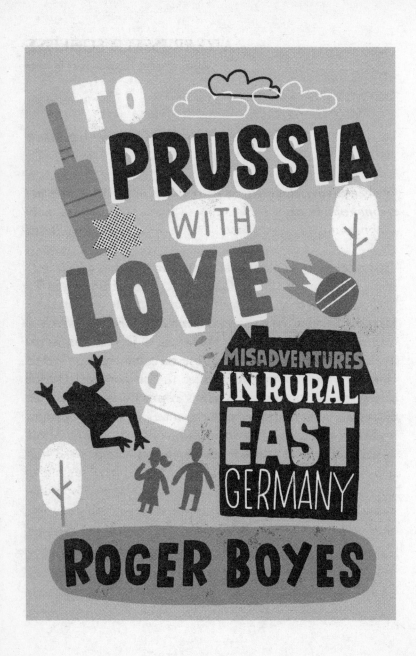

TO PRUSSIA

WITH

LOVE

MISADVENTURES IN RURAL EAST GERMANY

ROGER BOYES

TO PRUSSIA WITH LOVE
Misadventures in Rural East Germany

Roger Boyes

ISBN: 978 1 84953 125 2   Paperback   £8.99

'Roger Boyes' thigh-slapping account of a Brit's attempt to make it in rural Germany will leave you choking with laughter on your bratwurst'   Ben Hatch

'Boyes went to East Germany so no-one else has to. Danke!'   Henning Wehn

In a desperate attempt to save his relationship with girlfriend Lena and take a break from the world of journalism, Roger Boyes agrees to make a great escape from the easy urban lifestyle of Berlin and decamp to the countryside. He has hopes for Italy, but Lena has inherited a run-down old schloss in deepest, darkest Brandenburg.

Needing a form of income, they decide to set up a B & B with a British theme. Enter unhelpful Harry and his Trinidadian chef cousin, an unhinged Scot to advise them on re-branding Brandenburg, some suicidal frogs and a posse of mad tourists. It all culminates, naturally, in a cricket match between the Brits and the Germans on an old Russian minefield. Farce meets romance in this hilarious romp through East Germany's very own version of *Fawlty Towers*.

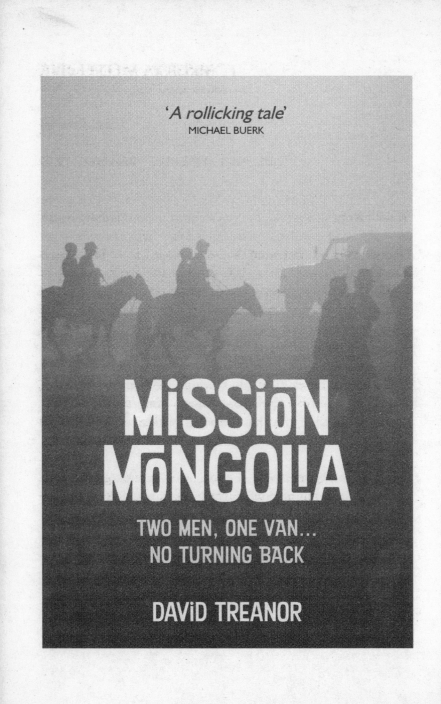

'*A rollicking tale*'
MICHAEL BUERK

MISSION
MONGOLIA

TWO MEN, ONE VAN...
NO TURNING BACK

DAVID TREANOR

MISSION MONGOLIA

Two Men, One Van... No Turning Back

David Treanor

ISBN: 978 1 84953 059 0   Paperback   £8.99

'A rollicking tale'   Michael Buerk

Fifty-something and tired of arguing with John Humphrys over the day's headlines, BBC journalists Geoff and David found themselves eagerly volunteering for redundancy. But rather than easing into retirement with the odd round of golf, they decided to buy a van and drive off to Mongolia. Well, it seemed like a good idea at the time...

In an epic journey through Ukraine, Russia, Kazakhstan, Siberia and across the Gobi Desert, they discover more about each other in a few weeks than they did sharing an office for years.

Lying in wait are crooked cops, bent border guards and terrible roads, but also welcoming and curious locals, eager to help the pair on their mission.

Have you enjoyed this book?
If so, why not write a review on your favourite website?
Thanks very much for buying this Summersdale book.

www.summersdale.com